I0018771

BLENDER MASTERY

From Fundamentals to Advanced Techniques

FIRST EDITION

Preface

Creating 3D graphics, animations, and visual effects has never been more accessible thanks to Blender, a free and open-source software that empowers creators across the globe. This book is designed to take you on a journey through the vast possibilities that Blender has to offer, whether you're a beginner exploring 3D graphics for the first time or an experienced user aiming to expand your knowledge.

Blender is a versatile tool for professionals in fields as diverse as animation, game development, and digital art. Throughout this book, each chapter systematically guides you through the essential features and tools available in Blender. The book begins with an overview of the software's history, setting the foundation for understanding why Blender has become a preferred choice for many. From there, we transition into the basics—how to install and set up Blender, and how to navigate the complex, yet fascinating user interface.

With Blender, understanding the fundamental concepts is key, and that's why the initial chapters cover topics such as workflow, essential tools, and object manipulation. Once you're familiar with the basics, the book leads you deeper into the world of 3D modeling, from creating basic shapes to employing advanced techniques like sculpting, retopology, and working with NURBS and curves.

Subsequent chapters focus on other crucial aspects of 3D content creation, such as texturing, lighting, and rendering. You'll learn how to use Blender's built-in engines, Eevee and Cycles, to create stunning visuals. We'll also delve into animation, covering everything from keyframe animation to physics-based animations, and more advanced rigging techniques to help bring your models to life.

The book doesn't stop there. We explore special effects, simulations, game asset creation, and optimizing workflows for collaborative projects. With sections on using version control systems, managing large projects, and network rendering, you'll find invaluable information for both solo and team endeavors. For those planning to use Blender in game development, this book includes a dedicated chapter on creating and preparing game assets for Unity and Unreal Engine.

The final chapters offer insight into workflow optimization, common pitfalls, and industry secrets that professionals use to streamline their projects. We conclude by encouraging readers to join the thriving Blender community, which is rich with resources and support for continued learning.

Our goal with this book is not just to teach you how to use Blender, but to help you think like a 3D artist, animator, or developer. By the end, you'll be equipped with the skills and knowledge to tackle your own creative projects, confident in your ability to harness the full potential of Blender. So, take this opportunity to learn, experiment, and become a part of this vibrant, creative community.

Table of Contents

Chapter 1: Introduction to Blender

The Evolution of Blender: A Brief History

Blender, the software at the heart of countless creative projects, has undergone an incredible transformation over the years. It has evolved from a niche tool to a powerful, feature-rich platform that competes with—and in some cases surpasses—industry-standard software. Understanding the history of Blender not only gives you insight into its development but also helps you appreciate the unique community-driven philosophy behind it.

Blender was first conceived in the mid-1990s by Ton Roosendaal, a Dutch software developer who originally worked for a company called NeoGeo, a Dutch animation studio. NeoGeo was, at the time, one of the largest 3D animation studios in the Netherlands. Roosendaal realized that the available commercial 3D tools were either too costly or lacked the flexibility required for their projects. In response, he began developing in-house software that would be faster, cheaper, and more versatile. This led to the creation of Blender, a piece of software that would eventually evolve into a versatile powerhouse for 3D graphics and animation.

Blender was officially launched in 1998 by Roosendaal's company, Not a Number (NaN). Initially, it was released as proprietary software with a free version available for non-commercial use. However, financial troubles led to NaN closing its doors in 2002. But that was not the end of Blender—far from it. Instead of letting Blender vanish into obscurity, Roosendaal initiated a unique campaign to save the software. He started the Blender Foundation and organized a crowdfunding campaign to make Blender open-source. The "Free Blender" campaign raised enough funds from supporters, enabling the release of Blender under the GNU General Public License (GPL). Since then, it has been developed by a community of contributors from around the world.

The open-source nature of Blender has been a key factor in its growth. The development community—comprised of volunteers, enthusiasts, professionals, and even studios—has contributed significantly to Blender's rapid advancement. The Blender Foundation and the Blender Institute have overseen this development, funding initiatives like the Blender Open Movie projects. These projects, such as "Elephants Dream," "Big Buck Bunny," and "Sintel," have showcased Blender's capabilities and driven the implementation of new features. By creating these open films, Blender has also helped establish itself as a viable tool for professional production.

Blender's major milestone came in 2019 with the release of version 2.80, a transformative update that overhauled its user interface and made it more accessible to newcomers. The 2.80 release also introduced Eevee, a real-time rendering engine that significantly expanded Blender's use cases, particularly for game developers and content creators who required instant feedback. Since then, Blender has continued to evolve rapidly, with new releases introducing cutting-edge features such as sculpting improvements, geometry nodes for procedural modeling, and significant performance optimizations.

One of the standout aspects of Blender's history is its community-driven ethos. Unlike commercial software, Blender's direction is determined by its community—artists, developers, and users from all walks of life. This collaborative approach has helped Blender grow into a highly flexible and adaptable tool that responds directly to the needs of its users. As a result, Blender has gained recognition from major industry players. Notably, companies like Epic Games, NVIDIA, and even Unity Technologies have supported Blender through grants and development contributions. These partnerships have allowed Blender to maintain its free and open nature while continuing to improve in terms of stability and feature set.

Another aspect worth noting is Blender's focus on cross-disciplinary workflows. Blender is not just a tool for modeling; it also encompasses sculpting, texturing, rigging, animation, rendering, compositing, and even video editing. The software's history reflects its growth into a "one-stop-shop" for content creators. This holistic approach has made it a popular choice for independent artists and small studios that cannot afford specialized software for each part of the production process. The addition of Grease Pencil, for example, allowed artists to combine 2D and 3D animation seamlessly, further expanding Blender's versatility.

The evolution of Blender has not been without challenges. The software's open-source model means that it lacks the marketing and sales teams that commercial software often relies on for widespread adoption. Instead, Blender's growth has been almost entirely organic, driven by passionate users who recognize its potential. This grassroots support is reflected in the Blender Conference, an annual event where developers, artists, and enthusiasts come together to share ideas, techniques, and innovations.

Blender's development is also supported through the Blender Development Fund, where individuals and companies can contribute financially to support Blender's ongoing development. This fund has been instrumental in enabling the Blender Foundation to hire full-time developers, ensuring that Blender can continue to evolve and keep pace with industry standards.

As of today, Blender is a mature and stable tool that can compete with industry giants like Autodesk Maya, 3ds Max, and Cinema 4D. It is used by a wide range of creators, from hobbyists to professionals at renowned studios. Major companies, such as Ubisoft and Netflix, have adopted Blender for various projects, proving that open-source software can thrive in professional environments. The use of Blender in these contexts has not only validated its capabilities but also attracted more professionals to contribute to its development, creating a positive feedback loop of growth and innovation.

Blender's journey from an in-house tool at NeoGeo to an industry-recognized, community-driven open-source platform is a testament to the power of collaboration and shared vision. Today, Blender stands as an example of what can be achieved when software is freely accessible, developed by a community, and fueled by the passion of its users. Whether you are interested in creating stunning animations, intricate models, or immersive game assets, Blender provides the tools you need—all without any cost.

The history of Blender is not just a story about software development; it's a story about creativity, community, and breaking down barriers. It's about challenging the status quo and proving that high-quality, professional tools can be accessible to everyone, regardless of budget. As you embark on your journey to learn Blender, remember that you are joining a community that values learning, sharing, and creativity above all else. Whether you're an artist, a developer, or someone entirely new to the world of 3D, there is a place for you in the Blender community, and countless resources to help you on your way.

Why Choose Blender? Key Features and Benefits

Blender stands out as a revolutionary tool in the world of 3D graphics, animation, and visual effects. Unlike many other software solutions that require substantial investments and subscriptions, Blender is completely free and open-source. This chapter will provide an in-depth look at why Blender is a compelling choice for artists, animators, game developers, and even visual effects professionals. We'll discuss its key features, highlight its numerous benefits, and explore what sets Blender apart from other tools in the industry.

Free and Open Source

One of the most attractive features of Blender is that it is free. Unlike other 3D software that requires expensive licenses, Blender is available to everyone without any restrictions. It is distributed under the GNU General Public License (GPL), which allows users to download, modify, and distribute the software as they see fit. This level of freedom is virtually unheard of in the professional 3D software market and makes Blender accessible to anyone with an interest in 3D graphics.

Blender's open-source nature has significant implications for its development and usability. Anyone can contribute to Blender, whether by writing code, creating documentation, or sharing their assets and experiences. This collaborative spirit has made Blender one of the most versatile and widely-used 3D tools available. Additionally, the open-source community means that users can expect a high level of transparency regarding development and an active, engaged community ready to offer support and resources.

All-in-One 3D Creation Suite

Blender is a complete 3D creation suite that provides tools for every stage of the production pipeline, from modeling to rendering and even video editing. Here are some of the core components that make Blender a truly comprehensive package:

1. **3D Modeling**: Blender's modeling tools are robust and intuitive, offering features like polygon modeling, sculpting, and procedural modeling using modifiers. Whether you are creating hard surface models or organic shapes, Blender has tools to fit your needs.
2. **Texturing and Shading**: Blender includes a powerful node-based shading system. The ability to create both procedural and image-based textures allows for incredible versatility when it comes to creating detailed, realistic surfaces.

3. **Animation and Rigging**: Blender is known for its powerful animation tools, including keyframe animation, inverse kinematics (IK), forward kinematics (FK), and a Nonlinear Animation (NLA) editor that allows for intricate, complex animations. Rigging tools, including bone-based systems, ensure that characters and objects are easy to animate.
4. **Rendering Engines**: Blender comes with two powerful rendering engines—Eevee and Cycles. Eevee is a real-time renderer, perfect for fast feedback and previews, while Cycles is a ray-traced engine that allows for photorealistic rendering.
5. **Compositing and Post-Processing**: Blender has an integrated compositor that allows artists to perform color grading, create visual effects, and more—all within Blender. The compositor is node-based, making it easy to create complex post-processing effects.
6. **Scripting with Python**: Blender's Python API makes it easy for users to create custom tools, automate repetitive tasks, or even develop full-fledged add-ons. This scripting capability greatly enhances Blender's flexibility and allows for significant customization.
7. **Video Editing**: The Video Sequence Editor (VSE) is a built-in non-linear editor that provides tools for cutting, splicing, and editing footage. This makes Blender a great choice for small studios and independent creators looking to complete an entire project within one software environment.

Customizability and Flexibility

Blender's interface is highly customizable, making it suitable for a wide range of workflows. Users can create custom workspaces tailored to specific tasks such as modeling, sculpting, or compositing. This flexibility helps streamline the production process, allowing artists to optimize their workspace for maximum efficiency.

Blender also supports a wide range of file formats for both import and export, which means that it can easily fit into any existing production pipeline. Whether you need to import models from other software or export assets to game engines like Unity or Unreal Engine, Blender makes the process straightforward. Additionally, Blender's add-on system further enhances its capabilities. There are numerous community-created add-ons available, ranging from modeling tools to asset libraries that further extend Blender's functionality.

For users with specific needs, Blender's Python scripting capabilities allow for the creation of entirely new tools or the automation of repetitive tasks. For instance, if you are working on a project that requires a specific operation to be performed repeatedly, you can use Python to automate it:

```python
import bpy

# Example: A script to create a row of cubes
def create_cubes(num_cubes):
    for i in range(num_cubes):
        bpy.ops.mesh.primitive_cube_add(location=(i * 2, 0, 0))
```

```
# Create a row of 10 cubes
create_cubes(10)
```

This level of flexibility and control is one of the reasons why Blender is favored by technical artists and developers who wish to create highly customized workflows.

Community Support and Learning Resources

Another reason to choose Blender is the strong community and abundance of learning resources. Blender's community is one of the most active and supportive groups in the world of 3D graphics. Whether you are a beginner looking for tutorials or an experienced artist seeking advice on a complex problem, the community is always willing to help. There are numerous forums, including Blender Artists and Blender Stack Exchange, where users can ask questions and share their knowledge.

In addition to forums, there are countless tutorials available, both free and paid, on platforms like YouTube, Udemy, and Blender Cloud. The Blender Foundation itself supports the community by creating high-quality training materials and open movies, which not only showcase what Blender can do but also provide valuable learning experiences for users.

The community's collaborative spirit is also evident in the Blender Market, where users can purchase add-ons, materials, and models. This ecosystem encourages artists to contribute to Blender's growth and also provides a way for talented creators to earn a living by selling assets or add-ons they've developed.

Industry Adoption and Professional Use

Blender is increasingly being adopted by professional studios and artists, and its usage is spreading throughout various industries, including animation, visual effects, gaming, and even architecture. While Blender was once viewed primarily as a tool for hobbyists and independent creators, its feature set and reliability have earned it a place in professional pipelines.

Studios like Ubisoft, Tangent Animation, and even Netflix have used Blender in their projects. The reason for this is simple—Blender has reached a level of maturity where it is capable of handling high-end production needs. Whether it's used for pre-visualization, modeling, texturing, or full animation and rendering, Blender's feature set is on par with many industry-standard tools.

Blender's real-time rendering engine, Eevee, has become particularly popular among game developers and artists who need to produce content quickly without sacrificing quality. The ability to create high-quality renders in real time makes Eevee ideal for pre-visualizations and quick iterations. On the other hand, Cycles, Blender's path-tracing engine, is used when photorealistic results are needed, making it perfect for high-quality visual effects and cinematic animations.

Cross-Disciplinary Application

Blender's versatility also means that it can be applied across many disciplines. Architects use Blender for visualization, allowing them to create detailed models of buildings and spaces that can be explored in real-time. Product designers use Blender to create visual prototypes of their products before they enter production. The fashion industry has even embraced Blender, using it for designing clothing and visualizing how garments would look on a model without the need for physical samples.

Blender's capability to work across disciplines without additional cost is a major benefit, especially for small businesses, startups, or freelance artists who cannot afford multiple specialized software packages. By learning Blender, an individual can acquire a skill set that is applicable in multiple industries, which not only enhances their versatility but also increases employment opportunities.

Cross-Platform Compatibility

Blender is available on multiple operating systems, including Windows, macOS, and Linux, and it runs well on all of them. This compatibility ensures that no matter which system you are using, Blender will work seamlessly. This is particularly important for studios and teams that may have artists working on different platforms. The consistent experience across all platforms ensures that everyone can work efficiently without worrying about software incompatibilities.

Integration with Other Tools and Game Engines

Blender's compatibility extends beyond operating systems—it integrates well with other tools and platforms, especially game engines like Unity and Unreal Engine. Blender offers dedicated export tools for these engines, which means that assets can be quickly transferred without the need for complex conversions.

Furthermore, Blender's FBX, OBJ, and glTF export capabilities mean that it can be used in conjunction with virtually any other 3D software. Whether you need to import models created in other applications or export Blender models to be used in a game engine, Blender's extensive support for different file formats ensures a smooth workflow.

Blender also supports VR viewing, allowing artists to view their models in a virtual reality environment using compatible VR headsets. This feature is incredibly useful for immersive design experiences, especially for those working in architectural visualization or interactive media.

Future-Proof and Continuously Improving

The Blender Foundation, along with a dedicated community of developers, ensures that Blender is continuously improving. New features are added on a regular basis, and the software is kept up to date with industry standards. The development cycle for Blender is rapid, with new releases approximately every three months, and Long Term Support (LTS) versions are also available for those who require more stability.

Blender's feature set today is a result of years of dedicated development, guided by the needs and feedback of its users. This level of commitment to constant improvement ensures that Blender remains relevant and competitive in a fast-evolving industry. The fact that it is open-source means that its growth is not dependent on any one company's financial interests but rather on the needs of its user community.

Summary

Blender is an exceptional choice for anyone interested in 3D graphics and animation. It's free, open-source, and offers a full range of features that can take you from the earliest stages of modeling through to final rendering and video editing. Its flexibility, customizability, and the power of its built-in tools make it a strong competitor to many expensive, industry-standard software packages.

Whether you are a hobbyist just getting started, a professional artist looking to add another tool to your belt, or a studio evaluating the cost-effectiveness of your pipeline, Blender provides a complete, versatile solution. By choosing Blender, you are also joining a thriving community that values creativity, collaboration, and continuous improvement. No matter your background or your project, Blender has the tools and the community to help you succeed.

Installing Blender: System Requirements and Setup

Getting Blender up and running on your computer is the first step toward creating 3D masterpieces. Installing Blender is generally straightforward, but it is important to understand the system requirements, the different options available for installation, and how to optimize your setup to get the best performance out of the software. This section will walk you through everything you need to know to successfully install Blender, whether you're using Windows, macOS, or Linux. Additionally, we'll look at some configurations that can enhance your experience and help you avoid common pitfalls during installation.

System Requirements

Before installing Blender, it is crucial to verify that your system meets the recommended specifications. Blender is a sophisticated application, and ensuring that you have a compatible system will make your experience smoother and more enjoyable.

Blender is available for all major operating systems, including Windows, macOS, and Linux, and it has different levels of hardware requirements based on what you want to achieve. Here are the recommended system requirements for running Blender smoothly:

Minimum Requirements

- **Processor (CPU)**: Dual Core 64-bit processor
- **Graphics Card (GPU)**: Integrated graphics such as Intel HD 5000
- **Memory (RAM)**: 4 GB
- **Storage**: At least 500 MB of available space for installation
- **Operating System**: Windows 8.1, macOS 10.13, or any Linux distribution that meets the GLIBC 2.17 requirement

Recommended Requirements

- **Processor (CPU)**: Quad Core 64-bit processor
- **Graphics Card (GPU)**: NVIDIA GeForce GTX 1060, AMD Radeon RX 480, or better
- **Memory (RAM)**: 16 GB or more
- **Storage**: SSD with at least 2 GB of free space for installation and project storage
- **Operating System**: Windows 10, macOS 11, or a recent Linux distribution

Blender's performance is significantly impacted by your hardware, especially your GPU. While Blender can run on integrated graphics, many of its features—such as rendering with Cycles—will perform much better with a dedicated graphics card. For professional work, a GPU with CUDA or OpenCL support (such as an NVIDIA or AMD card) is recommended to fully leverage Blender's capabilities.

Downloading Blender

Blender can be downloaded directly from its official website, blender.org. On the download page, you will find the latest stable release of Blender, as well as links to older versions if needed.

- **Stable Release**: The stable release is generally recommended for most users as it has been tested thoroughly for performance and stability. Blender Foundation updates the stable release every three months.
- **Beta Versions**: If you are interested in testing upcoming features, you can download beta or nightly builds. These are development versions and may contain bugs, so they are not recommended for production work.

The download page will automatically detect your operating system and provide you with the appropriate version, but you can also manually choose which version you need.

Installation on Different Operating Systems

Installing on Windows

1. **Download the Installer**: Once you've downloaded the `.exe` installer from Blender's website, double-click it to begin the installation process.
2. **Installation Wizard**: The installation wizard will guide you through the steps. You can choose to install Blender for all users of the computer or just for your own account.
3. **Choose the Installation Location**: By default, Blender will be installed in the `C:\Program Files\` directory, but you can choose a different location if needed.
4. **Customizing the Installation**: You have the option to create a desktop shortcut, add Blender to the system PATH (recommended if you want to run Blender from the command line), and configure file associations so `.blend` files open automatically in Blender.
5. **Completing the Installation**: After you click "Install," the wizard will complete the installation, and you can then launch Blender immediately.

For users who prefer not to go through an installation process, Blender also offers a **portable version** for Windows. This version can be unzipped and run directly without any need for installation, which is handy if you want to carry Blender on a USB drive.

Installing on macOS

1. **Download the DMG File**: Download the .dmg file from Blender's website.
2. **Mount the DMG**: Double-click the .dmg file to mount it. You will see the Blender application icon.
3. **Drag to Applications**: Drag the Blender icon to the Applications folder. This will install Blender on your system.
4. **Security Settings**: When opening Blender for the first time, you might see a warning from macOS about Blender being from an "unidentified developer." You can bypass this by right-clicking on the Blender icon, selecting "Open," and then confirming that you want to open it.

macOS users should note that Blender works best with more recent versions of macOS due to the need for updated OpenGL support.

Installing on Linux

Blender installation on Linux offers more flexibility, and there are several options depending on your preferences.

Official Tarball: Download the .tar.xz file from Blender's website, extract it, and run the executable.
bash

```
tar -xvf blender-<version>-linux64.tar.xz
cd blender-<version>-linux64
./blender
```

1.

Snap Package: Blender is available as a Snap package. This is the easiest way to install Blender on most Linux distributions:
bash

```
sudo snap install blender --classic
```

2.

APT for Ubuntu: Blender can be installed using the APT package manager on Ubuntu-based systems:
bash

```
sudo apt install blender
```

3. However, the version available through APT might not be the latest one. It is often recommended to download Blender directly from the official website for the most up-to-date version.

Regardless of the method you choose, ensure that you have the necessary permissions to install software on your Linux system. For the best performance, you may also need to install additional drivers for your graphics card, especially if you are using NVIDIA or AMD hardware.

Setting Up Blender for First-Time Use

Once you have installed Blender, there are a few initial configurations that you can make to ensure that the software works smoothly and meets your preferences.

Launching Blender

After launching Blender for the first time, you will be greeted with the **Splash Screen**, which provides quick access to recently opened projects, links to learning resources, and the option to start a new project. The splash screen is also where you can choose from various **preset workspaces** depending on the type of work you intend to do (e.g., Modeling, Sculpting, Animation).

Configuring Preferences

1. **Edit > Preferences**: Open the Preferences window by navigating to `Edit > Preferences` in the top-left menu bar. Here you can configure various settings, including:
   - **Interface**: You can customize the theme and appearance of Blender's interface. Blender comes with several built-in themes, and you can also create your own.
   - **Navigation**: Adjust how you navigate the 3D Viewport, such as enabling or disabling the option for continuous zooming, changing the orbit style, or setting up shortcuts for common actions.
   - **Input**: You can customize keyboard shortcuts or configure Blender to use different mouse preferences. Blender's input configuration allows users coming from other software, such as Maya, to switch to familiar key mappings.
   - **Add-ons**: Blender comes with many pre-installed add-ons that extend its functionality. By default, only essential add-ons are enabled, but you can explore and enable other add-ons depending on your needs. For example, the "Node Wrangler" add-on is particularly useful when working with shaders, and the "Loop Tools" add-on enhances modeling capabilities.

GPU Configuration

If you have a dedicated GPU, you will want to enable it for rendering in Blender:

1. **Preferences > System**: In the Preferences window, go to the `System` tab. Here, you can select the rendering device.

2. **Cycles Rendering**: Under the `Cycles` render engine settings, you can select between CPU and GPU rendering. Choose your GPU (NVIDIA CUDA, AMD OpenCL, or OptiX) to significantly improve rendering speeds compared to using the CPU.
3. **Eevee Settings**: If you're using Eevee, Blender will automatically use your GPU, but you can still tweak the performance settings for better results in real-time previews.

Testing Your Installation

To verify that Blender is working correctly, you can create a simple project. A great starting point is rendering the default cube:

1. **Open Blender** and use the default scene, which includes a cube, a light, and a camera.
2. Press `F12` to render the image. If the render completes without errors, you can be confident that Blender is installed correctly and that your system meets the necessary requirements.
3. **Save Your Render**: To save the rendered image, click `Image > Save As` in the render window.

Updating Blender

Blender's development is rapid, and new versions are released approximately every three months. It is essential to keep Blender updated to take advantage of the latest features and performance improvements.

- **Automatic Updates**: Blender does not include an automatic update feature in the application, so you will need to download updates from the Blender website manually.
- **Multiple Versions**: You can have multiple versions of Blender installed simultaneously. This can be useful if you want to test new features in the latest version while maintaining stability in a production environment using an older, well-tested version.

Troubleshooting Common Installation Issues

Missing DLL Files on Windows

A common issue on Windows systems is missing DLL files, particularly when Blender depends on certain Microsoft Visual C++ Redistributable packages. If you encounter an error indicating that a DLL file is missing, download and install the appropriate version of the Microsoft Visual C++ Redistributable from Microsoft's website.

Permissions on Linux

Linux users might face issues related to file permissions, especially when trying to execute the Blender binary. Make sure the executable has the correct permissions:

```
chmod +x blender
```

Additionally, ensure that you have installed the necessary graphics drivers for your system. The open-source drivers included in many distributions may not provide the best performance, especially for rendering tasks, so installing proprietary drivers from NVIDIA or AMD might be necessary.

macOS Security Restrictions

macOS users might face issues with security restrictions when launching Blender for the first time. To bypass this, you can go to `System Preferences > Security & Privacy` and select "Open Anyway" after attempting to launch Blender. This will allow macOS to recognize Blender as a trusted application.

Conclusion

Installing Blender is a relatively simple process, but configuring your system to get the best performance out of Blender can make a world of difference. From understanding the system requirements to customizing your preferences, each step plays a crucial role in ensuring that you have the best experience possible when working with Blender.

Blender's strength lies not only in its powerful tools but also in its flexibility and accessibility. By taking the time to properly install and set up Blender, you are setting the foundation for a rewarding journey into the world of 3D graphics, animation, and beyond. Whether you're creating stunning visuals, intricate models, or engaging animations, Blender is a tool that can bring your ideas to life—all starting with the right setup.

Navigating Blender's Interface

Blender's interface can be intimidating at first glance, but once you become familiar with its layout and navigation controls, it becomes an intuitive and powerful environment for 3D content creation. This section will guide you through Blender's interface, explain its major components, and provide useful tips on how to effectively navigate within Blender. Understanding the interface is foundational, as every action—from modeling to animation—requires working efficiently within Blender's various editors and panels.

Overview of Blender's Interface

Blender's interface is composed of different sections called **editors**, each serving a specific purpose. The layout is designed to provide a flexible workspace, which can be customized based on the task at hand, whether it's modeling, animation, texturing, or rendering. The interface is organized into the following primary components:

1. **Topbar**: The topmost section of Blender includes the main menu, tool settings, and quick access to different workspaces.

2. **Info Editor**: Below the Topbar, you'll find menus for managing files, rendering, and editing preferences.
3. **3D Viewport**: This is the main workspace where you interact with and manipulate your 3D models.
4. **Sidebar and Tool Shelf**: On the left side of the 3D Viewport is the tool shelf, and on the right side, you have the sidebar, which provides additional settings.
5. **Outliner**: This panel shows the hierarchical structure of your scene, listing all objects within it.
6. **Properties Editor**: Located typically on the right, the Properties Editor allows you to access and modify settings for objects, materials, textures, and rendering.
7. **Timeline**: The Timeline at the bottom is primarily used for animation, displaying keyframes and providing playback controls.
8. **Additional Editors**: Blender also includes other specialized editors, such as the Shader Editor, Image Editor, Video Sequence Editor, and Node Editor, each serving a distinct purpose.

The default workspace layout contains a combination of these editors that are most commonly used. However, Blender allows you to customize and save your own workspaces depending on your workflow preferences.

Workspaces in Blender

Blender comes with several **predefined workspaces** designed for different tasks, such as Layout, Modeling, Sculpting, Shading, Animation, and Rendering. You can switch between workspaces using the tabs at the top of the interface. Each workspace is a collection of editors configured to streamline a specific part of the 3D creation pipeline.

For example:

- **Layout Workspace**: This workspace is for basic scene management and object interaction.
- **Modeling Workspace**: It has additional editors such as the Modifiers panel and focuses on tools useful for 3D modeling.
- **Shading Workspace**: This workspace includes a Shader Editor for working with materials and textures, alongside the 3D Viewport.
- **Animation Workspace**: This layout emphasizes the Timeline and Graph Editor, making it easier to create and adjust animations.

The flexibility to switch between different workspaces helps streamline the 3D creation process, as each workspace has tools relevant to the specific stage of your workflow.

Navigating the 3D Viewport

The **3D Viewport** is the heart of Blender, where you spend most of your time interacting with your scene. Navigating the viewport efficiently is crucial, and Blender provides several methods for doing so:

Orbiting, Panning, and Zooming

- **Orbit**: You can orbit around your scene by holding down the middle mouse button (MMB) and dragging. If you're using a trackpad, two-finger dragging usually achieves the same effect.
- **Pan**: To pan the view, hold down `Shift` + MMB and drag the mouse. Panning allows you to move the camera view up, down, left, or right.
- **Zoom**: Scrolling the mouse wheel will zoom in and out. You can also zoom by holding `Ctrl` and pressing MMB, then moving the mouse.

Alternatively, you can use the **Numpad** to navigate the 3D Viewport:

- **Numpad 1**: Front view
- **Numpad 3**: Right view
- **Numpad 7**: Top view
- **Numpad 5**: Toggle between orthographic and perspective view
- **Numpad 0**: Camera view

For users without a Numpad, Blender provides an option to emulate the Numpad in the Preferences under `Edit > Preferences > Input`.

Viewport Shading Modes

Blender's 3D Viewport has several **shading modes** that change the way objects are displayed:

- **Wireframe**: Shows only the edges of objects. This is useful when modeling, as it allows you to see through and manipulate geometry more easily.
- **Solid**: Displays the objects as shaded solids without any lighting effects.
- **Material Preview**: Displays the objects with the applied materials and lighting, using Eevee in real-time. This is great for getting a quick preview of your materials.
- **Rendered**: Shows a fully rendered view of your scene using either Eevee or Cycles. This mode provides a realistic preview, including lighting, shadows, and materials.

You can switch between these modes using the icons in the top-right corner of the 3D Viewport or by pressing `Z` to bring up a shading pie menu.

Understanding Editors and Their Functionality

Blender is composed of multiple **editors**, each with a specialized role. Let's dive into some of the commonly used editors that form the interface.

3D Viewport

The **3D Viewport** is the editor where all the magic happens. Whether you're modeling, sculpting, animating, or rendering, the 3D Viewport is where you interact with your scene. Here are some key aspects of working in the 3D Viewport:

- **Object Mode and Edit Mode**: By default, Blender starts in Object Mode, where you can select, move, and transform entire objects. To modify the geometry of an object, switch to **Edit Mode** by pressing Tab. In Edit Mode, you can select vertices, edges, and faces to make changes to your mesh.

- **Transform Tools**: The 3D Viewport includes several basic transform tools, such as **Move (G)**, **Rotate (R)**, and **Scale (S)**. You can constrain these transformations along specific axes by pressing X, Y, or Z after initiating the transformation.

Outliner

The **Outliner** editor displays all objects in your scene as a hierarchical list. It allows you to:

- **Select and Hide**: Click on objects in the Outliner to select them, or click the eye icon to hide/unhide objects.
- **Organize**: You can rename objects, group them into collections, or even parent objects to organize complex scenes.
- **Filter**: The filter options in the Outliner make it easy to locate specific types of objects, such as lights or cameras.

The Outliner is especially useful when managing large scenes with many objects, as it allows you to keep track of everything in your project.

Properties Editor

The **Properties Editor** is located on the right side of the interface and contains tabs for managing object properties, material settings, modifiers, and render settings. Here are some of the key sections:

- **Object Properties**: This tab allows you to modify the object's location, rotation, and scale, as well as set object visibility.
- **Material Properties**: This is where you create and adjust materials for your objects, using Blender's powerful node-based shader system.
- **Modifiers**: Blender's **Modifiers** are non-destructive tools that allow you to modify objects without permanently altering their geometry. For example, you can use a **Subdivision Surface** modifier to add extra detail to a model, or a **Boolean** modifier to cut or combine objects.

Timeline and Animation Editors

At the bottom of the default interface is the **Timeline** editor. This is primarily used for animation:

- **Playhead**: The playhead is the red line in the Timeline that indicates the current frame.
- **Keyframes**: You can insert keyframes by selecting an object, pressing I, and choosing which property to keyframe, such as location, rotation, or scale. Keyframes are displayed as diamonds on the Timeline.

In addition to the Timeline, Blender has other animation editors, such as the **Graph Editor** and the **Dope Sheet**, which allow for more refined control over animations and keyframe interpolation.

Customizing Blender's Interface

Blender's interface is highly **customizable**, allowing you to adapt it to your workflow. You can split or join editors, create custom workspaces, and save those as defaults.

Splitting and Joining Editors

- **Split an Editor**: Move your cursor to the corner of any editor until it turns into a crosshair, then click and drag to split the editor into two.
- **Join Editors**: To merge two editors, drag one editor's corner over the other until the arrow changes direction, then release.

This flexibility means you can create as many editor windows as you need, giving you complete control over your workspace. For example, you might want to have both the 3D Viewport and the Shader Editor open simultaneously while working on materials.

Custom Workspaces

Blender comes with pre-configured workspaces, but you can also create your own:

1. **Create a New Workspace**: Click the + button in the workspace tabs at the top, and choose "General > New Workspace."
2. **Customize the Layout**: Arrange editors as needed by splitting or joining them, and then save the layout.
3. **Save Startup File**: If you want Blender to always open with your custom workspace, go to `File > Defaults > Save Startup File`.

Custom workspaces can significantly speed up your workflow by allowing you to switch between specialized setups for different tasks.

Quick Access Tools and Shortcuts

Blender's interface offers several **shortcuts and quick access tools** to improve efficiency:

- **Search Function**: Press `F3` (or `Space` depending on your settings) to bring up the **search menu**. This allows you to search for any operation, making it much easier to find tools without having to browse through menus.
- **Pie Menus**: Pie menus are radial context menus that can be accessed with shortcuts like `Z` (Shading Mode), `Shift + S` (Snap), or `Ctrl + Tab` (Switch Mode). Pie menus make selecting options faster and more intuitive compared to linear menus.
- **Tool Shelf and Sidebar**: On the left side of the 3D Viewport, you'll find the **Tool Shelf**, which contains commonly used tools like Move, Rotate, and Scale. The right side contains the **Sidebar**, which shows contextual information about selected objects, including transform values and custom properties.

Learning Blender's shortcuts is essential to becoming proficient with the software, as it drastically reduces the time spent navigating menus and panels.

Blender Preferences

Blender's **Preferences** can be accessed by navigating to `Edit > Preferences`. Here you can adjust a variety of settings to customize Blender's interface and functionality to suit your needs.

- **Keymap**: You can modify **keyboard shortcuts** to suit your workflow. Blender comes with several keymaps, including an industry-compatible keymap for users coming from other 3D software.
- **Add-ons**: The Add-ons tab allows you to enable or disable various plugins that extend Blender's capabilities. Some essential add-ons, such as **LoopTools** and **Node Wrangler**, come pre-installed with Blender and can be activated here.

Conclusion

Understanding Blender's interface and becoming comfortable navigating it is key to making the most out of the software. The 3D Viewport, the Outliner, the Properties Editor, and other essential editors form the foundation for creating in Blender. Blender's flexibility in workspace customization, combined with a plethora of shortcuts and quick-access menus, ensures that you can configure the interface to suit your specific needs and workflow.

Investing time in understanding the interface, workspaces, and navigation controls will pay off greatly as you move forward in your Blender journey. Whether you are modeling, animating, texturing, or rendering, an efficient workflow starts with a thorough understanding of the tools at your disposal and how to navigate them with ease.

Chapter 2: Understanding the Basics

Blender's Workflow: An Overview

Blender's workflow is a critical aspect of becoming proficient in the software. Understanding how the various components of Blender work together will significantly improve your ability to create complex and visually impressive projects. In this section, we'll explore Blender's workflow from a high-level perspective, covering everything from modeling to rendering. We'll also discuss how these components interconnect, creating a seamless process from conception to the final output.

Understanding the Blender Workflow

Blender's workflow is a flexible and versatile process that allows artists to transform ideas into fully realized digital projects. It encompasses several phases, including modeling, texturing, lighting, animation, and rendering. Each phase requires different tools and techniques, and Blender integrates these elements in a way that encourages both exploration and precision.

To begin with, it's helpful to have a general understanding of the major components of Blender's workflow:

1. **Modeling**: The first step in most 3D projects involves creating the shapes and structures that form your scene. This may include organic models like characters or hard-surface models like buildings or vehicles.
2. **Texturing and Materials**: Once the models are created, the next step is to add materials and textures to give them a realistic or stylized appearance. This can be accomplished using Blender's material and UV mapping tools.
3. **Lighting**: Lighting can dramatically affect the look of your scene. Whether it's a natural sunlight look or a dramatic studio light setup, Blender's lighting tools provide the flexibility needed to achieve your desired effect.
4. **Animation**: If your project involves movement, animation tools come into play. Animation in Blender can involve simple keyframing or more complex rigging and physics-based simulations.
5. **Rendering**. Finally, rendering is where everything comes together. Blender has powerful rendering engines like Cycles and Eevee, each with their strengths depending on the needs of the project.
6. **Compositing and Post-Processing**: After rendering, compositing allows you to adjust elements like color balance, add effects, or perform other types of post-production tasks.

These steps are interconnected, and a typical Blender artist will move back and forth between them frequently. For example, changes to the lighting setup might necessitate modifications in the materials or even the models themselves.

Blender's Non-Linear Workflow

A significant advantage of Blender is its non-linear workflow. Unlike some other applications where you need to follow a rigid sequence, Blender allows you to move fluidly between different stages of the project. This means you can start with simple shapes, add basic lighting to understand how the scene reads, and refine details in any order as the project progresses.

Example: Iterating with Blender's Workflow

Consider a simple example of creating a 3D character. You might start by sculpting the basic form of the character using Blender's sculpting tools. At this stage, you're focused purely on the shape and silhouette without worrying too much about fine details. Once you're happy with the overall shape, you might switch to a more precise mesh editing mode to add finer details, such as facial features.

After refining the character model, you might move to texturing. This step involves using Blender's UV mapping tools to unwrap the character's mesh so you can apply image textures or procedural materials. As you start to texture the model, you might realize that the lighting setup isn't highlighting your textures effectively. Instead of waiting until later to solve this, you can immediately switch to lighting and make adjustments.

This ability to freely move between modeling, texturing, lighting, and other phases is what makes Blender so powerful. It allows for iterative improvements and ensures that changes can be made without disrupting the entire project.

Blender's Interface and How It Supports Workflow

Blender's interface is designed to support a seamless workflow. It includes various editors that are specialized for different tasks, and understanding how to navigate between these editors efficiently is crucial for maintaining productivity.

The key editors in Blender include:

1. **3D Viewport**: This is where you'll spend most of your time, whether you're modeling, animating, or sculpting. The 3D Viewport provides visual feedback on the elements you're working on, making it the center of Blender's workflow.
2. **Shader Editor**: When working with materials, the Shader Editor is where you'll create and fine-tune the nodes that define the appearance of your surfaces.
3. **UV Editor**: This editor is used during texturing to unwrap models and create UV maps. Proper UV mapping is essential for applying textures accurately.
4. **Animation Editors**: Blender includes several editors for animation, including the Dope Sheet and Graph Editor. These tools allow you to control keyframes and animations precisely, ensuring that movements are smooth and realistic.
5. **Timeline**: The Timeline editor provides a straightforward way to control animation sequences. You can easily navigate between keyframes, making it simpler to refine animations.
6. **Compositor**: The Compositor is used for post-processing. You can add effects, perform color correction, and create final tweaks before rendering the final output.

These editors are not isolated. Blender allows you to split your workspace into multiple areas so that you can have, for example, the 3D Viewport and Shader Editor open simultaneously. This setup helps facilitate the iterative workflow that Blender encourages.

Key Concepts in Blender's Workflow

Scenes and Collections

Blender projects are organized into **scenes** and **collections**. A scene is a complete environment, which can include objects, cameras, lights, and other elements. You might have multiple scenes in a single Blender file for different shots or different stages of a project.

Collections, on the other hand, are used to organize the elements within a scene. Think of collections as folders. They make it easier to manage complex projects by grouping similar objects together. For example, you might have separate collections for "Environment," "Characters," and "Props." Collections can be turned on or off in the viewport and during rendering, making them invaluable for focusing on specific parts of your scene without distraction.

Object Modes

Blender features various **object modes** that support different stages of the workflow. Some of the most important ones include:

- **Object Mode**: Used for positioning, scaling, and rotating entire objects.
- **Edit Mode**: Used for detailed modeling work, such as editing vertices, edges, and faces.
- **Sculpt Mode**: Ideal for organic modeling where you push and pull the mesh to create smooth shapes.
- **Pose Mode**: Used for rigging and animating characters. Once a rig (or skeleton) is in place, Pose Mode allows you to manipulate the bones to create animation sequences.

Switching between these modes is quick, and each mode provides specialized tools to help you accomplish the task at hand efficiently.

Transform Tools and Shortcuts

Mastering Blender's transform tools is crucial for an efficient workflow. These tools include:

- **Grab (G)**: Moves an object or vertex around.
- **Rotate (R)**: Rotates the selected object or elements.
- **Scale (S)**: Scales an object or component up or down.

Blender relies heavily on keyboard shortcuts to speed up the workflow. For example:

- Pressing **G**, **R**, or **S** in the 3D Viewport lets you grab, rotate, or scale the selected object respectively.
- **Shift + D** duplicates objects.

- **Ctrl + Z** undoes the last action.

Blender's extensive use of shortcuts is one of the keys to a fast and efficient workflow, and taking the time to learn these shortcuts can dramatically improve productivity.

Practical Tips for a Smooth Workflow

Setting Up Custom Workspaces

Blender allows you to create **custom workspaces** that are tailored to different tasks. For instance, you might set up a workspace specifically for modeling, with a large 3D Viewport, an outliner, and a smaller shader editor. Another workspace might be tailored for animation, with the Timeline editor, Dope Sheet, and 3D Viewport all easily accessible.

To create a new workspace, you can start from an existing template and then split or join areas to fit your preferences. These custom workspaces can be saved as part of your default startup file, so they're available every time you open Blender.

Using Add-ons for Workflow Efficiency

Blender's open-source nature means that it has a thriving community creating add-ons to enhance its capabilities. Some of these add-ons can significantly streamline your workflow. For example:

- **LoopTools**: Adds a set of tools for easier mesh modeling, such as bridge, curve, and flatten tools.
- **Node Wrangler**: A must-have when working with materials, Node Wrangler provides shortcuts for connecting nodes and creating more complex shader networks faster.
- **BlenderKit**: Provides an extensive library of free assets, including materials, models, and HDRs, to jump-start your projects.

To enable these add-ons, go to **Edit > Preferences > Add-ons** and search for the tools you need.

Iterative Workflow: Blocking Out First

For most projects, it's a good idea to start by blocking out the basic shapes before focusing on details. This iterative approach allows you to test proportions, composition, and camera angles early, making it easier to make changes before you get too deep into the finer aspects of modeling and texturing.

For example, if you're working on an interior scene, start by creating simple boxes to represent walls, furniture, and other large elements. You can quickly adjust the layout and make sure everything fits together visually. Once you're satisfied with the composition, you can move on to adding details like bevels, materials, and lighting.

Saving and Versioning

Because Blender projects can become complex very quickly, it's crucial to save often and maintain versions of your project. Blender has an **incremental save** feature that allows you to quickly create numbered versions of your file by pressing **Ctrl + Shift + S** and adding a new version number. This helps you to go back to a previous state if you decide that recent changes aren't working.

Another option for version control is integrating Blender with Git. While Git is traditionally used for code, it can also be very effective for managing the incremental progress of Blender projects, especially if multiple artists are working on the same project.

Conclusion

Blender's workflow is a dynamic and iterative process, encompassing several stages such as modeling, texturing, lighting, and rendering. Each of these stages requires different tools, and Blender's user-friendly interface and non-linear capabilities make it possible to navigate between them fluidly.

By understanding the overarching structure of Blender's workflow and familiarizing yourself with the various editors and modes, you can dramatically improve your efficiency and produce high-quality work. Customizing workspaces, making use of shortcuts, and leveraging the power of add-ons are all effective ways to make your time in Blender more productive.

Ultimately, the key to mastering Blender's workflow is practice. The more you experiment with the different stages of a project, the more comfortable and proficient you will become. Whether you're blocking out basic shapes, fine-tuning shaders, or creating complex animations, Blender provides a versatile set of tools that can adapt to your needs.

Essential Tools and Functions

Blender provides a variety of essential tools and functions that form the foundation for all creative work within the software. Mastering these tools will enable you to efficiently perform tasks such as modeling, sculpting, texturing, animating, and rendering. In this section, we will go through some of Blender's core tools, including basic manipulation tools, selection techniques, and specialized functions that are crucial for any Blender project.

Blender's Transform Tools

Blender's transform tools are some of the most fundamental and commonly used tools. These tools allow you to move, rotate, and scale objects or specific parts of an object. They provide precise control over the placement and orientation of elements in your scene, allowing you to build complex models and arrange objects to achieve your desired look.

The transform tools are:

1. **Grab (G)**: Moves the selected object or vertex freely in the 3D space.
2. **Rotate (R)**: Rotates the selected element about an axis.
3. **Scale (S)**: Changes the size of the selected object or component.

You can access these tools using their respective hotkeys (**G**, **R**, and **S**), or you can use the tool icons in the left-hand toolbar of the 3D Viewport.

Moving, Rotating, and Scaling Along Axes

One of the most powerful features of Blender's transform tools is the ability to constrain transformations along specific axes. For example, if you want to move an object only along the X-axis, you can press **G** and then **X**. Similarly, pressing **R** followed by **Z** will rotate the object about the Z-axis, and pressing **S** followed by **Y** will scale the object along the Y-axis.

You can also combine axis constraints. For instance, pressing **G** followed by **Shift + Z** will move an object only along the X and Y axes, constraining movement along the Z-axis.

Precision Modeling with Snapping

Blender includes powerful **snapping** tools that allow you to align objects and vertices precisely. Snapping is useful when you need to position objects relative to each other or align elements in a highly accurate manner. To enable snapping, click the magnet icon in the 3D Viewport toolbar or press **Shift + Tab**.

Blender provides several snapping options, such as:

- **Vertex Snapping**: Snap to the vertices of other objects.
- **Edge Snapping**: Snap to the edges of objects.
- **Face Snapping**: Snap to the faces of other objects.
- **Increment Snapping**: Snap to grid increments for precise movement.

You can also adjust snapping settings to align rotation or scale transformations, making it easy to create perfectly aligned models and achieve professional-grade precision.

Selection Tools

Selecting elements in Blender is one of the first skills you need to master. Whether you are dealing with whole objects or working in **Edit Mode** to adjust vertices, edges, or faces, effective selection is essential.

Basic Selection Techniques

- **Left-Click Select**: By default, you can use the left mouse button to select objects or components.
- **Box Select (B)**: Press **B** and then click and drag to draw a box around the elements you wish to select.
- **Circle Select (C)**: Press **C** to enter a selection mode where you can "paint" over elements to select them.
- **Lasso Select (Ctrl + Left-Click Drag)**: You can also use the lasso selection tool by pressing **Ctrl** and dragging with the left mouse button.

Advanced Selection Techniques

- **Selecting Linked (L)**: In **Edit Mode**, pressing **L** while hovering over a mesh will select all linked vertices, edges, or faces. This is helpful for selecting entire parts of a mesh that are connected.
- **Select Similar (Shift + G)**: You can select elements with similar properties, such as selecting all vertices that share the same bevel weight. This can be accessed by pressing **Shift + G**.
- **Edge Loops and Rings**: Pressing **Alt + Left-Click** on an edge will select an edge loop, while **Ctrl + Alt + Left-Click** will select an edge ring. These tools are useful for quickly selecting large areas of a mesh for editing.

The **3D Cursor** is another powerful tool for selection and positioning. You can position the 3D Cursor anywhere in the scene by left-clicking, and then use it as a reference point for various operations, such as object transformations and adding new objects.

Edit Mode Tools

Edit Mode is where you modify the internal components of a mesh, such as vertices, edges, and faces. It's a critical part of the modeling workflow, allowing you to create detailed shapes and refine your models. Below are some of the essential Edit Mode tools that you'll need to master for effective modeling.

Extrude Tool (E)

The **Extrude** tool is one of the most commonly used tools in Edit Mode. It allows you to create new geometry by extending existing faces or edges. To use the extrude tool, select a face or edge and press **E**. You can then move the new geometry in the desired direction.

For example, if you have a cube and you select one of its faces, you can press **E** to extend that face outward, effectively adding a new section to your model.

Inset Faces (I)

The **Inset** tool allows you to create a new face within an existing face, effectively adding an edge loop that outlines the shape. To use the inset tool, select a face and press **I**. You can then adjust the size of the inset to create a smaller, concentric face within the original.

This is especially useful for creating details like window frames or control panels on your models.

Loop Cut (Ctrl + R)

The **Loop Cut** tool adds edge loops around your mesh, allowing you to divide the geometry for further editing. This is an essential tool for adding detail to models, as it creates new vertices, edges, and faces that you can manipulate.

To use the Loop Cut tool, press **Ctrl + R** and hover over your mesh. You will see a preview of the cut, which you can then confirm and move to your desired location.

```python
# Loop Cut Example in Python API (bpy)
import bpy

# Create a new cube
bpy.ops.mesh.primitive_cube_add()

# Enter edit mode
bpy.ops.object.editmode_toggle()

# Add a loop cut
bpy.ops.mesh.loopcut_slide(MESH_OT_loopcut={"number_cuts": 1,
"smoothness": 0},
                           TRANSFORM_OT_edge_slide={"value": 0.5})
```

Knife Tool (K)

The **Knife** tool allows you to cut new edges into your mesh, which can be used to create custom shapes and add detail. To use the knife tool, press **K** and then click on the points where you want to make cuts. Once you're satisfied with the cuts, press **Enter** to confirm.

The Knife tool is excellent for adding geometry precisely where you need it, especially in organic models or when creating custom cuts that don't align with the existing edge loops.

Proportional Editing

Proportional Editing is a feature that allows you to move, scale, or rotate a selection while affecting nearby geometry in a smooth, proportional manner. This tool is particularly useful for creating organic shapes and making natural-looking deformations.

To enable Proportional Editing, click the circular icon in the 3D Viewport toolbar or press **O**. You can then adjust the influence radius using the scroll wheel, controlling how much of the surrounding geometry is affected.

For example, if you are modeling a landscape, you can use Proportional Editing to create rolling hills by selecting and moving individual vertices while smoothly adjusting the surrounding area.

Modifiers: Non-Destructive Modeling

Modifiers are powerful tools that allow you to apply non-destructive changes to your models. They let you add detail, deform shapes, and automate repetitive tasks without permanently altering the underlying geometry.

Some essential modifiers include:

- **Subdivision Surface**: Adds smoothness and detail to your model by subdividing its geometry. This is commonly used for organic shapes like characters and animals.
- **Mirror Modifier**: Allows you to mirror geometry across an axis, making it easy to create symmetrical models like characters or vehicles.
- **Array Modifier**: Creates duplicates of an object in a specified pattern. This is useful for creating things like railings, fences, or repetitive architectural features.

Sculpting Tools

Blender's **Sculpt Mode** provides tools for creating organic models by "sculpting" the mesh as if it were digital clay. Sculpt Mode is ideal for characters and other organic shapes where smooth, flowing surfaces are necessary.

Some of the key sculpting brushes include:

- **Draw Brush**: Adds volume to the mesh by "drawing" on the surface.
- **Crease Brush**: Creates creases and folds, useful for detailing things like skin or fabric.
- **Smooth Brush**: Smooths out the surface of the mesh, making it useful for refining the shape after other sculpting operations.

Sculpt Mode also includes advanced features like **Dynamic Topology**, which adds geometry dynamically as you sculpt, allowing you to create intricate details without worrying about the underlying topology.

Material and Shading Tools

Blender's material and shading tools are essential for giving your models their final appearance. The **Shader Editor** allows you to create complex materials using a node-based system, giving you the ability to create everything from basic colors to realistic metals, glass, and more.

Assigning Materials

To assign a material to an object, first, select the object in the 3D Viewport and then navigate to the **Material Properties** tab in the properties panel. Click **New** to create a new material and assign it to your object.

You can adjust basic properties like color, roughness, and metallic values to create a wide variety of materials. For more advanced effects, you can use the Shader Editor to create custom node networks.

```python
# Example: Assigning a material using Python API
import bpy

# Create a new material
material = bpy.data.materials.new(name="NewMaterial")
```

```
material.diffuse_color = (0.8, 0.1, 0.1, 1)  # Red color

# Assign material to the active object
bpy.context.object.data.materials.append(material)
```

Using the Outliner and Collections

The **Outliner** is a hierarchical view of all the objects in your Blender scene. It allows you to quickly find, select, and organize objects. By using **Collections**, you can group related objects together, making it easier to manage large projects.

For example, in a scene with multiple characters, props, and environment assets, you can create separate collections for each type of object. This not only helps in organizing your project but also allows you to hide, select, or isolate entire groups of objects at once.

Practical Example: Creating a Simple Scene

To bring together many of the tools and functions discussed in this section, let's go through a simple practical example of creating a basic room scene.

1. **Create the Walls**: Start by adding a cube to the scene (**Shift + A > Mesh > Cube**). Scale it along the X and Y axes to form the basic shape of the room. Use **Edit Mode** to delete the top face, creating an open box.
2. **Add a Table**: Add another cube and scale it to form a tabletop. Use the **Extrude** tool to create legs for the table. You can use the **Mirror Modifier** to make sure all legs are identical.
3. **Add a Chair**: Similar to the table, create a chair by scaling a cube. Use the **Inset** and **Extrude** tools to add details like the backrest and seat.
4. **Add Lighting**: Add a point light to the scene and position it above the table. Adjust its **Strength** and **Radius** in the light properties panel to achieve a soft, warm light.
5. **Assign Materials**: Create a wood material in the **Shader Editor** and assign it to the table and chair. Use a different color for the walls to differentiate them from the furniture.
6. **Arrange Using Snapping**: Enable **Vertex Snapping** to make sure the chair is positioned correctly relative to the table. This ensures that all elements in the scene are properly aligned.
7. **Rendering the Scene**: Switch to **Rendered View** in the 3D Viewport to preview how the scene looks with materials and lighting. Once satisfied, configure the render settings and render an image using the **Render** menu.

Conclusion

The tools and functions in Blender are designed to provide a balance of precision, flexibility, and speed. Mastering these essential tools, from transform and selection techniques to advanced features like modifiers and sculpting, will enable you to tackle a wide variety of projects with confidence. By understanding how these tools fit into Blender's broader workflow, you can create compelling 3D models and scenes that bring your creative visions to life.

Mastering the 3D Viewport

The 3D Viewport is at the core of your work in Blender—it's where you create, modify, and visualize your models and scenes. It is one of the most critical parts of the Blender interface and understanding how to effectively navigate and use it is essential for maximizing productivity and achieving high-quality results. In this section, we will explore how to master the 3D Viewport by discussing navigation techniques, view modes, overlays, shading options, and the use of specialized tools.

Navigating the 3D Viewport

Effective navigation is key to efficiently modeling and working in Blender. The 3D Viewport allows you to see your models and scenes from different angles and distances, enabling you to make precise adjustments. There are several navigation tools that you need to master to fully harness the potential of Blender's Viewport.

Orbiting, Panning, and Zooming

- **Orbiting (Middle Mouse Button)**: By pressing and holding the **Middle Mouse Button (MMB)**, you can orbit around the selected object or the scene. This is essential for getting a better view of your model from different angles.
- **Panning (Shift + MMB)**: To move the view side-to-side or up-and-down, hold **Shift** and drag with the **Middle Mouse Button**. Panning helps you to navigate through large scenes and focus on different areas without changing the camera angle.
- **Zooming (Scroll Wheel)**: To zoom in and out of the scene, you can use the mouse **Scroll Wheel**. You can also hold **Ctrl** and drag with the **Middle Mouse Button** to zoom more precisely. Zooming is crucial when you need to focus on small details or get an overview of a larger scene.

These three functions—orbiting, panning, and zooming—form the foundation of 3D navigation, and mastering them will make working in Blender much more intuitive.

Navigation Gizmo and Shortcuts

Blender also features a **Navigation Gizmo** in the top right corner of the 3D Viewport. The gizmo provides a visual reference for the orientation of your scene, and you can click on the different axis handles (X, Y, Z) to quickly align the view to those axes.

Additionally, Blender provides useful shortcuts for aligning the view:

- **Numpad 1**: Front view
- **Numpad 3**: Right view
- **Numpad 7**: Top view
- **Numpad 5**: Toggles between orthographic and perspective view
- **Numpad 0**: Camera view

These shortcuts are invaluable when you need to work from specific angles, such as when modeling symmetric objects or precisely positioning elements.

View Modes

Blender's 3D Viewport offers several **View Modes** that allow you to visualize your scene in different ways. Each view mode has a specific purpose and is suited for different stages of the modeling process.

Wireframe Mode

Wireframe Mode displays only the edges of the models without any surfaces, making it easier to see through objects and view overlapping geometry. This is particularly useful when selecting or editing complex meshes, as it allows you to see all of the geometry at once.

To switch to Wireframe Mode, press **Z** and select **Wireframe**, or you can use the **Viewport Shading** dropdown in the top right corner of the 3D Viewport.

Solid Mode

Solid Mode is the default view mode in Blender. It shows the surfaces of your models with basic shading, allowing you to easily perceive the form and volume of objects. Solid Mode is ideal for general modeling tasks and assessing the shape and structure of your models.

In Solid Mode, Blender can also display the normals and shading differences, helping you evaluate the smoothness of the surfaces and identify any issues such as flipped normals.

Material Preview Mode

Material Preview Mode allows you to preview how materials and textures look on your models without doing a full render. It's an excellent way to see the effects of lighting, textures, and material properties in real-time. This mode uses the **Eevee** render engine to provide a high-quality preview that balances performance with visual fidelity.

Rendered Mode

Rendered Mode shows a fully rendered view of the scene using the active render engine, either **Eevee** or **Cycles**. This mode is useful for getting an accurate preview of how the final render will look, including lighting, shadows, and reflections. However, Rendered Mode can be resource-intensive, especially when using the Cycles render engine, which is why it's often used for final checks rather than continuous modeling.

Shading and Overlays

Blender offers several shading options and overlays that enhance the visibility and help you work efficiently within the 3D Viewport. Understanding how to use these tools effectively will greatly improve your workflow.

Shading Options

The **Shading Options** in the 3D Viewport toolbar provide control over how objects are displayed in Solid Mode. You can access different shading properties such as **MatCap** and **Cavity**.

- **MatCap**: MatCap (Material Capture) is a shading method that uses predefined lighting setups to make it easier to see the form of your model. This is particularly helpful when sculpting, as it highlights details like creases and bumps.
- **Cavity**: The **Cavity** option enhances the visibility of creases and edges on the model, making it easier to identify fine details. Cavity shading is especially useful when working with detailed models or during sculpting, as it gives a better sense of depth and volume.

Viewport Overlays

Overlays are additional visual elements that help you understand what's happening in the 3D Viewport. You can toggle overlays on and off using the **Overlays** button in the top right of the 3D Viewport.

Some common overlays include:

- **Wireframe Overlay**: Displays the wireframe on top of the solid geometry, making it easier to see the underlying structure.
- **Face Orientation**: This overlay is used to visualize the orientation of faces. It helps identify flipped normals, where the front and back sides of faces are incorrectly oriented.
- **Normals Display**: You can also display **normals** to understand the direction each face is pointing. Normals are important for ensuring that shading, lighting, and other effects behave correctly on your model.

The 3D Cursor

The **3D Cursor** is a unique tool in Blender that serves as a reference point for a wide range of operations. Understanding how to effectively use the 3D Cursor can greatly speed up the modeling process and help you perform complex tasks with precision.

Positioning the 3D Cursor

To place the 3D Cursor in the 3D Viewport, simply left-click at the desired location. You can also manually position the 3D Cursor by entering its coordinates in the **3D Cursor** section of the **N-panel** (press **N** to open the panel).

The 3D Cursor can be used as the pivot point for transformations, the location for adding new objects, or the reference for certain alignment operations. Mastering the 3D Cursor will allow you to position objects with precision and perform operations that are otherwise cumbersome.

Practical Uses of the 3D Cursor

One common use of the 3D Cursor is setting the **origin point** of an object. By placing the 3D Cursor at a specific location and then setting the origin of the object to the cursor, you can easily define how the object behaves during transformations.

Another use is when adding new objects. Instead of always adding new objects to the center of the scene, you can position the 3D Cursor wherever you need and add the new geometry at that specific point, which is particularly useful for precise modeling tasks.

Using the Numpad for View Control

The **Numpad** is an essential tool for controlling the view in Blender, especially for those who need to work from specific orthographic views or control the camera view with precision. Here is a summary of useful Numpad shortcuts:

- **Numpad 1**: Front view
- **Ctrl + Numpad 1**: Back view
- **Numpad 3**: Right view
- **Ctrl + Numpad 3**: Left view
- **Numpad 7**: Top view
- **Ctrl + Numpad 7**: Bottom view
- **Numpad 5**: Toggles between perspective and orthographic views
- **Numpad 0**: Camera view

If you do not have a physical numpad, you can enable the **Numpad Emulation** option in the **Preferences** to use the standard number keys as a substitute.

Local and Global View

Local View allows you to isolate the selected object from the rest of the scene, making it easier to work on specific elements without distractions. This can be activated by pressing **Numpad / (Slash)**. When in Local View, all other objects are hidden, and you can focus on the selected object in full detail.

To exit Local View and return to the standard view with all objects visible, press **Numpad / (Slash)** again.

Camera Navigation in the Viewport

In Blender, the **Camera** is what ultimately defines the final view of your rendered scene. Navigating and positioning the camera can be challenging, but Blender provides several tools to make this easier.

Aligning the Camera to View

One useful feature is **Align Camera to View (Ctrl + Alt + Numpad 0)**, which positions the active camera to match your current viewport perspective. This is useful when you have found a good angle for your scene and want the camera to capture it.

Once the camera is aligned, you can use **G** (grab) to move the camera and **R** (rotate) to adjust the angle. You can also lock the camera to view by enabling **Lock Camera to View** in the **N-panel**. This allows you to navigate the viewport while keeping the camera view active, making it much easier to frame your scene.

View Layers and Collections

Blender uses **View Layers** and **Collections** to organize the scene and control the visibility of different elements. This system is highly effective for managing complex scenes with many objects, as it allows you to focus on specific parts of the scene without clutter.

Using Collections

Collections are like folders that contain objects. You can create new collections and move objects between them using the **M** key. Collections can be toggled on and off in the **Outliner**, which helps to declutter the viewport.

For example, if you are working on a character model that consists of the body, clothing, and accessories, you could create separate collections for each part. This way, you can work on the body without the distractions of the clothing and accessories, improving both performance and focus.

View Layers

View Layers work alongside collections to create different configurations of visibility for rendering. You can create multiple view layers that include different combinations of collections. This is particularly useful in complex projects where different elements need to be rendered separately, such as background, characters, and visual effects.

Clipping Border

When working on large scenes, it can be helpful to hide parts of the scene that you are not working on. Blender offers a feature called **Clipping Border** (**Alt + B**), which allows you to define a section of the scene to make visible while clipping everything else. This can make it much easier to focus on specific details without the distraction of other elements.

To define a clipping border, press **Alt + B** and drag to draw a rectangle around the area you want to keep visible. To clear the clipping border and make everything visible again, press **Alt + B** a second time.

Using the Pie Menus for Faster Navigation

Blender includes **Pie Menus**, which are radial menus that provide faster access to common tools and options. These menus are context-sensitive and help to streamline workflow by reducing the number of keystrokes needed to perform actions.

For example, pressing **Z** opens the **Shading Pie Menu**, where you can quickly switch between Wireframe, Solid, Material Preview, and Rendered modes. Similarly, pressing **Shift**

+ **S** opens the **Snap Pie Menu**, where you can set the 3D Cursor, snap the selection to the cursor, or align objects in the scene.

Pie menus are customizable, and many artists prefer them for their speed and efficiency. You can enable additional pie menus in the **Preferences** under the **Add-ons** tab.

Conclusion

The 3D Viewport is the heart of Blender, and mastering it is essential for efficient modeling, sculpting, texturing, and rendering. From understanding the navigation tools and view modes to using overlays, the 3D Cursor, and camera alignment techniques, the Viewport provides a rich set of features that can significantly enhance your productivity.

By taking full advantage of the Viewport's capabilities—such as using the numpad shortcuts, local view, collections, and clipping border—you can navigate through complex scenes with ease and create highly detailed and organized models. Becoming comfortable with the 3D Viewport is a crucial step on your journey to mastering Blender, and it will pay off immensely as your projects grow in complexity and scope.

The Basics of Object Manipulation

Object manipulation in Blender is one of the foundational skills that every 3D artist must master. It involves positioning, rotating, and scaling objects to create and arrange the elements in a scene. In this section, we'll cover the essential aspects of object manipulation, including transformation tools, pivot points, advanced snapping, and useful techniques for achieving precision in your projects.

Understanding Transformations: Move, Rotate, Scale

The three basic types of transformations in Blender are **Move (Grab)**, **Rotate**, and **Scale**. These operations allow you to adjust the position, orientation, and size of an object in 3D space. You can access these tools using the toolbar icons or by using their respective hotkeys:

- **Move (G)**: Moves the object along the X, Y, or Z axis.
- **Rotate (R)**: Rotates the object around a specified axis.
- **Scale (S)**: Changes the size of the object in a uniform or non-uniform manner.

Moving Objects

The **Move** tool, also called **Grab**, allows you to reposition objects within the 3D space. After selecting an object, press **G** to activate the Move tool. You can then move the object freely or constrain movement along a specific axis.

- **Axis Constraints**: To constrain movement along an axis, press **G** and then the desired axis key (**X**, **Y**, or **Z**). For example, pressing **G**, then **Z** will move the object only along the Z-axis.

- **Free Movement**: If you press **Shift** along with an axis key, the movement will be constrained to the two other axes. For example, pressing **G** followed by **Shift + Z** will move the object along the X and Y axes, while constraining movement along the Z-axis.

This level of control allows you to precisely position objects within your scene. Moving objects along specific axes is crucial for creating well-aligned models, whether it's architectural models or organic forms.

Rotating Objects

To **Rotate** an object, press **R**. By default, the object will rotate based on your viewport orientation, but you can also constrain rotation to a specific axis.

- **Rotation Around Axis**: Press **R** followed by an axis key (**X**, **Y**, or **Z**) to rotate the object around that axis. For example, pressing **R**, then **X** will rotate the object around the X-axis.
- **Two-Axis Rotation**: Similar to the Move tool, pressing **Shift** and an axis key allows you to exclude that axis from rotation. For example, **R + Shift + Z** will rotate the object in the X and Y axes while ignoring the Z-axis.

The **Rotate** tool is essential for orienting objects in the desired direction, whether you're setting up camera angles or adjusting elements in a mechanical assembly.

Scaling Objects

The **Scale** tool is activated by pressing **S**. You can scale objects uniformly or along specific axes:

- **Uniform Scaling**: Press **S** and move the mouse to scale the object uniformly along all axes.
- **Axis Constraints**: To scale along a specific axis, press **S** followed by an axis key (**X**, **Y**, or **Z**). For example, **S**, then **Y** will scale the object along the Y-axis only.

Scaling is useful for adjusting the proportions of objects, such as resizing a character's arm or stretching a building to the correct height.

Combining Transformations for Complex Manipulation

In most modeling workflows, you will use combinations of **Move**, **Rotate**, and **Scale** to create and refine your objects. For instance, if you are modeling a chair, you might start by adding a cube, scaling it to create the seat, and then adding more cubes for the legs and backrest, rotating and positioning them as needed.

Practical Example: Creating a Table

Let's go through a practical example of creating a simple table using basic transformations.

1. **Add the Tabletop**: Start by adding a **Cube** to the scene (**Shift + A > Mesh > Cube**). Scale the cube along the **X** and **Y** axes to create a flat rectangular tabletop.

- ○ Press **S**, then **X** to scale the cube along the X-axis.
- ○ Press **S**, then **Y** to scale along the Y-axis.
- ○ Finally, press **S**, then **Z** and scale down to make it flat.
2. **Add Table Legs**: Add another **Cube** and scale it to create one of the table legs. Use the **Move** tool (**G**) to position the leg under one corner of the tabletop. Then, duplicate the leg (**Shift + D**) and move it to the other corners.
    - ○ Use axis constraints while moving the legs to ensure they are positioned accurately.
3. **Refine the Layout**: Rotate and scale the legs as needed to create a balanced, realistic table. You can use the **Snap** function (explained below) to align the legs perfectly with the tabletop.

By using combinations of move, rotate, and scale, you can quickly create complex objects like furniture, machinery, or even entire environments.

Pivot Points and Their Importance

The **Pivot Point** determines the point around which transformations (like rotation and scaling) occur. By default, the pivot point is set to the **Median Point**, which is the center of the selected object or group of objects. However, Blender provides several pivot point options, each suitable for different modeling situations:

- **Median Point**: The default pivot point, located at the center of the selected objects.
- **3D Cursor**: Uses the 3D Cursor as the pivot point. This is useful for rotating or scaling objects around a custom point.
- **Individual Origins**: Allows each selected object to transform around its own origin. This is helpful when scaling multiple objects simultaneously without affecting their relative positions.
- **Active Element**: Uses the active element (the last selected object) as the pivot point.

To change the pivot point, use the dropdown menu in the 3D Viewport toolbar or press **Period (.)** to bring up the **Pivot Point** pie menu.

Using the 3D Cursor as a Pivot Point

The **3D Cursor** can be placed anywhere in the 3D Viewport and used as the pivot point for transformations. For example, if you want to rotate a door around its hinge, you can place the 3D Cursor at the hinge location and set it as the pivot point before rotating the door.

- **Positioning the 3D Cursor**: To position the 3D Cursor precisely, you can use the **Shift + Right-Click** or manually input coordinates in the **3D Cursor** section of the **N-panel** (press **N** to open the panel).
- **Setting Pivot to 3D Cursor**: After positioning the cursor, press **Period (.)** and select **3D Cursor** as the pivot point.

This technique allows you to perform transformations around specific points, giving you greater control over your models.

Snapping for Precision

The **Snap** tool is essential for precision modeling, allowing you to align objects or elements accurately without manually adjusting their position. Blender offers several snapping options, which can be activated by clicking the **magnet icon** in the 3D Viewport toolbar or by pressing **Shift + Tab**.

Types of Snapping

- **Vertex Snapping**: Aligns objects or components to the vertices of other objects. This is useful when connecting two pieces of geometry precisely.
- **Edge Snapping**: Allows you to snap to the edges of other objects.
- **Face Snapping**: Enables you to align objects to the faces of other objects.
- **Increment Snapping**: Snaps to grid increments, which is useful for maintaining a clean and organized layout.

Practical Use Case: Aligning Objects

Suppose you are modeling a building and need to position a window exactly on the wall. You can use **Face Snapping** to move the window and align it precisely with the wall surface:

1. **Select the Window**: Click on the window object to select it.
2. **Enable Face Snapping**: Click the magnet icon or press **Shift + Tab**, then choose **Face** as the snapping target.
3. **Move the Window**: Press **G** to move the window, and hover over the wall. The window will snap to the wall's surface, ensuring perfect alignment.

Snapping ensures that your models are built with accuracy, preventing gaps, overlaps, or misaligned elements.

Advanced Techniques: Proportional Editing

Proportional Editing is a tool that allows you to transform objects or components while affecting nearby geometry in a smooth, proportional manner. This tool is useful for creating natural-looking deformations, such as adjusting the terrain or bending organic shapes.

Enabling Proportional Editing

Press **O** to enable **Proportional Editing**. Once enabled, any transformation you make will also influence nearby geometry, creating a smooth transition.

- **Adjusting Influence Radius**: Use the mouse **scroll wheel** to increase or decrease the radius of influence during the transformation.
- **Falloff Types**: Blender offers several falloff types, such as **Smooth, Sharp, Constant**, and **Random**, each of which determines how the transformation influences surrounding geometry.

For example, if you are modeling a landscape and want to create a hill, you can select a vertex, enable Proportional Editing, and move the vertex upwards. The surrounding vertices will also move, creating a natural hill shape.

Manipulating Object Origins

The **origin** of an object is the point that serves as the reference for all transformations. By default, the origin is located at the geometric center of the object, but you may need to adjust it depending on your modeling requirements.

Setting the Object Origin

To change the origin of an object, select the object and then go to **Object > Set Origin** in the menu. You will see several options:

- **Origin to Geometry**: Moves the origin to the center of the object's geometry.
- **Origin to 3D Cursor**: Sets the origin at the location of the 3D Cursor. This is useful for repositioning the pivot point for rotations and scales.
- **Origin to Center of Mass**: Moves the origin to the object's center of mass, which can be useful for physical simulations.

Aligning and Mirroring Objects

Blender provides several tools for **aligning** and **mirroring** objects, which can be helpful for creating symmetrical models and ensuring that elements are evenly distributed.

Align Tool

The **Align Tool** allows you to align objects along specific axes. To use the tool:

1. Select the objects you want to align.
2. Press **F3** to open the **Search Menu** and type **Align Objects**.
3. Choose the axis along which you want to align the objects (X, Y, or Z).

This tool is particularly useful when you need to create a row of objects that are perfectly aligned, such as pillars or fence posts.

Mirroring Objects

The **Mirror Modifier** is a powerful tool for creating symmetrical objects. It allows you to model one half of an object while automatically generating the other half. This is especially useful when creating characters, vehicles, or other objects that require perfect symmetry.

- **Add a Mirror Modifier**: Select the object, go to the **Modifiers** tab in the properties panel, and add a **Mirror Modifier**.
- **Choose the Axis**: Specify the axis along which to mirror the object (X, Y, or Z).
- **Adjust Settings**: You can enable options like **Clipping** to ensure that the mirrored halves join seamlessly at the center.

The Mirror Modifier not only saves time but also ensures that your model remains symmetrical, which is crucial for character modeling and other symmetrical designs.

Practical Example: Modeling a Symmetrical Object

Suppose you want to model a symmetrical vase. Here's how you can use the Mirror Modifier and basic transformations:

1. **Add a Cylinder**: Press **Shift + A** > **Mesh** > **Cylinder** to add a cylinder to the scene.
2. **Enter Edit Mode**: Press **Tab** to enter **Edit Mode** and select the top face of the cylinder.
3. **Extrude and Scale**: Press **E** to extrude and **S** to scale the top face, creating the flared shape of the vase.
4. **Add Mirror Modifier**: Exit **Edit Mode**, add a **Mirror Modifier**, and ensure that it mirrors along the correct axis.
5. **Fine-Tune the Shape**: Continue to extrude, scale, and move vertices to create the desired shape of the vase. The Mirror Modifier will automatically update the other half, ensuring perfect symmetry.

Conclusion

Mastering object manipulation in Blender is crucial for any 3D artist, as it forms the foundation for all modeling, animation, and scene arrangement tasks. By understanding and effectively using transformations—Move, Rotate, and Scale—along with advanced tools like pivot points, snapping, proportional editing, and the Mirror Modifier, you can create complex and precise models with ease.

The key to efficient object manipulation is practice. The more you work with Blender's transformation tools and experiment with different techniques, the more intuitive and productive your modeling workflow will become. Whether you're creating a simple table, a detailed character, or an entire environment, object manipulation is at the heart of bringing your creative visions to life.

Chapter 3: Modeling Fundamentals

Introduction to 3D Modeling

3D modeling is one of the core skills required to create content in Blender, whether you're designing characters, environments, objects, or anything in between. At its core, modeling involves creating a representation of a real or imagined object in a 3D space, building up its shape using vertices, edges, and faces. This chapter is designed to introduce you to the essential concepts and practices involved in 3D modeling within Blender.

What is 3D Modeling?

3D modeling is the process of creating a three-dimensional representation of an object. This object can be anything from a simple box to an intricate architectural structure, or a character for animation. Blender offers a diverse range of tools and methods for modeling, allowing you to create just about anything you can imagine. Whether you are creating a simple low-poly environment or a highly detailed character model, Blender's capabilities can meet your needs.

In Blender, the structure of a 3D object is defined by its geometry, which includes vertices, edges, and faces:

- **Vertices** are the individual points in 3D space.
- **Edges** are lines connecting two vertices.
- **Faces** are the polygons that define the surface of an object, created when three or more vertices are joined.

Types of 3D Modeling Techniques

There are several methods used for 3D modeling in Blender, each suitable for different tasks:

1. **Polygonal Modeling**: This is the most common technique, where models are built using vertices, edges, and faces to form the geometry.
2. **Sculpting**: This technique is akin to digital clay modeling, allowing for a more organic approach that is suitable for characters and complex forms.
3. **NURBS and Curves**: These techniques are used to create smooth surfaces using mathematical curves rather than polygonal meshes.
4. **Parametric Modeling**: This involves using modifiers and procedural methods to generate geometry.

Understanding which method to use and when is crucial for efficient modeling. For example, creating hard surface models like buildings or machinery is often best done with polygonal modeling, while organic modeling (such as characters or natural objects) benefits from sculpting.

Getting Started with Basic Shapes

Blender offers several basic shapes to get you started. These include the **Cube**, **Sphere**, **Cylinder**, **Cone**, and **Torus**. You can add these shapes by pressing Shift + A and selecting the desired object from the "Mesh" menu. Each of these shapes serves as a starting point that you can further manipulate.

Here's an example of adding a cube and modifying it:

1. **Add a Cube**: Press Shift + A > Mesh > Cube.
2. **Enter Edit Mode**: Press Tab to enter Edit Mode.
3. **Select and Modify**: You can select vertices (1 key), edges (2 key), or faces (3 key) and move (G key), rotate (R key), or scale (S key) them to shape the cube.

For example, to create a basic table, you could start with a cube and scale it to form the tabletop, then add and scale cylinders to form the legs.

Understanding Edit Mode

Blender's **Edit Mode** is where most of your modeling work will take place. You can toggle between Object Mode (where you interact with entire objects) and Edit Mode (where you work on the components of a mesh) using the Tab key.

Once in Edit Mode, you'll primarily work with vertices, edges, and faces:

- **Vertex Select**: Select individual points in the mesh.
- **Edge Select**: Select and manipulate lines between vertices.
- **Face Select**: Select entire polygons to manipulate larger sections.

Extrude, Inset, and Loop Cut

Three essential tools in Edit Mode are **Extrude**, **Inset**, and **Loop Cut**:

1. **Extrude**: This is used to add new geometry by extending faces or edges outward. To extrude, select a face or edge, press E, and then drag to create new geometry. Extrusion is especially useful for adding depth or extending parts of a model, like creating the legs of a table from the top surface.
2. **Inset**: The **Inset** tool (I key) is used to create a smaller, inset version of a face. This is useful for adding detail, such as windows or panel lines on a surface.
3. **Loop Cut**: The **Loop Cut** tool (Ctrl + R) allows you to add additional edge loops to refine your geometry. Adding loops is useful for increasing the resolution of your model and ensuring smooth deformations during animation.

Modeling Practice: Creating a Simple Chair

Let's walk through a practical example to help you understand how to put these tools into action—modeling a simple chair.

1. **Start with a Cube**:
    - Press `Shift + A` > Mesh > Cube to add a cube to the scene.
    - Press `S` to scale it and `Z` to constrain the scaling to the vertical axis, creating a flat seat for the chair.
2. **Create the Legs**:
    - Enter **Edit Mode** (`Tab` key).
    - Select the bottom face of the cube.
    - Press `E` to **Extrude** and pull down to create four legs.
    - Press `S` to scale down the extruded section to create four distinct legs.
3. **Add a Backrest**:
    - Select the back face of the seat.
    - Press `E` to extrude upward to form the backrest.
4. **Refine the Shape**:
    - Use **Loop Cut** (`Ctrl + R`) to add edge loops where more detail is needed, like reinforcing the corners or adjusting the backrest.

This simple project demonstrates how you can combine basic shapes and tools to create more complex models. As you become comfortable, you can add more details, such as rounding the edges using the **Bevel** tool (`Ctrl + B`) or applying modifiers to enhance the form.

Using Modifiers to Simplify Complex Tasks

Modifiers are powerful tools in Blender that help to automate and simplify complex modeling tasks. Some commonly used modifiers for modeling include:

1. **Subdivision Surface Modifier**: Adds more geometry and smooths out the object's shape. It's particularly useful when working on organic models to make them appear more rounded.
2. **Mirror Modifier**: Allows you to work symmetrically by mirroring geometry along an axis. This is helpful for modeling symmetrical objects like characters or vehicles, as you only need to model half of the object.
3. **Boolean Modifier**: Used to perform operations like union, difference, or intersection between two objects. For instance, if you need to cut a hole through an object, the Boolean modifier can make that process much easier.

To add a modifier:

- Select your object in Object Mode.
- Go to the **Modifiers** tab (wrench icon) on the right-hand panel.
- Click **Add Modifier** and select the modifier you need.

Here's an example of using a **Mirror Modifier** to model a symmetrical object:

1. Start by creating a basic shape like a cube.
2. Enter **Edit Mode** (`Tab` key) and delete one half of the cube using **Box Select** (`B`) and the `X` key to delete.

3. Add a **Mirror Modifier** and select the appropriate axis. Now, any edits you make on one side will be mirrored to the other, maintaining symmetry.

Common Modeling Challenges

Topology is a critical aspect of modeling. Good topology refers to how well your mesh is structured in terms of edge flow and polygon distribution, which affects how easily it can be modified or animated later. Here are a few tips:

- **Avoid N-gons**: Try to keep your mesh composed of quads (four-sided polygons). N-gons (polygons with more than four sides) can cause issues during deformation and shading.
- **Use Edge Loops for Deformation**: When modeling something that will be animated, make sure the **edge loops** are placed to facilitate natural movement. For example, loops around joints allow for more realistic bending.
- **Maintain Uniform Geometry**: Avoid having areas that are overly dense with vertices next to areas with very few. This can lead to unpredictable results during rendering or deformation.

Practical Exercise: Modeling a Wine Glass

For another practice, let's model a simple wine glass using the **Spin Tool**, which is ideal for objects with radial symmetry.

1. **Add a Reference Image**:
   - Press `Shift` + `A` > Image > Reference to add a reference image of a wine glass to your scene. This helps guide the modeling process.
2. **Create a Basic Profile**:
   - In **Edit Mode**, delete all vertices from the default cube (`X` key).
   - Switch to the **Vertex Select** mode and press `Ctrl` + `Left Mouse Button` to create the profile of half the wine glass. This profile should follow the outline of the glass as closely as possible.
3. **Spin Tool**:
   - Select the profile and press `Alt` + `R` to bring up the **Spin Tool**.
   - Adjust the settings to spin the profile 360 degrees around the vertical axis. This should complete the model of the wine glass.
4. **Apply Modifiers**:
   - Apply a **Subdivision Surface Modifier** to smooth out the shape.
   - Optionally, use the **Solidify Modifier** to add thickness to the glass.

Applying Materials to the Model

After modeling, applying the right materials can significantly enhance the appearance of your model. For the wine glass:

1. Go to the **Materials** tab.
2. Create a new material and adjust the **Transmission** property to give it a glass-like appearance.

3. Adjust the **Roughness** to control how reflective or frosted the glass appears.

Summary

3D modeling is a foundational skill that takes time and practice to master. This section introduced you to the basics of Blender's modeling tools and concepts. By understanding the different methods of creating geometry, using modifiers to simplify tasks, and employing best practices for topology, you can build both simple and complex models effectively.

The exercises presented—creating a chair and a wine glass—are designed to help you get hands-on experience with Blender's tools and understand the practical applications of these techniques. With practice, these foundational skills will enable you to take on more ambitious projects, setting the stage for advanced modeling and animation.

Creating Basic Shapes

In Blender, basic shapes serve as the building blocks for most 3D models. They provide a starting point for creating more complex geometry by transforming, extruding, or modifying these primitive shapes. This section will take an in-depth look at Blender's basic geometric shapes and how you can effectively use them to begin building models. Understanding the fundamentals of basic shapes is crucial for efficiently creating a wide range of objects, from simple props to complex structures.

Adding Basic Shapes to Your Scene

Blender provides a variety of primitive shapes, such as the **Cube**, **Sphere**, **Cylinder**, **Cone**, and **Torus**. These primitives can be added to your scene easily, and each one has unique properties that make it suitable for different purposes.

To add a basic shape in Blender:

1. Press Shift + A to open the **Add** menu.
2. Navigate to **Mesh** to view the list of available shapes.
3. Select the shape you want to add.

Alternatively, you can access the **Add** menu from the 3D Viewport's top bar.

Here are some of the most commonly used primitive shapes:

- **Cube**: A six-sided, uniform shape that serves as a versatile base for many models.
- **UV Sphere**: A rounded shape made up of horizontal and vertical segments, useful for creating spherical objects.
- **Cylinder**: A shape with a circular base, ideal for modeling columns, pipes, and other cylindrical items.
- **Cone**: A shape with a circular base that tapers to a point, useful for a variety of objects like cones and spikes.
- **Torus**: A donut-like shape that's commonly used to create rings, tires, and other rounded objects.

Example: Adding and Transforming a Cube

Let's start by adding a **Cube** to the scene, then transforming it to create a basic table:

1. **Add a Cube**:
   - Press `Shift + A` > **Mesh** > **Cube**.
   - The cube appears at the cursor's position.
2. **Scale the Cube**:
   - Press `S` to scale the cube uniformly.
   - Press `S` followed by `Z` to scale along the Z-axis and flatten the cube, creating the tabletop.
3. **Duplicate and Transform**:
   - Press `Shift + D` to duplicate the cube.
   - Use `S` and `Z` again to adjust the size for the table legs.
   - Position the legs accordingly by pressing `G` to move them to the corners of the table.

Understanding Transformations: Move, Rotate, and Scale

To manipulate these basic shapes effectively, you need to understand the **Move, Rotate, and Scale** operations, collectively known as the **Transformation Tools**.

1. **Move (G)**: Moving an object in Blender is done with the `G` key. You can use this to drag objects to new positions. Once you press `G`, you can constrain the movement along a specific axis by pressing `X`, `Y`, or `Z`.
   Example:
   - Select a shape and press `G`, followed by `X`, to move it along the X-axis only.
   - You can also type in a number to move it a specific distance, such as `G > X > 2`, which moves the object 2 units along the X-axis.
2. **Rotate (R)**: Rotating is done with the `R` key. Like moving, you can constrain the rotation to a specific axis by pressing `X`, `Y`, or `Z` after pressing `R`.
   Example:
   - Press `R` to enter rotation mode.
   - Press `Z` to constrain the rotation along the Z-axis, and then drag or type an angle (e.g., `90` degrees).
3. **Scale (S)**: Scaling an object is done with the `S` key This allows you to change the size of an object either uniformly or along a specific axis.
   Example:
   - Press `S` to scale uniformly.
   - Press `S` followed by `X` to scale the object along the X-axis.

These tools are fundamental to manipulating and modifying the primitive shapes you add to your scene.

Origin and Pivot Points

When transforming objects in Blender, it's important to understand the concept of the **Origin** and **Pivot Points**.

- **Origin**: The origin is the point around which transformations such as rotation and scaling occur. By default, the origin is set to the center of the object. However, you can move the origin using the **Object > Set Origin** menu to change where rotations and scaling happen.
- **Pivot Point**: The pivot point determines how transformations affect a group of selected objects or elements. You can choose different pivot points like **Bounding Box Center**, **Median Point**, or **3D Cursor**. Changing the pivot point allows for more complex transformations, such as rotating multiple objects around a shared center.

Combining Basic Shapes to Create Complex Objects

To create more complex models, you can combine multiple primitive shapes by positioning them relative to each other and joining them into a single mesh. Let's look at an example to illustrate this concept:

Example: Modeling a Simple Castle Tower

1. **Create the Tower Base**:
   - Add a **Cylinder** (Shift + A > **Mesh** > **Cylinder**).
   - Scale it along the Z-axis (S > Z) to make it taller, representing the tower's main structure.
2. **Add a Parapet**:
   - Add a **Cube** (Shift + A > **Mesh** > **Cube**).
   - Scale it down (S), and then duplicate it (Shift + D) multiple times to create a row of battlements around the top of the cylinder.
   - Use G to position each cube along the perimeter of the cylinder.
3. **Union with Boolean Modifier**:
   - If you want to merge the battlements with the main tower, you can use a **Boolean Modifier**:
     - Select the cylinder, go to the **Modifiers** tab, and add a **Boolean Modifier**.
     - Choose **Union** as the operation, and select one of the cubes as the object to merge.
4. **Apply the Modifier**:
   - Once you're satisfied with the layout, **Apply** the Boolean Modifier to join the battlements with the main tower.
5. **Refine with Bevel**:
   - Add a **Bevel Modifier** to the tower to smooth out some edges, making the model look more polished.

Object Modifiers for Procedural Modeling

Modifiers are non-destructive operations you can apply to an object, meaning that you can adjust them at any time without permanently altering the geometry. They are particularly useful for creating complex shapes from simple primitives. Some commonly used modifiers include:

1. **Subdivision Surface Modifier**: Adds geometry to smooth out an object's surface. This is useful when working with rounded objects like a sphere or when modeling organic shapes.
2. **Bevel Modifier**: Adds bevels to the edges of an object, making them less sharp. This is great for hard surface modeling where realistic edges are necessary.
3. **Array Modifier**: Creates multiple copies of an object in a linear or radial arrangement. You can use this to easily create patterns or repeating elements.
4. **Boolean Modifier**: This modifier allows you to use one object to cut, combine, or intersect with another. For example, you could use a cube to cut a hole through another shape.

Example: Creating a Complex Gear

To create a gear, you can start with a simple **Cylinder** and use modifiers to add details procedurally:

1. **Create the Base**:
   - Add a **Cylinder** (Shift + A > **Mesh** > **Cylinder**).
   - Scale it along the Z-axis to create the thickness of the gear.
2. **Add Teeth with Array and Boolean Modifiers**:
   - Add a **Cube** and position it at the perimeter of the cylinder to represent one gear tooth.
   - Apply an **Array Modifier** to duplicate the cube around the cylinder. Adjust the count and offset to create evenly spaced teeth.
   - Use a **Boolean Modifier** to join the teeth with the base cylinder.
3. **Bevel the Edges**:
   - Add a **Bevel Modifier** to the gear to make the edges smoother.

Practical Exercise: Modeling a Coffee Mug

This exercise will help you practice combining and manipulating basic shapes to create a practical object—a coffee mug.

1. **Add a Cylinder**:
   - Press Shift + A > **Mesh** > **Cylinder**.
   - Scale it along the Z-axis to make it taller, forming the mug body.
2. **Hollow Out the Mug**:
   - Add another cylinder inside the first one, slightly smaller.
   - Use a **Boolean Modifier** (set to **Difference**) to subtract the inner cylinder from the larger one, creating a hollow interior.
3. **Create the Handle**:
   - Add a **Torus** (Shift + A > **Mesh** > **Torus**).
   - Scale and position the torus to the side of the mug, then delete part of it to create the handle shape.
   - Use **Loop Cut** (Ctrl + R) to add more geometry if needed for shaping.

4. **Join the Handle to the Mug**:
   - Apply a **Boolean Modifier** to join the handle to the mug body.
   - Use the **Smooth** shading option (`Object Context Menu` > **Shade Smooth**) to make the mug look more polished.
5. **Refine the Mesh**:
   - Add a **Subdivision Surface Modifier** to the mug to smooth out the surface.
   - Apply a **Bevel Modifier** to round the edges slightly for a more realistic appearance.

Summary

In Blender, basic shapes form the foundation of nearly all 3D models. By learning how to add, manipulate, and transform these shapes, you can quickly create a variety of objects and use them as the starting point for more detailed models. The **Move**, **Rotate**, and **Scale** tools allow you to control the placement and size of these shapes, while **Modifiers** provide procedural methods to create complex geometry non-destructively.

By practicing the creation of objects like a simple table, a castle tower, and a coffee mug, you develop a deeper understanding of how to use Blender's primitive shapes effectively. As you continue to experiment with these tools and concepts, you'll be able to take on more advanced modeling challenges and develop your skills further.

Modifiers: Simplifying Complex Tasks

Blender's **Modifiers** are powerful tools that allow you to alter geometry in a non-destructive manner. They provide an efficient way to perform complex modeling tasks without permanently affecting the base mesh, enabling you to experiment and adjust settings until you are satisfied with the result. This section explores different types of modifiers available in Blender, their practical applications, and how they can simplify complex tasks.

What Are Modifiers?

Modifiers are operations that automatically affect an object's geometry in Blender. They allow you to perform advanced modeling tasks such as subdivision, deformation, and duplication without directly modifying the object's mesh. Using modifiers is like adding a layer of effects to an object—these effects can be adjusted or removed at any time, which makes working with modifiers very flexible.

To add a modifier in Blender:

1. Select the object you want to modify.
2. Go to the **Modifiers** tab in the properties panel (represented by a wrench icon).
3. Click **Add Modifier** and select the modifier you need from the list.

Types of Modifiers

Blender offers a wide range of modifiers that can be grouped into several categories based on their functionality:

- **Generate Modifiers**: These create new geometry or alter existing geometry, such as **Array**, **Mirror**, and **Subdivision Surface** modifiers.
- **Deform Modifiers**: These change the shape of an object without adding new geometry, like **Simple Deform**, **Lattice**, and **Wave** modifiers.
- **Simulate Modifiers**: These are used to create physical simulations, such as **Cloth** and **Fluid** modifiers.

Each modifier can be applied to achieve different modeling goals, and they can be combined to create intricate effects. Let's dive into some of the most commonly used modifiers and their practical applications.

Subdivision Surface Modifier

The **Subdivision Surface Modifier** is one of the most commonly used modifiers in Blender. It subdivides the geometry of an object to create a smoother surface. This is particularly useful when working on organic models, such as characters or creatures, where smooth and rounded shapes are essential.

Using the Subdivision Surface Modifier

1. **Add a Basic Shape**:
   - Start by adding a **Cube** to the scene (`Shift + A` > **Mesh** > **Cube**).
2. **Apply the Subdivision Surface Modifier**:
   - Select the cube, go to the **Modifiers** tab, and choose **Subdivision Surface**.
3. **Adjust the Levels**:
   - In the modifier properties, you can adjust the **Levels Viewport** and **Render** settings to control how many times the geometry is subdivided. Higher levels result in smoother surfaces but increase the polygon count.

For example, if you are modeling a character's head, you would start with a basic sphere and then use the **Subdivision Surface Modifier** to add detail gradually, ensuring the surface remains smooth.

Practical Exercise: Creating a Smooth Vase

1. **Add a Cylinder**:
   - Press `Shift + A` > **Mesh** > **Cylinder** to add a cylinder to the scene.
2. **Shape the Vase**:
   - Enter **Edit Mode** (`Tab` key) and select the top face of the cylinder.
   - Press `S` to scale down the top face, giving it a narrower neck.
   - Use **Extrude** (`E` key) to extend the neck upward and shape it into a vase.
3. **Apply the Subdivision Surface Modifier**:
   - Add a **Subdivision Surface Modifier** to smooth out the vase.
   - Increase the **Viewport Levels** to see a smoother version of the vase.

The **Subdivision Surface Modifier** makes it easy to create smooth, flowing shapes without manually adding edge loops or adjusting vertices.

Mirror Modifier

The **Mirror Modifier** is another powerful tool in Blender that is particularly useful when modeling symmetrical objects, such as characters, vehicles, or architectural structures. Instead of modeling both sides of an object, you can model only half and use the **Mirror Modifier** to automatically create the other half.

Using the Mirror Modifier

1. **Add a Basic Shape**:
   o Start by adding a **Cube** (Shift + A > **Mesh** > **Cube**).
2. **Delete Half of the Cube**:
   o Enter **Edit Mode** (Tab key) and select half of the vertices.
   o Press X and choose **Vertices** to delete the selected half.
3. **Apply the Mirror Modifier**:
   o In **Object Mode**, select the cube, go to the **Modifiers** tab, and add a **Mirror Modifier**.
4. **Adjust the Mirror Settings**:
   o Ensure the **Axis** is set to mirror across the desired axis (e.g., **X**).

Example: Modeling a Character's Head

To model a character's head efficiently:

1. **Start with a Sphere**:
   o Add a **UV Sphere** (Shift + A > **Mesh** > **UV Sphere**).
2. **Delete One Half**:
   o Enter **Edit Mode** and delete the vertices on one side of the sphere.
3. **Add Mirror Modifier**:
   o Apply the **Mirror Modifier** to mirror the remaining half, ensuring symmetry as you model.
4. **Refine the Shape**:
   o Use **Proportional Editing** (0 key) to adjust the shape smoothly, and the changes will be mirrored automatically.

The **Mirror Modifier** saves significant time when modeling symmetrical objects and ensures that both sides are identical, which is crucial for character modeling.

Array Modifier

The **Array Modifier** is used to create multiple copies of an object in a specific pattern. This is particularly useful when creating repetitive structures, such as fences, railings, or columns.

Using the Array Modifier

1. **Add a Basic Shape**:
   - Start by adding a **Cube** (`Shift + A` > **Mesh** > **Cube**).
2. **Apply the Array Modifier**:
   - Select the cube, go to the **Modifiers** tab, and add an **Array Modifier**.
3. **Adjust the Count and Offset**:
   - In the **Array Modifier** settings, adjust the **Count** to determine how many copies are created.
   - Use the **Relative Offset** to control the spacing between the copies.

Practical Exercise: Creating a Set of Stairs

1. **Add a Step**:
   - Start by adding a **Cube** to represent a single step.
2. **Apply the Array Modifier**:
   - Add an **Array Modifier** to the cube.
   - Set the **Count** to the number of steps you need (e.g., 10).
   - Adjust the **Relative Offset** values to create a staircase pattern, ensuring that each step is positioned slightly higher and forward compared to the previous one.

The **Array Modifier** allows you to create complex, repetitive structures with minimal effort, making it an essential tool for architectural and environmental modeling.

Boolean Modifier

The **Boolean Modifier** allows you to perform operations like **Union**, **Difference**, and **Intersection** between two objects. This is especially useful for cutting holes, combining meshes, or creating complex geometry by merging simple shapes.

Using the Boolean Modifier

1. **Add Two Shapes**:
   - Start by adding a **Cube** and a **Cylinder** (`Shift + A` > **Mesh** > **Cube** and **Cylinder**).
2. **Position the Cylinder**:
   - Move the **Cylinder** so that it intersects with the **Cube**.
3. **Apply the Boolean Modifier**:
   - Select the cube, go to the **Modifiers** tab, and add a **Boolean Modifier**.
   - Set the **Operation** to **Difference** and select the **Cylinder** as the target object.
4. **Apply and Inspect**:
   - Apply the modifier, and the cylinder will be subtracted from the cube, creating a hole.

Example: Creating a Doorway in a Wall

1. **Create the Wall**:
   - Add a **Cube** and scale it to form a wall.
2. **Add a Door Shape**:
   - Add another **Cube** and position it where you want the doorway.

3. **Apply Boolean Modifier**:
   ○ Select the wall, add a **Boolean Modifier**, and choose **Difference** with the second cube as the target.

The **Boolean Modifier** makes it easy to perform complex modeling operations that would otherwise require extensive manual editing.

Bevel Modifier

The **Bevel Modifier** is used to create beveled edges on an object, which helps to eliminate sharp edges and make the object look more realistic. Beveling is essential for hard surface modeling, especially when creating objects that need to have smooth transitions between surfaces.

Using the Bevel Modifier

1. **Add a Basic Shape**:
   ○ Start by adding a **Cube** to the scene.
2. **Apply the Bevel Modifier**:
   ○ Select the cube, go to the **Modifiers** tab, and add a **Bevel Modifier**.
3. **Adjust the Width**:
   ○ In the modifier settings, adjust the **Width** to control how much of the edge is beveled.
4. **Increase Segments**:
   ○ Increase the **Segments** to create a smoother bevel.

Example: Beveling the Edges of a Table

1. **Add a Tabletop**:
   ○ Add a **Cube** and scale it to create a flat tabletop.
2. **Add Table Legs**:
   ○ Add four **Cylinders** for the legs and position them accordingly.
3. **Apply Bevel Modifier**:
   ○ Apply a **Bevel Modifier** to the tabletop and the legs to give them a polished, realistic look.

The **Bevel Modifier** helps to soften the edges of your models, adding a professional touch that improves the overall appearance of hard surface objects.

Combining Modifiers for Complex Effects

One of the most powerful aspects of Blender's modifiers is that you can stack them to create complex effects. Each modifier in the stack is applied in sequence, which allows you to build intricate models with minimal manual effort.

Example: Modeling a Detailed Pillar

1. **Add a Cylinder**:
   ○ Start with a **Cylinder** to create the basic shape of the pillar.

2. **Add an Array Modifier**:
   - ○ Apply an **Array Modifier** to create multiple grooves along the length of the pillar.
3. **Apply a Bevel Modifier**:
   - ○ Add a **Bevel Modifier** to soften the edges and make the grooves more polished.
4. **Add a Subdivision Surface Modifier**:
   - ○ Finally, add a **Subdivision Surface Modifier** to smooth out the entire pillar.

By stacking these modifiers, you can create a detailed pillar with grooves and smooth surfaces without manually modeling every detail.

Summary

Blender's **Modifiers** are powerful tools that simplify complex modeling tasks, allowing you to create intricate models without permanently altering the base geometry. From the **Subdivision Surface Modifier** for smooth surfaces to the **Boolean Modifier** for cutting and combining shapes, each modifier has unique capabilities that make it invaluable for different modeling scenarios.

Modifiers not only save time but also add flexibility to your modeling workflow, enabling you to experiment and iterate more effectively. By mastering modifiers like **Mirror**, **Array**, **Boolean**, and **Bevel**, you can create detailed, polished models that meet professional standards while maintaining a non-destructive workflow.

Experiment with these modifiers in your projects, combining them to create complex forms, and you'll find that many previously daunting modeling tasks become straightforward and even enjoyable.

Building Precision with Edit Mode

Blender's **Edit Mode** is the workspace where you take a model from its basic form to a refined, intricate version, adding details, adjusting geometry, and creating complex structures. This mode allows you to work directly with the components of a mesh—**vertices**, **edges**, and **faces**—providing full control over the geometry of your model. In this section, we'll explore Edit Mode's tools and techniques that help you build models with precision, covering fundamental aspects like vertex manipulation, edge operations, face creation, and more advanced tools like loop cuts, snapping, and proportional editing.

Understanding Edit Mode

In Blender, **Edit Mode** is accessed by selecting an object and pressing the Tab key. This mode allows you to modify the actual mesh geometry, whereas **Object Mode** is used for moving, scaling, or rotating entire objects. In Edit Mode, you can select different elements of the mesh: **vertices**, **edges**, or **faces**.

- **Vertex Select (1)**: Allows you to manipulate individual points in the mesh.
- **Edge Select (2)**: Lets you select the lines that connect two vertices.

- **Face Select (3)**: Allows you to select and modify the entire face of a mesh.

Switching between these selection modes helps you to precisely control the structure of your model, whether you need to adjust a single point or manipulate larger sections of the geometry.

Vertex, Edge, and Face Manipulation

Blender provides several fundamental tools to manipulate vertices, edges, and faces in Edit Mode. These operations form the basis of all modeling in Blender, giving you the ability to create and refine the shape of any model.

Vertex Manipulation

Vertices are the building blocks of any 3D object. In Edit Mode, you can manipulate vertices to precisely adjust the shape of your model. Here are some common operations:

1. **Move (G)**: Select a vertex and press G to move it freely. To constrain movement along an axis, press X, Y, or Z after pressing G.
2. **Merge Vertices (M)**: Sometimes, you need to merge two or more vertices into a single point. Select the vertices you want to merge, press M, and choose how you want to merge them—e.g., **At Center**, **At First**, or **At Last**.
3. **Snap Vertices**: Blender allows you to snap a vertex to another element in the scene for precise alignment. Enable **Snap** (Shift + Tab) and choose the element to snap to, such as **Vertex** or **Edge**.

Edge Operations

Edges are lines that connect vertices, forming the framework of your model. Edge operations help you shape the geometry by adding or refining details:

1. **Extrude Edge (E)**: You can extend an edge by selecting it and pressing E. This is particularly useful for creating new faces or extending geometry along a path.
2. **Edge Bevel (Ctrl + B)**: To smooth out sharp edges or create rounded corners, use the **Bevel** tool. Select the edge, press Ctrl + B, and drag to adjust the bevel width. You can also increase the number of segments with the mouse wheel to create a smoother curve.
3. **Edge Slide (G, G)**: The **Edge Slide** tool allows you to move an edge along its adjacent geometry. Select an edge and press G twice to slide it along its connected vertices. This is useful for adjusting geometry without distorting the shape.

Face Manipulation

Faces are the surfaces of a model, created by connecting three or more vertices. Manipulating faces allows you to define the shape and detail of your model:

1. **Extrude Face (E)**: Similar to edge extrusion, you can extrude faces to add new geometry. This is often used to create features like walls, pillars, or mechanical parts.

2. **Inset Faces (I)**: The **Inset** tool allows you to create a smaller face within a selected face. Press I to inset a face, which is useful for adding details like windows or panels.
3. **Delete Faces (X)**: You can delete faces to create holes or remove unwanted geometry. Select the face and press X, then choose **Delete Faces**.

Precision Tools in Edit Mode

To build models with precision, Blender provides several tools that help you make exact adjustments and alignments. Here, we'll cover some of these precision tools, including **Loop Cut**, **Knife Tool**, **Snapping**, and **Proportional Editing**.

Loop Cut and Slide

The **Loop Cut and Slide** tool (Ctrl + R) is one of the most important tools for adding detail to a model. It allows you to insert new edge loops into a mesh, which is essential for controlling the topology and adding resolution where needed.

1. **Add an Edge Loop**:
   o Press Ctrl + R and hover over the mesh. You will see a preview of where the edge loop will be placed.
   o Click to confirm the position, and then move your mouse to slide the edge loop along the surface. Click again to finalize its position.

Edge loops are crucial for adding detail to specific areas without affecting the rest of the model. For example, if you're modeling a character, you might add edge loops around the joints to ensure smooth deformations during animation.

Knife Tool

The **Knife Tool** (K) allows you to make custom cuts in the mesh, giving you precise control over the geometry. This tool is especially useful for creating complex shapes or adding specific details that aren't possible with standard edge loops.

1. **Activate the Knife Tool**:
   o Press K to activate the Knife Tool. Click on the mesh to start cutting, and continue clicking to define the cut path.
   o Press Enter to finalize the cut.

The **Knife Tool** is highly flexible and allows you to add geometry exactly where you need it, making it ideal for creating intricate details or modifying the flow of topology.

Snapping for Accurate Placement

Blender's **Snapping** feature (Shift + Tab) is a powerful tool for ensuring precise alignment of vertices, edges, and faces. You can snap elements to the **Grid**, **Vertices**, **Edges**, or **Faces**, making it easy to align parts of your model accurately.

1. **Enable Snapping**:
    - Press `Shift + Tab` to toggle snapping on or off.
    - In the **Snapping Options** (found in the 3D Viewport header), choose the type of element to snap to, such as **Vertex** or **Edge**.

Snapping is particularly useful when modeling mechanical parts or architectural elements where exact placement is critical.

Proportional Editing

Proportional Editing (`O` key) allows you to transform selected vertices, edges, or faces while smoothly affecting surrounding geometry. This tool is essential for creating organic shapes, such as character features or natural environments.

1. **Enable Proportional Editing**:
    - Press `O` to toggle **Proportional Editing** on or off.
    - Select a vertex and press `G`, `R`, or `S` to move, rotate, or scale it. Use the mouse wheel to adjust the radius of influence.

For example, when modeling a hill or a face, **Proportional Editing** helps you make adjustments that affect the surrounding vertices in a natural, smooth way, creating realistic deformations without hard edges.

Practical Example: Modeling a Chair with Edit Mode

To put these tools into practice, let's model a simple chair using **Edit Mode**. This example will demonstrate how to use vertex, edge, and face manipulation, as well as the precision tools we discussed.

1. **Create the Chair Seat**:
    - Add a **Cube** (`Shift + A` > **Mesh** > **Cube**).
    - Scale the cube along the X and Y axes (`S` > `X`, then `S` > `Y`) to create a rectangular seat.
2. **Extrude the Legs**:
    - Enter **Edit Mode** (`Tab` key) and switch to **Face Select** mode (`3` key).
    - Select the four bottom faces of the cube.
    - Press `E` to **Extrude** downward to create the chair legs.
3. **Add the Backrest**:
    - Select the back face of the seat.
    - Press `E` to **Extrude** upward, forming the backrest of the chair.
4. **Refine the Edges**:
    - Use the **Bevel Tool** (`Ctrl + B`) to add slight bevels to the edges of the seat and backrest, making the chair look more polished and realistic.
5. **Use Loop Cuts for Detail**:
    - Press `Ctrl + R` to add **Loop Cuts** along the legs and backrest. This will allow you to add more detail and refine the shape.
6. **Proportional Editing for Comfort**:

- Enable **Proportional Editing** (O key) and select the top vertices of the backrest.
- Press G to move them slightly backward, giving the backrest a more ergonomic curve.

Managing Topology for Clean Geometry

Topology refers to the arrangement of vertices, edges, and faces in a mesh. Good topology is crucial for creating models that deform well during animation and look clean when rendered. Here are some tips for managing topology in Edit Mode:

1. **Use Quads Instead of N-gons**: Try to keep your geometry composed of **quads** (four-sided faces) rather than **N-gons** (faces with more than four sides) or **triangles**. Quads deform more predictably during animation and make the model easier to edit.
2. **Maintain Edge Flow**: **Edge flow** refers to the direction of edges in a mesh and how they follow the form of the model. Good edge flow is essential for creating natural deformations, especially in organic models. Use **Loop Cuts** (Ctrl + R) to add edge loops that follow the contours of your model.
3. **Avoid Stretching**: When extruding or scaling, be mindful of stretching the geometry, which can cause shading issues. Use tools like **Loop Cut** to add geometry where needed and maintain even face distribution.

Advanced Techniques: Knife Project and Edge Crease

Knife Project

The **Knife Project** tool allows you to use one object to cut another in Edit Mode. This is useful for adding complex details or patterns to a model.

1. **Add a Cutting Object**:
   - Create the shape you want to use for cutting, such as a **Circle**.
2. **Position and Project**:
   - Position the cutting object above the target mesh.
   - Select both objects, enter **Edit Mode**, and press Knife Project to project the shape onto the target mesh, creating new edges.

Edge Crease

The **Edge Crease** tool (Shift + E) allows you to control the sharpness of edges when using a **Subdivision Surface Modifier**. This is useful for maintaining sharp edges on specific parts of a model while keeping other areas smooth.

1. **Select Edges to Crease**:
   - Enter **Edit Mode** and select the edges you want to remain sharp.
2. **Apply Edge Crease**:
   - Press Shift + E and drag to adjust the crease value, making the edges sharper or softer.

Practical Exercise: Modeling a Simple Table with Edit Mode

1. **Create the Tabletop**:
   - Add a **Cube** (Shift + A > **Mesh** > **Cube**).
   - Scale it along the X and Y axes to create a flat, rectangular tabletop.
2. **Add the Legs**:
   - Enter **Edit Mode** and select the four bottom corners of the tabletop.
   - Press E to **Extrude** downward to create the table legs.
3. **Add Loop Cuts for Support**:
   - Use **Loop Cuts** (Ctrl + R) along the legs to add additional geometry, making the legs look more detailed.
4. **Bevel the Edges**:
   - Select the edges of the tabletop and apply a **Bevel** (Ctrl + B) to round them slightly, giving the table a polished appearance.

Summary

Edit Mode in Blender is a powerful environment where you can take a basic mesh and refine it into a detailed, precise model. By using tools like **Extrude**, **Loop Cut**, **Knife Tool**, and **Proportional Editing**, you can manipulate vertices, edges, and faces to achieve the desired level of detail. Precision tools like **Snapping** and **Edge Slide** help you align and adjust geometry accurately, while modifiers like **Bevel** and **Subdivision Surface** add a finishing touch to your model.

Mastering Edit Mode is essential for creating clean, detailed, and well-structured models. The techniques and tools discussed in this section form the foundation of efficient 3D modeling in Blender, enabling you to build everything from simple props to complex characters with precision and ease. Practice these skills, combine them creatively, and you'll be well on your way to becoming a proficient 3D artist.

Chapter 4: Advanced Modeling Techniques

Mesh Modeling: Sculpting and Retopology

Introduction to Advanced Mesh Modeling

Mesh modeling in Blender is an essential skill for creating highly detailed and refined 3D models. It involves working with various techniques, from sculpting organic shapes to using retopology for optimal geometry. Sculpting is a powerful tool for creating intricate details and organic forms, while retopology ensures that your model remains efficient for animation or real-time applications. In this section, we will dive deep into the techniques for mesh sculpting and the principles of retopology that help create clean, manageable meshes.

Sculpting in Blender

Sculpting is a crucial step when creating organic models, such as characters, animals, or other natural forms. Blender provides a sculpting environment with a wide array of brushes, tools, and modifiers, similar to specialized sculpting software like ZBrush. Here, we will explore the essential tools, techniques, and workflows for effective sculpting in Blender.

Setting Up for Sculpting

Before beginning any sculpting project, it is important to prepare your model properly. Blender has a "Sculpting" workspace that can be accessed from the top toolbar, which provides a streamlined interface with all the necessary sculpting tools.

- **Dynamic Topology (Dyntopo)**: Dynamic Topology is a key feature that allows you to dynamically adjust the resolution of your mesh as you sculpt. It can be enabled by pressing the "Dyntopo" button on the top panel while in Sculpt Mode. This feature allows you to add finer details to areas that need it without significantly increasing the poly count across the entire model.
- **Multi-Resolution Modifier**: Another way to handle sculpting is through the Multi-Resolution Modifier. This allows you to work at multiple levels of detail, similar to subdivision surfaces, which is especially useful when you need to create different levels of sculpted detail.
- **Brushes**: Blender offers a wide variety of brushes such as the Clay, Clay Strips, Smooth, Inflate, Grab, and Snake Hook brushes. Understanding the application of each brush is key to successful sculpting. The **Clay Strips** brush, for instance, is useful for adding volume in broad strokes, while the **Smooth** brush is essential for reducing harsh edges and blending different areas.

Workflow Tips for Sculpting

1. **Blocking Out Basic Forms**: Start with broad, large-scale forms before moving on to finer details. Blocking out helps establish the proportions of your model, which is critical to achieving a natural look.
2. **Use Reference Images**: Having a clear reference to guide your sculpting is crucial. You can load reference images directly into Blender by using the "Background Images" option in the Properties panel.
3. **Symmetry and Mirroring**: Sculpting usually involves working with symmetrical models, especially for characters. Blender's symmetry options allow you to sculpt both sides of your model simultaneously, ensuring consistency in your design. You can enable symmetry from the "Symmetry" section in the Sculpting toolbar.
4. **Detail Management with Dyntopo**: When working on different parts of the mesh, adjust the detail size in Dynamic Topology settings based on the need for detail in that particular area. Use lower resolution for general areas and higher resolution for intricate parts like facial features.
5. **Avoid Overworking Areas**: Sculpting can be quite intuitive, and it's easy to spend too much time on a single part of the model. To avoid overworking, it's helpful to rotate the model frequently and ensure that all sides are being worked on proportionally.

Practical Exercise: Sculpting a Character Head

To get started with sculpting, let's take a simple exercise—sculpting a character head.

1. **Start with a Base Mesh**: Begin with a basic UV Sphere or a modified cube. You can use the Mirror Modifier to sculpt only one side and have Blender automatically mirror the changes on the other side.
2. **Block Out Main Forms**: Use the **Grab** brush to pull the general shape of the head and establish features like the brow ridge, nose, and jawline. It's crucial to get the silhouette and proportions right at this stage.
3. **Refine with Detail**: Switch to the **Clay Strips** brush to start adding more form to the features. Gradually add detail to areas like the nose and eye sockets. Use the **Crease** brush to define edges and lines around features like the lips and eyes.
4. **Fine Detailing**: Once the primary forms are in place, add details such as wrinkles or pores using **Alpha Textures** with the **Draw** or **Inflate** brush. Adjust the brush strength and size as you work on different details.
5. **Smooth Transitions**: Use the **Smooth** brush to soften transitions between different areas. This is especially important for organic models to avoid unnatural-looking geometry.

Retopology in Blender

Retopology is the process of recreating the topology of your sculpted model to make it more animation-friendly and optimized for rendering. High-polygon models are great for sculpting but may be too heavy for practical use in animation or real-time applications.

Why Retopology Matters

1. **Efficient Geometry**: High-resolution meshes are not suitable for animation or game engines. Retopology creates efficient geometry that retains the original sculpt's shape but has fewer polygons.
2. **Improved Deformation**: Models with optimized topology deform more naturally during animation. Retopology helps in creating proper edge loops around joints, which is crucial for believable character movement.
3. **Compatibility with Texturing and Rigging**: Clean topology is also essential for UV unwrapping and skinning, which are required steps for adding textures and rigging your model.

Tools for Retopology in Blender

- **Shrinkwrap Modifier**: One of the easiest ways to begin retopologizing in Blender is by using the Shrinkwrap Modifier. You create a new, low-poly mesh over your sculpted model and use the Shrinkwrap Modifier to "wrap" it onto the high-poly version.
- **Poly Build Tool**: Blender has a built-in **Poly Build** tool that makes manual retopology much easier. This tool allows you to extrude and place faces directly on the surface of your sculpt, offering precise control over edge loops and polygon flow.
- **Bsurfaces Add-on**: The **Bsurfaces** add-on (which needs to be enabled from the preferences) is an excellent tool for creating smooth, flowing topology on complex shapes. It allows you to draw curves over your high-poly sculpt, which are then converted into geometry.

Retopology Workflow

1. **Create a Base Mesh**: Start by creating a basic low-poly mesh that you will use to generate new geometry. This could be anything from a simple plane to a cylinder, depending on the part of the model you are working on.
2. **Use the Shrinkwrap Modifier**: Apply the Shrinkwrap Modifier to your low-poly mesh, and set your high-poly sculpt as the target. This will help the new mesh conform to the surface of your sculpt.
3. **Build Edge Loops**: When retopologizing a character, focus on building clean edge loops around key features such as the eyes, mouth, and joints. Proper edge flow is critical to ensure that your character deforms naturally during animation.
4. **Poly Build for Manual Adjustments**: Use the Poly Build tool to manually adjust the topology where necessary. This allows you to create more specific edge loops and ensure that the geometry flows smoothly across your model.
5. **Subdivision Testing**: After you've completed retopology, apply a **Subdivision Surface Modifier** to check how your new topology holds up under higher resolution. This helps identify areas that may need more geometry for smoother deformation.

Conclusion

Mastering mesh sculpting and retopology in Blender takes practice, patience, and a good understanding of both organic forms and efficient geometry. Sculpting allows for creative expression and intricate detail work, while retopology ensures that your models are practical for animation, rendering, and real-time use. By combining these skills, you can create professional-level models that are both visually impressive and technically optimized.

Whether sculpting a character or designing a complex organic structure, always keep in mind the balance between detail and efficiency. Sculpt freely and creatively, but always consider the end-use of your model—retopology is the bridge that brings your sculpted creations into practical applications.

NURBS and Curves: Beyond the Basics

Introduction to NURBS and Curves

Blender provides multiple modeling methods to achieve various outcomes, and one of the most effective ways to create smooth, flowing surfaces is through NURBS and curves. Unlike mesh modeling, where models are created from polygons, curves allow for more control and precision in creating complex, mathematically defined surfaces. NURBS (Non-Uniform Rational B-Splines) and Bezier curves play an essential role in workflows involving architecture, industrial design, or even character animation for more flexible and flowing designs.

In this section, we will cover what NURBS and curves are, how they differ from traditional mesh modeling, and how you can use them to create highly sophisticated models. We will also delve into some advanced applications of these tools in Blender and how they can significantly enhance your modeling projects.

Understanding NURBS and Bezier Curves

What Are NURBS?

NURBS, or Non-Uniform Rational B-Splines, are a type of curve or surface used in 3D modeling that allows for high precision and smooth surfaces. Unlike meshes that are made up of vertices, edges, and faces, NURBS are defined mathematically, making them an excellent choice for creating smooth curves and flowing shapes. This is especially important in fields like automotive and aerospace design, where mathematical precision is critical.

NURBS curves are defined by control points that influence their shape. The more control points you have, the greater your ability to manipulate the curve. NURBS can represent both simple and complex shapes, from circles to intricate freeform surfaces.

What Are Bezier Curves?

Bezier curves are another type of curve that is used extensively in Blender for creating paths, text, and many other elements. Unlike NURBS, which use control points that influence the entire curve, Bezier curves have handles attached to each control point that allow you to directly manipulate the curve's tangents. This provides intuitive control over the shape, making them ideal for animation paths and other creative uses where hands-on manipulation is beneficial.

Setting Up Curves in Blender

To get started with NURBS or Bezier curves in Blender, follow these steps:

1. **Add a Curve**: To add a curve in Blender, press `Shift + A` and select `Curve`. You will have several options, including `Bezier`, `Circle`, `NURBS Curve`, and `Path`. For this example, we'll start with a simple Bezier curve.
2. **Switch to Edit Mode**: Press `Tab` to enter Edit Mode. Here you can see the control points and handles that define the shape of the curve.
3. **Manipulate Control Points**: Select the control points and use `G` (grab), `R` (rotate), and `S` (scale) to manipulate them, just like you would in mesh modeling.
4. **Extrude the Curve**: You can extrude the curve by selecting an endpoint and pressing `E`. This adds new segments and extends the curve.

NURBS vs. Bezier Curves

The primary difference between NURBS and Bezier curves is in their control methods and applications:

- **NURBS Curves** are best suited for creating complex, smooth surfaces that require precise control. They are mathematically defined, which means they can create very smooth and accurate surfaces without the need for dense geometry.
- **Bezier Curves** offer a more hands-on approach, allowing the artist to control tangents and create custom paths. This makes them ideal for animation, typography, and artistic modeling.

Using NURBS Surfaces

Blender allows not only the creation of NURBS curves but also **NURBS surfaces**, which are 3D shapes created by extending NURBS curves into surfaces. NURBS surfaces are very powerful in generating smooth forms that would be difficult to create using mesh-based techniques.

To create a NURBS surface:

1. **Add a NURBS Surface**: Press `Shift + A`, navigate to `Surface`, and choose an option like `NURBS Surface` or `NURBS Sphere`.
2. **Edit the Surface**: Enter Edit Mode by pressing `Tab`. You'll see control points similar to those for NURBS curves, which can be manipulated to adjust the surface.
3. **Refine the Surface**: By adjusting the control points, you can create complex, smooth, flowing surfaces. NURBS surfaces are particularly useful for applications like car body panels, aircraft fuselages, or any organic, flowing structure that benefits from smooth, continuous surfaces.

Practical Applications of NURBS and Curves

Creating Pipes and Cables

One of the most common uses of curves in Blender is creating pipes, cables, and wires. This can be done by using a **Bezier or NURBS curve** as the path and then using a profile curve to generate the 3D mesh.

1. **Create the Path**: Add a Bezier or NURBS curve and shape it into the path that the pipe or cable should follow.
2. **Add a Circle Profile**: Press `Shift + A` to add a `Curve > Circle`. This circle will serve as the profile for the pipe.
3. **Use the Curve as a Bevel Object**: Select the path curve, go to the properties panel, and under the **Geometry** tab, set the `Bevel` object to be the circle. This will sweep the circle along the path, creating a pipe.

This method is incredibly flexible, as it allows you to make adjustments to the curve and automatically update the pipe's shape without having to modify the mesh.

Lofting with NURBS

Lofting is the process of creating a surface between two or more curves, and it is a powerful technique when using NURBS in Blender. You can create a lofted surface by defining multiple NURBS curves and then using a surface generation tool.

- **Create Multiple NURBS Curves**: Start by adding multiple NURBS curves (`Shift + A > Curve > NURBS`). Arrange them in the 3D space to outline the profile of the surface you wish to create.
- **Use Lofting Add-ons**: Blender doesn't have a direct lofting feature out-of-the-box, but there are several add-ons available that can accomplish this task, such as the **Surface Sketching** add-on. With the add-on, you can create a smooth surface connecting the curves you have defined.

Python Scripting with Curves

Blender's Python API allows you to create, manipulate, and automate curves and NURBS surfaces, which is highly beneficial for repetitive tasks or generating parametric models.

For example, to create a simple Bezier curve using Python:

```python
import bpy
from mathutils import Vector

# Create a new curve and object
curve_data = bpy.data.curves.new(name='BezierCurve', type='CURVE')
curve_data.dimensions = '3D'

# Add a spline to the curve
spline = curve_data.splines.new('BEZIER')
spline.bezier_points.add(1)
```

```python
# Set the points of the Bezier curve
spline.bezier_points[0].co = Vector((0.0, 0.0, 0.0))
spline.bezier_points[1].co = Vector((2.0, 2.0, 0.0))

# Create an object with the curve
curve_obj = bpy.data.objects.new('BezierObject', curve_data)

# Link to the current scene
scene = bpy.context.scene
scene.collection.objects.link(curve_obj)
```

This script demonstrates how you can create a Bezier curve, set its control points, and add it to the current scene. Using Python scripting, you can easily automate the creation and manipulation of complex curves.

Advanced Techniques with Curves

Taper and Bevel Objects

Blender allows you to use other curves as **taper** and **bevel** objects for more advanced shaping of your curves. This is useful when creating objects like musical instruments, where you want the shape to change along the length of the curve.

- **Taper Object**: To taper a curve, create another curve that represents the variation in radius along the length of the original curve. In the original curve's properties panel, set this new curve as the `Taper Object`.
- **Bevel Object**: Similarly, you can use a curve as a **Bevel Object** to define the profile of your main curve. This gives you precise control over the cross-sectional shape of the curve, which is very useful for creating decorative molding or other architectural details.

Converting Curves to Meshes

Once you are happy with the shape of your curve, you may want to convert it to a mesh for further editing. This can be done easily in Blender:

1. **Select the Curve**: Click on the curve you want to convert.
2. **Convert to Mesh**: Press `Alt + C` and select `Convert to Mesh from Curve`. This will turn the curve into mesh object that you can further refine with Blender's mesh modeling tools.

Conclusion

NURBS and curves are powerful tools in Blender that provide a level of flexibility and precision that is difficult to achieve with traditional polygonal modeling. By understanding the fundamentals of NURBS, Bezier curves, and their applications, you can take your modeling skills to new heights.

Whether you are creating sleek architectural forms, intricate character details, or practical models like pipes and cables, NURBS and curves allow you to achieve smooth, complex, and highly controlled shapes. Their integration into Blender, combined with tools like Python scripting and advanced bevel and taper options, gives you a vast toolkit for creating detailed, professional-quality models.

Practicing these techniques and experimenting with different curve types will help you understand the nuances and capabilities of Blender's curve-based modeling system, ultimately enhancing your overall 3D modeling proficiency.

Hard Surface Modeling: Tools and Tips

Introduction to Hard Surface Modeling

Hard surface modeling in Blender refers to the creation of objects that are typically non-organic, mechanical, and made up of rigid, well-defined shapes. This can include models like vehicles, weapons, buildings, and robots. Unlike organic modeling, which often involves fluid and complex curves, hard surface modeling requires a different approach focused on precise edges, sharp details, and clean geometry.

In this section, we'll explore the tools, techniques, and best practices for creating high-quality hard surface models in Blender. We will cover key topics such as mesh manipulation, Boolean operations, beveling, and the use of modifiers to achieve professional-level results.

Key Principles of Hard Surface Modeling

Hard surface models are often defined by their need for **sharp edges**, **consistent topology**, and **clean geometry**. Here are a few key principles to keep in mind:

1. **Use Bevels to Avoid Sharp Transitions**: In the real world, very few surfaces are perfectly sharp. Adding subtle bevels to your edges will help to make your models look more realistic by catching highlights in rendered images. Blender's **Bevel Modifier** is a powerful tool for this purpose.
2. **Efficient Use of Geometry**: Unlike organic modeling where polygon density can vary greatly, hard surface models need consistent edge flow and clean topology. Avoid unnecessary subdivisions and focus on placing edges where they are needed to define the structure.
3. **Utilize Modifiers**: Modifiers are non-destructive tools in Blender that allow you to perform a wide range of modeling tasks. Commonly used modifiers for hard surface modeling include the **Bevel Modifier**, **Subdivision Surface Modifier**, and **Boolean Modifier**.

Essential Tools for Hard Surface Modeling

Mesh Editing Tools

Blender's **Edit Mode** is the primary workspace for manipulating geometry. Here are some of the most important tools for hard surface modeling:

- **Extrude (E)**: This is one of the most commonly used tools in hard surface modeling. It allows you to pull out new geometry from a face, which is particularly useful for creating mechanical details like panels, buttons, or other protrusions.
- **Inset (I)**: The **Inset** tool allows you to create a new face that is inset from the selected face. This is very useful for adding details like panels or vent grilles.
- **Loop Cut and Slide (Ctrl + R)**: Adding **loop cuts** helps you control the flow of your geometry, which is crucial for creating clean models. Loop cuts can also be used to define areas where you need sharper edges or to add detail.
- **Knife Tool (K)**: The **Knife Tool** is used to cut new edges into your geometry. This is especially useful for creating custom geometry that fits specific design needs.

Boolean Operations

Boolean operations are essential in hard surface modeling, as they allow you to combine or subtract shapes in ways that would be difficult to achieve otherwise.

- **Union**: The **Union** Boolean operation allows you to merge two objects together. This can be helpful when combining multiple parts into a single cohesive model.
- **Difference**: The **Difference** Boolean is perhaps the most commonly used Boolean operation in hard surface modeling. It allows you to subtract one object from another, which is perfect for creating cutouts, vents, or holes.
- **Intersect**: The **Intersect** operation keeps only the overlapping part of two objects. This can be useful for creating details that are part of two intersecting structures.

Practical Example of a Boolean Operation:

1. Create a **cylinder** and a **cube** in your scene.
2. Position the cube so that it intersects with the cylinder.
3. With the cylinder selected, add a **Boolean Modifier**.
4. Set the **Operation** to Difference and select the cube as the target object.
5. Apply the modifier, and then delete the cube to reveal the cut-out in the cylinder.

```
import bpy

# Example: Creating a cylinder and using Boolean to subtract a cube
bpy.ops.mesh.primitive_cylinder_add(radius=1, depth=2, location=(0,
0, 0))
cylinder = bpy.context.object

bpy.ops.mesh.primitive_cube_add(size=1, location=(0.5, 0.5, 0))
cube = bpy.context.object
```

```python
# Boolean Modifier setup
bool_mod = cylinder.modifiers.new(name="Boolean", type='BOOLEAN')
bool_mod.operation = 'DIFFERENCE'
bool_mod.object = cube

# Apply the modifier
bpy.context.view_layer.objects.active = cylinder
bpy.ops.object.modifier_apply(modifier="Boolean")

# Delete the cube
bpy.data.objects.remove(cube, do_unlink=True)
```

Using the Bevel Modifier for Detail

One of the most crucial elements in hard surface modeling is the **Bevel Modifier**. Beveling creates a chamfer or rounded edge along the sharp edges of your model, which is critical for adding realism.

- **Applying the Bevel Modifier**: Start by selecting your object and adding a **Bevel Modifier** from the modifiers tab. You can adjust the **width** and **segments** to control the size and smoothness of the bevel.
- **Bevel Weight**: For more control, you can use **bevel weights** on specific edges. Enter **Edge Select Mode (2)**, select the edges you want to bevel, and assign a bevel weight by pressing Ctrl + E and selecting **Edge Bevel Weight**.

Practical Tips for Beveling

- **Consistent Bevels**: Maintain consistent bevel widths throughout your model. This will give your hard surface models a more polished and cohesive appearance.
- **Manual Bevels**: While the **Bevel Modifier** is powerful, sometimes manual beveling is necessary for precise control. In **Edit Mode**, select an edge and press Ctrl + B to perform a manual bevel.

Subdivision Surface and Control of Edge Sharpness

The **Subdivision Surface Modifier** can be used to add smoothness to your model, but in hard surface modeling, it's essential to control where the smoothing occurs.

- **Edge Loops for Control**: To maintain sharp edges while using the **Subdivision Surface Modifier**, add **supporting edge loops** close to the edges that you want to remain sharp. This will limit the effect of the subdivision and help maintain the model's hard edges.
- **Crease Tool**: Another option is to use **Edge Creasing**. In **Edit Mode**, select the edges you want to sharpen, press Shift + E, and drag to adjust the crease. A value of 1 will make the edge perfectly sharp under subdivision.

Creating Panels and Surface Details

Hard surface models often feature panels, vents, and surface details. Here's a simple workflow to create such details:

1. **Create a Base Mesh**: Start with a basic cube or other primitive shape that serves as the foundation of your model.
2. **Use the Inset Tool**: Select a face, press I to inset the face slightly, then press E to extrude it inward or outward. This creates a panel that's either recessed or protruding from the base.
3. **Adding Bolts and Screws**: For additional realism, add small details like bolts and screws. These can be created as separate objects (using cylinders, for instance) and then placed appropriately around the model.

Using Arrays and Mirror Modifiers

Array and **Mirror Modifiers** are incredibly useful for adding repeating elements and ensuring symmetry.

- **Mirror Modifier**: This modifier allows you to work on one side of your model and have Blender mirror your actions to the other side. This is especially useful for symmetrical models like vehicles or robots. Add a **Mirror Modifier** to your object, and ensure the mirror axis aligns correctly to create symmetry.
- **Array Modifier**: The **Array Modifier** allows you to create multiple instances of an object along an axis. For example, if you're modeling a spaceship with repeating hull plating, use the **Array Modifier** to duplicate the plating along a specified axis.

Practical Example of Using the Array Modifier:

1. Create a simple panel by adding a **cube** and scaling it to a flat rectangle.
2. Add an **Array Modifier** to the cube.
3. Set the **Count** to define how many instances you want.
4. Adjust the **Offset** to control the spacing between the panels.

```
import bpy

# Create a panel object
bpy.ops.mesh.primitive_cube_add(size=1, location=(0, 0, 0))
panel = bpy.context.object
panel.scale = (1, 0.2, 0.1)

# Add an Array Modifier to create repeating panels
array_mod = panel.modifiers.new(name="Array", type='ARRAY')
array_mod.count = 5
array_mod.relative_offset_displace = (1.5, 0, 0)
```

Advanced Techniques: Kitbashing

Kitbashing is the practice of using pre-made parts to build complex models quickly. This technique is widely used in concept design, especially for creating sci-fi models, as it allows artists to produce highly detailed results efficiently.

- **Building a Kitbash Library**: Collect and organize a library of reusable assets like bolts, gears, panels, and mechanical elements. These can be appended or linked into new projects, significantly speeding up the modeling process.
- **Using Add-ons**: There are several add-ons available for Blender, such as **HardOps** and **BoxCutter**, that facilitate kitbashing and hard surface modeling by providing advanced Boolean tools, cutting mechanisms, and pre-made components.

Shading and Materials for Hard Surfaces

Hard surface models benefit from thoughtful shading and texturing that highlight their sharp edges and details. Here are a few tips for applying materials:

- **Edge Wear and Tear**: Use a procedural **ambient occlusion mask** to add edge wear to your materials. This simulates wear and tear, making your model look more realistic. In **Blender's Shader Editor**, combine the **Ambient Occlusion** node with a mix shader to blend between different materials, such as clean metal and worn edges.
- **Bump and Normal Maps**: Adding **normal maps** or **bump maps** can enhance the perception of detail on your hard surface model without adding more geometry. For example, add a normal map with subtle patterns to create the illusion of panel lines, bolts, or scratches.

```python
import bpy

# Assigning a simple material with edge wear effect
mat = bpy.data.materials.new(name="EdgeWearMaterial")
mat.use_nodes = True

nodes = mat.node_tree.nodes
links = mat.node_tree.links

# Adding ambient occlusion for edge wear effect
ao_node = nodes.new(type='ShaderNodeAmbientOcclusion')
mix_shader = nodes.new(type='ShaderNodeMixShader')
diffuse = nodes.new(type='ShaderNodeBsdfDiffuse')
glossy = nodes.new(type='ShaderNodeBsdfGlossy')

links.new(ao_node.outputs['Color'], mix_shader.inputs['Fac'])
links.new(diffuse.outputs['BSDF'], mix_shader.inputs[1])
```

```
links.new(glossy.outputs['BSDF'], mix_shader.inputs[2])
links.new(mix_shader.outputs['Shader'], nodes.get('Material
Output').inputs['Surface'])
```

Conclusion

Hard surface modeling is an essential skill for creating mechanical, architectural, and product design models. By mastering Blender's tools such as **Boolean operations**, **Bevel Modifier**, **Array Modifier**, and leveraging advanced techniques like **kitbashing**, you can create highly detailed and realistic models.

The key to successful hard surface modeling lies in maintaining clean topology, using modifiers effectively, and adding details that enhance realism. By practicing the concepts discussed in this section and applying them to your projects, you'll be well-equipped to handle any hard surface modeling task, from designing futuristic vehicles to intricate mechanical devices.

Organic Modeling: Crafting Characters and Natural Forms

Introduction to Organic Modeling

Organic modeling in Blender focuses on creating models that resemble living beings or natural forms, such as animals, characters, plants, and even landscapes. Unlike hard surface modeling, organic modeling deals with fluid, irregular shapes, requiring different techniques and tools to produce believable forms. In this section, we will cover the essential techniques for modeling organic characters, discuss best practices for sculpting natural forms, and explore how Blender's tools can be leveraged to create dynamic, naturalistic models.

The Importance of Organic Modeling

Organic models are characterized by complex, flowing curves and non-linear shapes. They require a greater emphasis on **proportions**, **anatomy**, and **deformation** to ensure they look natural and are suitable for animation. Key elements in organic modeling include:

1. **Understanding Anatomy**: Whether modeling humans, animals, or fantastical creatures, a solid understanding of the anatomy is crucial. Proper anatomical proportions help create a believable model that can be effectively animated.
2. **Dynamic Forms**: Organic forms are rarely symmetrical or repetitive. This means your model needs to have a natural variance in its shapes and curves to feel alive. This is especially true for characters, where asymmetry in facial features or musculature adds personality.
3. **Sculpting Over Box Modeling**: Unlike mechanical models, organic modeling typically benefits from sculpting rather than traditional polygonal modeling. Sculpting

allows for greater control over subtle shapes, which is essential for creating muscles, facial features, and other organic details.

Setting Up for Organic Sculpting

Blender offers a variety of tools and workflows to assist with organic modeling, primarily centered around its **Sculpt Mode** and **Dynamic Topology**.

1. **Starting with a Base Mesh**: A base mesh is essential for organic modeling. It can be as simple as a UV sphere or a cube. The base mesh serves as the foundation for the sculpting process and should be properly subdivided for effective sculpting.
2. **Sculpting Brushes**: Blender has a rich set of brushes that are specifically designed for organic modeling:
   - **Clay Strips**: This brush is ideal for building up muscle structure or defining major forms.
   - **Crease Brush**: Perfect for adding definition, such as wrinkles or sharp folds.
   - **Grab Brush**: The **Grab** brush allows you to move large parts of your mesh, which is crucial during the early stages of sculpting when defining overall proportions.
3. **Dynamic Topology (Dyntopo)**: **Dynamic Topology** (Dyntopo) enables you to dynamically add or remove geometry as you sculpt. This means you can add details in areas where you need more resolution and keep other areas simple, ensuring your model remains manageable.

Blocking Out Primary Forms

The first stage of organic modeling is to block out the primary forms of the model. This involves establishing the overall shape and major volumes before adding any fine details.

- **Focus on Silhouette**: Start by focusing on the silhouette of the model. Rotate the model frequently to evaluate its profile from different angles. The silhouette should convey the general character or nature of the model.
- **Use the Grab Brush**: The **Grab Brush** is perfect for moving large portions of your model without adding additional geometry. This brush allows you to adjust the proportions quickly without affecting the topology too much.
- **Broad Strokes with Clay Strips**: Use the **Clay Strips** brush to begin building up mass. At this stage, you want to define where major anatomical elements such as muscles, bone structures, or other defining features are located.

Anatomy Considerations in Character Modeling

An essential part of organic modeling is creating models that adhere to the underlying anatomical structure. Even if you are modeling a creature from your imagination, understanding the basics of anatomy will help your model look more realistic.

Human Anatomy

For character modeling, understanding human anatomy is critical. Here are some tips to keep in mind:

1. **Bone Structure**: Start by defining the skeletal landmarks, such as the rib cage, pelvis, and spine. These form the foundation of your model.
2. **Muscle Groups**: Once the bone structure is established, begin defining the larger muscle groups. Pay attention to the natural flow of muscle fibers. For example, muscles such as the **pectorals** should connect from the shoulder to the sternum.
3. **Facial Features**: Faces are one of the most complex parts to model due to their many subtle forms. Use reference images to identify key landmarks, such as the **brow ridge**, **cheekbones**, **nose**, and **jawline**. Use a combination of **Smooth** and **Crease** brushes to create realistic facial features.

Animal Anatomy

Modeling animals requires a similar approach but with a focus on different anatomical elements. The following aspects are important:

- **Skeletal Differences**: Understand the anatomy of the animal you are modeling. For example, quadrupeds have a different leg structure than bipeds, including **digitigrade** versus **plantigrade** stances.
- **Muscle Structure**: Animals have different muscle groups based on their movement type. For example, a cat's back muscles are very flexible, allowing for a greater range of motion, which must be reflected in your model.

Detailing and Refining

Once the primary forms are in place, you can begin refining your model by adding smaller details. This includes muscles, veins, wrinkles, and surface textures that add realism to your model.

Adding Secondary Forms

Secondary forms refer to medium-sized details such as the definition of specific muscles, fat deposits, and bone landmarks.

- **Crease Brush for Definition**: The **Crease Brush** is perfect for accentuating areas such as muscle striations or defining bone features like the collarbone.
- **Inflate Brush for Volume**: Use the **Inflate Brush** to give volume to areas that need more mass. This is helpful when adding muscle definition or rounding out forms that are too flat.

Surface Detailing

The final pass involves adding small details that give character to your model. This includes skin textures, pores, wrinkles, and other fine features.

- **Detailing with Alpha Brushes**: Blender allows you to use **alpha textures** with your brushes to add surface details like skin pores or scales. You can import an image texture and use it as an alpha map to imprint those details onto the surface.
- **Smooth Brush for Transitions**: Use the **Smooth Brush** to blend areas and soften transitions between different parts of the model. This is especially important for making muscles appear to flow naturally under the skin.

Retopology for Animation

After the sculpting phase is complete, your model may have a very high polygon count, which is impractical for animation. **Retopology** is the process of creating a new, simplified mesh that retains the details of the sculpt while having a manageable polygon count.

- **Use the Shrinkwrap Modifier**: Create a low-poly version of your model and use the **Shrinkwrap Modifier** to conform it to the high-resolution sculpt. This allows you to create clean, animation-ready topology.
- **Edge Loop Placement**: Proper edge loop placement is crucial for effective deformation during animation. Place edge loops around key areas such as **joints** (elbows, knees) and **facial features** to ensure they deform naturally.

Using Multi-Resolution for Detail

The **Multi-Resolution Modifier** is another powerful tool in Blender for adding detail without sacrificing overall model performance.

- **Lower Resolution for Broad Strokes**: Start at a lower resolution to adjust the overall form, then gradually increase the resolution to add finer details. This approach keeps the model manageable and avoids adding unnecessary geometry too early in the process.
- **Baking Details**: Once you have completed the sculpt, use the **Bake** tool to capture the high-resolution details as **normal maps** or **displacement maps**. These maps can be applied to your low-poly model, allowing it to retain the detailed look without the high polygon count.

Shading and Material Considerations for Organic Models

To make your organic models look even more realistic, it's essential to consider how you apply materials and shading.

- **Subsurface Scattering (SSS)**: Organic materials such as skin, leaves, and certain plants often exhibit **subsurface scattering**, where light penetrates the surface and scatters inside the material. Blender's **Principled BSDF Shader** has a **Subsurface** parameter to help achieve this effect, making skin and other organic materials look more lifelike.
- **Bump and Normal Maps**: Use **bump maps** and **normal maps** to add surface imperfections like skin pores or scales. This adds depth and detail to your material without additional geometry.

```python
import bpy

# Example of adding subsurface scattering to a character material
material = bpy.data.materials.new(name="SkinMaterial")
material.use_nodes = True

# Accessing nodes
nodes = material.node_tree.nodes
links = material.node_tree.links

# Principled BSDF for skin
principled = nodes.get("Principled BSDF")
principled.inputs['Subsurface'].default_value = 0.2
principled.inputs['Subsurface Radius'].default_value = (1.0, 0.8,
0.5)
principled.inputs['Subsurface Color'].default_value = (0.8, 0.5,
0.4, 1)

# Assigning the material to an object
character = bpy.context.object
if character:
    if character.data.materials:
        character.data.materials[0] = material
    else:
        character.data.materials.append(material)
```

Sculpting Natural Forms and Environments

Organic modeling isn't limited to characters and animals; it also includes natural forms like rocks, trees, and terrain.

Creating Trees and Foliage

- **Use Curves for Branches**: Blender's **Bezier Curves** are very useful for creating tree branches. Convert the curves into meshes, and then use the **Skin Modifier** to give them thickness.
- **Add Leaf Geometry**: Create a simple leaf model and use the **Particle System** to distribute it across the branches. This method provides realistic-looking foliage with minimal effort.
- **Tree Add-ons**: Blender has several add-ons, such as **Sapling Tree Gen**, that can generate trees procedurally. These add-ons allow you to control parameters like branch growth, leaf density, and overall tree shape.

Sculpting Terrain

- **Start with a Plane**: Begin with a subdivided plane. Use **Proportional Editing** (O) to pull up mountains or hills.
- **Sculpt Brushes for Detailing**: Use the **Draw Brush** to add elevation, the **Smooth Brush** to soften transitions, and the **Flatten Brush** to create plateaus.
- **Add Rocks and Details**: Use Blender's **Rock Generator** or manually sculpt rocks to scatter across the terrain. Scatter these objects to add realism and break up the monotony of the landscape.

Conclusion

Organic modeling in Blender is an art form that requires a deep understanding of natural shapes, anatomy, and proportion. By leveraging Blender's sculpting tools, modifiers, and careful attention to detail, you can create characters, creatures, and environments that are both compelling and believable.

The process begins with blocking out the basic shapes, refining the forms, adding anatomical details, and finally, using retopology and texture maps to make the model suitable for animation and rendering. Mastery of these techniques takes time and practice, but by continually studying anatomy and experimenting with Blender's tools, you will gain the skills needed to craft stunning organic models.

Chapter 5: Texturing and Materials

Understanding UV Mapping

UV mapping is a fundamental technique in 3D graphics that involves wrapping a 2D image texture onto a 3D model. In Blender, mastering UV mapping is essential for creating realistic textures and materials. This section will guide you through the principles, workflows, and tools necessary to understand and effectively use UV mapping in your projects.

What is UV Mapping?

In 3D space, every vertex on a 3D model corresponds to a specific point on a 2D texture. These correspondences are defined by UV coordinates, where "U" and "V" are the axes of the 2D texture (analogous to X and Y in 3D space). UV mapping ensures that every part of a 3D object is associated with a particular section of a texture image.

UV mapping allows artists to:

- Precisely control how textures appear on a 3D object.
- Minimize stretching and distortion in textures.
- Create seamless and accurate materials for rendering and game assets.

UV Unwrapping Workflow

To begin UV mapping in Blender, you need to unwrap the model, which is the process of projecting its 3D surface onto a 2D plane. Follow these steps:

1. **Prepare Your Model**
   Ensure your model is complete and has a clean topology. It's best to apply transformations (Ctrl+A > Apply > All Transforms) to avoid scaling issues.
2. **Switch to Edit Mode**
   Select the object in Object Mode, then switch to Edit Mode (Tab). Select the faces, edges, or vertices you want to unwrap.
3. **Mark Seams**
   Seams define where the model will be "cut" during the UV unwrapping process. To mark a seam:
   - Select the edges (2 for edge select mode).
   - Press Ctrl+E > Mark Seam. Seams act as guides for Blender's unwrapping algorithm.
4. **Unwrap the Model**
   With the desired faces selected, press U to open the UV Mapping menu. Choose an unwrapping method:
   - **Unwrap**: Best for complex models with well-placed seams.

- ○ **Smart UV Project**: Automatically determines seams and unwraps the model (useful for quick results).
- ○ **Cube Projection**, **Cylinder Projection**, or **Sphere Projection**: For specific geometric shapes.

5. **Adjust UV Islands**
   Open the UV Editor (Shift+F10 or select it from the workspace). Here, you can view and modify the UV layout. Use G, S, and R to move, scale, and rotate UV islands for better alignment and scaling.

Best Practices for UV Mapping

1. **Minimize Stretching**
   Check for stretching in the UV Editor. Use the "Display Stretch" option (N > View > Display Stretch) to visualize distortions. Adjust UV islands as needed.

2. **Uniform Scaling**
   Ensure UV islands have consistent scaling. This is particularly important for tiling textures. Use the "Average Island Scale" option in the UV Editor (UV > Average Island Scale).

3. **Efficient Packing**
   Optimize UV space usage by packing UV islands efficiently. Use the "Pack Islands" tool (UV > Pack Islands) to minimize wasted space.

4. **Maintain Proportions**
   For organic models, like characters or plants, prioritize proportional mapping to preserve detail. For hard-surface models, focus on alignment and symmetry.

5. **Check the Result**
   Apply a checker texture to preview the UV layout. Create a new material, add a procedural checker texture in the Shader Editor, and assign it to the model. Look for uniform squares and adjust the UV layout if necessary.

UV Mapping Example in Blender

Here's an example of UV unwrapping a basic cube with seams:

1. Create a cube (Shift+A > Mesh > Cube).
2. Select the cube and switch to Edit Mode (Tab).
3. Select the edges where you want to create seams (e.g., edges around one face of the cube).
4. Mark seams (Ctrl+E > Mark Seam).
5. Select all faces (A) and unwrap the cube (U > Unwrap).
6. Open the UV Editor and view the resulting UV map.

Advanced Techniques and Tools

1. **Live Unwrap**
   Enable Live Unwrap (UV > Live Unwrap) to see real-time changes as you adjust seams and unwrap settings.

2. **UDIM Workflow**
   Blender supports UDIM (U-Dimension), which allows for multi-tile UV mapping. This is useful for high-resolution textures or when working on large-scale projects. Enable UDIM by creating a new UV map and selecting the UDIM grid layout.
3. **Seamless Textures**
   To create seamless textures, ensure the UV edges align appropriately and avoid stretching at the seams. Use image editing software to create tileable textures.
4. **Pinning UVs**
   Pin specific UV vertices (P) to lock them in place during further adjustments. This is helpful for precise alignment.

Common Challenges in UV Mapping

- **Overlapping UVs**: This occurs when two or more UV islands occupy the same space. Fix this by separating and repositioning the islands.
- **Distortion**: Stretching or compression in the UV layout leads to texture inaccuracies. Adjust seams and UV island scaling to resolve this.
- **Large UV Maps**: For detailed models, splitting the UV map into multiple tiles or using UDIM can prevent excessive resolution requirements.

Conclusion

Understanding UV mapping is crucial for creating realistic and professional-quality 3D assets. With Blender's robust tools, you can achieve precise control over textures and materials, whether you're working on games, animations, or visual effects. Practice these techniques on various models to refine your skills and produce stunning results.

Material Nodes: The Basics of Shader Creation

Material nodes are a cornerstone of Blender's powerful node-based shading system. They allow for creating complex and visually stunning materials by combining various node types to define surface properties. This section explores the foundational concepts, workflows, and practical applications of material nodes in Blender.

Introduction to the Shader Editor

The Shader Editor is where material nodes are managed and configured. To access it.

1. Select your object.
2. Switch to the Shader Editor workspace (Shift+F3 or select it from the workspace menu).
3. Ensure the object has a material assigned. If not, click the **New** button in the Shader Editor to create a material.

Materials in Blender consist of a network of nodes that define how the object interacts with light, controls its surface appearance, and even affects its physical properties.

The Node System

Nodes are individual components that represent specific functions or properties. Blender's material node system is composed of:

- **Input Nodes**: Provide basic information like textures, coordinates, or values.
- **Shader Nodes**: Define how light interacts with a surface (e.g., diffuse, glossy, transparent).
- **Mix and Math Nodes**: Combine or modify input and shader data.
- **Output Nodes**: Connect the material to the object's surface or volume.

Building a Basic Material

Let's start by creating a simple material:

1. **Add a Principled BSDF Node**
   The Principled BSDF node is Blender's all-in-one shader for creating realistic materials. It combines multiple shader properties into a single node.
   - Press `Shift+A` in the Shader Editor.
   - Navigate to **Shader > Principled BSDF**.
   - Connect it to the **Material Output** node.
2. **Adjust Basic Properties**
   The Principled BSDF node offers various parameters:
   - **Base Color**: Defines the surface's primary color.
   - **Metallic**: Simulates metallic surfaces.
   - **Roughness**: Controls surface smoothness.
   - **Specular**: Adjusts light reflection intensity.
3. **Preview the Material**
   Switch to the Material Preview or Rendered view in the 3D Viewport to see changes in real-time.

Here's a Python script to automate the creation of a basic material:

```python
import bpy

# Create a new material
material = bpy.data.materials.new(name="BasicMaterial")
material.use_nodes = True

# Access the material's node tree
nodes = material.node_tree.nodes
links = material.node_tree.links

# Clear existing nodes
for node in nodes:
```

```
    nodes.remove(node)

# Add Principled BSDF node
bsdf = nodes.new(type='ShaderNodeBsdfPrincipled')
bsdf.location = (0, 0)

# Add Material Output node
output = nodes.new(type='ShaderNodeOutputMaterial')
output.location = (300, 0)

# Link nodes
links.new(bsdf.outputs['BSDF'], output.inputs['Surface'])
```

Assign this material to an object by selecting the object and setting its active material.

Enhancing with Textures

Textures add complexity and realism to materials. Blender supports both procedural and image-based textures.

Adding an Image Texture

1. Add an **Image Texture** node (Shift+A > **Texture** > **Image Texture**).
2. Load a texture image by clicking **Open**.
3. Connect the **Color** output of the Image Texture node to the **Base Color** input of the Principled BSDF.

To properly align the texture:

- Add a **Texture Coordinate** node (Shift+A > **Input** > **Texture Coordinate`**).
- Add a **Mapping** node (Shift+A > **Vector** > **Mapping`**).
- Connect the **UV** output of the Texture Coordinate node to the **Vector** input of the Mapping node, then link the Mapping node's output to the Image Texture node's input.

Procedural Textures

Procedural textures are generated using algorithms and do not rely on external image files. Blender offers nodes like **Noise Texture**, **Voronoi Texture**, and **Wave Texture** for procedural effects.

Example: Creating a marble-like material using procedural textures:

1. Add a **Noise Texture** node and a **ColorRamp** node.
2. Connect the **Noise Texture** node's output to the **ColorRamp** node.
3. Link the **ColorRamp** output to the **Base Color** input of the Principled BSDF.

4. Adjust the ColorRamp to achieve the desired effect.

Mixing Shaders

To create complex materials, you can combine multiple shaders using the **Mix Shader** node.

Example: A glassy metallic material:

1. Add a **Glass BSDF** node and a **Glossy BSDF** node.
2. Add a **Mix Shader** node.
3. Connect the outputs of the Glass and Glossy nodes to the Mix Shader inputs.
4. Link the Mix Shader output to the Material Output node.

Control the blend using the Mix Shader's **Fac** input. Use a texture or procedural node to dynamically vary the factor.

Using Material Nodes for Animation

Material nodes can be animated to create dynamic effects. For instance:

- Animate the color of a material by keyframing the **Base Color**.
- Add a **Value** node and animate its output. Connect it to various properties like Roughness or Emission Strength.

Example code for animating material color:

```
import bpy

# Access the active material
material = bpy.context.object.active_material
nodes = material.node_tree.nodes
bsdf = nodes.get("Principled BSDF")

# Animate the base color
for frame, color in [(1, (1, 0, 0, 1)), (50, (0, 1, 0, 1)), (100,
(0, 0, 1, 1))]:
    bsdf.inputs['Base Color'].default_value = color
    bsdf.inputs['Base ·
Color'].keyframe_insert(data_path="default_value", frame=frame)
```

Conclusion

Mastering material nodes in Blender unlocks endless possibilities for creating visually rich and dynamic 3D assets. By experimenting with different node combinations and workflows, you can achieve materials that rival those seen in professional productions. Start simple, build your understanding, and progressively incorporate advanced techniques to take your projects to the next level.

Procedural Textures vs. Image Textures

Creating realistic materials in Blender often involves texturing, a process that defines the surface detail and appearance of 3D models. Textures can be either procedural or image-based, each offering unique advantages and workflows. This section explores these two approaches, their differences, and practical applications to help you decide when and how to use them effectively.

What Are Procedural Textures?

Procedural textures are algorithmically generated textures created using Blender's node-based system. They are resolution-independent, meaning they are defined mathematically rather than being limited to a fixed pixel size. Procedural textures are ideal for creating patterns, gradients, and other effects that require scalability or dynamic adjustments.

Key Features of Procedural Textures:

- **Infinite Detail**: Procedural textures don't lose quality when zoomed in.
- **Customizability**: Parameters like scale, distortion, and color can be dynamically adjusted.
- **Seamlessness**: Procedural textures are inherently seamless, making them ideal for tiling.
- **No External Files**: They don't rely on external image files, reducing project dependencies.

Example: Creating a Procedural Wood Texture

1. Open the Shader Editor and create a new material.
2. Add a **Wave Texture** node (Shift+A > **Texture** > **Wave Texture`).
3. Add a **ColorRamp** node (Shift+A > **Converter** > **ColorRamp`).
4. Connect the Wave Texture's **Color** output to the ColorRamp's input.
5. Link the ColorRamp's output to the **Base Color** input of a **Principled BSDF** node.

Adjust the Wave Texture's **Scale**, **Distortion**, and **Detail** properties to achieve a wood-like pattern. Use the ColorRamp to fine-tune the color variation.

What Are Image Textures?

Image textures are raster-based images applied to 3D models. They are typically created in external software, such as Photoshop or Substance Painter, and imported into Blender. Image textures are perfect for achieving photorealistic results, especially when precise details or real-world references are needed.

Key Features of Image Textures:

- **Realism**: They capture intricate details like scratches, wear, and imperfections.
- **Versatility**: Can include albedo, normal maps, roughness maps, and more for physically-based rendering (PBR).
- **Ease of Use**: Pre-made textures save time and are readily available from online libraries.

Example: Applying an Image Texture

1. Create a new material in the Shader Editor.
2. Add an **Image Texture** node (Shift+A > **Texture** > ****Image Texture`**).
3. Click **Open** to load your image file.
4. Connect the Image Texture's **Color** output to the Principled BSDF's **Base Color** input.

For a complete PBR workflow, connect additional maps (e.g., Normal, Roughness, Metallic) to their respective inputs on the Principled BSDF node.

Differences Between Procedural and Image Textures

Feature	Procedural Textures	Image Textures
Resolution	Infinite detail	Limited by image resolution
Customization	Fully adjustable	Fixed once created
File Dependency	No external files required	Requires image files
Seamlessness	Always seamless	May require manual editing
Realism	Stylized or abstract patterns	Photorealistic
Performance	Higher computational cost	Faster rendering after preprocessing

Combining Procedural and Image Textures

A hybrid approach often yields the best results. For example:

- Use a procedural texture for base patterns and an image texture for detailed imperfections.
- Combine a procedural noise texture with a dirt mask to add subtle variation to an image-based material.

Example: Hybrid Texture Workflow

1. Add a **Noise Texture** node and a **ColorRamp** node.
2. Add an **Image Texture** node for your primary texture.
3. Use a **MixRGB** node to blend the Noise Texture and Image Texture.
4. Connect the MixRGB's output to the Principled BSDF's **Base Color** input.

Adjust the MixRGB's **Fac** value to control the influence of each texture.

Creating Tileable Image Textures

One challenge with image textures is ensuring they tile seamlessly. Here's how to make a tileable texture in Blender:

1. Open your texture in the Image Editor.
2. Enable **UV Editing** mode and adjust the UV map to ensure no visible seams.
3. Use a **Mapping** node in the Shader Editor to tile the image texture. Connect the Mapping node's output to the Image Texture's input and adjust the scaling.

Alternatively, use external tools like Photoshop or GIMP to edit the image directly.

Advanced Procedural Techniques

Blender's procedural system can produce highly detailed and complex effects. For instance:

- **Noise Texture**: Great for adding randomness and subtle surface variation.
- **Voronoi Texture**: Used for cell-like patterns, water ripples, or cracks.
- **Wave Texture**: Ideal for linear patterns like wood grains or water waves.

Example: Creating a Procedural Marble Texture

1. Add a **Noise Texture** node and a **Wave Texture** node.
2. Use a **MixRGB** node to blend them.
3. Connect the output to a **ColorRamp** node to control contrast.
4. Link the ColorRamp's output to the Principled BSDF's **Base Color**.

Adjust the Noise and Wave Texture properties to achieve a realistic marble effect.

Optimizing Texture Performance

Large textures or complex procedural setups can strain your system. To optimize:

- Use lower-resolution image textures for preview renders.
- Bake procedural textures into image textures for faster performance.
- Minimize the number of nodes in complex setups.

Baking Textures in Blender

1. Switch to the **Cycles** render engine.
2. Add an **Image Texture** node and create a new blank texture.
3. Select your object and go to the **Bake** settings in the Properties panel.

4. Choose a bake type (e.g., Diffuse, Normal) and click **Bake**.

Save the baked texture and use it in place of procedural nodes.

Conclusion

Procedural and image textures each offer unique strengths, and understanding their differences allows for more informed decisions when creating materials. Procedural textures excel in flexibility and scalability, while image textures shine in realism and detail. By leveraging both approaches and combining them effectively, you can achieve stunning results tailored to your specific project needs. Experimenting with these techniques will expand your texturing skills and enhance your creative workflow.

Creating Realistic Materials

Realistic materials are essential for producing convincing 3D renders in Blender. They bring life to models, making them appear tactile and believable. This section will delve into techniques and workflows for creating materials that mimic real-world surfaces, leveraging Blender's powerful node-based shader system and rendering engines.

Understanding Physically-Based Rendering (PBR)

Physically-Based Rendering (PBR) is a standard approach to material creation that simulates how light interacts with surfaces in the real world. Blender's Principled BSDF shader is a cornerstone for PBR workflows.

Key Properties of PBR:

- **Base Color**: Defines the primary color of the material.
- **Metallic**: Determines whether the surface behaves like a metal or a non-metal.
- **Roughness**: Controls the surface's smoothness and how light is reflected.
- **Specular**: Adjusts the intensity of light reflection on non-metal surfaces.
- **Normal/Bump Maps**: Add surface detail without increasing geometry.
- **Subsurface Scattering (SSS)**: Simulates light penetration in translucent materials like skin or wax.

Creating a Realistic Material: A Step-by-Step Guide

1. **Setup Your Scene**
    - Ensure adequate lighting in your scene. Use an HDRI environment for natural lighting and reflections.
    - Switch to the Cycles render engine for more accurate light calculations.
2. **Create a Base Material**
    - In the Shader Editor, create a new material.
    - Add a **Principled BSDF** node (Shift+A > **Shader** > **Principled BSDF`**) and connect it to the **Material Output** node.
3. **Define the Base Color**

- o Choose a realistic color for the material. For example, a wooden surface might have a warm brown tone.
4. **Add Roughness and Metallic Properties**
   - o Adjust the Roughness slider based on the surface type. A mirror has low roughness, while a rough stone has high roughness.
   - o If the material is metallic, set the Metallic slider to 1. Non-metals like wood or plastic should have a Metallic value of 0.

Example Code to Create a PBR Material in Python:

```python
import bpy

# Create a new material
material = bpy.data.materials.new(name="RealisticMaterial")
material.use_nodes = True
nodes = material.node_tree.nodes

# Add Principled BSDF
bsdf = nodes.new(type='ShaderNodeBsdfPrincipled')
bsdf.location = (0, 0)

# Assign properties
bsdf.inputs['Base Color'].default_value = (0.8, 0.5, 0.3, 1)  #
Example color
bsdf.inputs['Roughness'].default_value = 0.5
bsdf.inputs['Metallic'].default_value = 0.0

# Connect to material output
output = nodes.get("Material Output")
material.node_tree.links.new(bsdf.outputs['BSDF'],
output.inputs['Surface'])
```

Enhancing Realism with Texture Maps

Texture maps add details like color variations, surface imperfections, and depth. Common texture maps include:

- **Albedo/Color Map**: Defines the surface's primary color and pattern.
- **Roughness Map**: Specifies areas of varying smoothness.
- **Normal Map**: Simulates fine details like scratches or grooves.
- **Displacement Map**: Alters geometry to add depth.
- **Specular Map**: Controls reflection intensity.

Workflow for Adding Texture Maps

1. **Import Texture Maps**
   - Add an **Image Texture** node for each map (Shift+A > **Texture** > **Image Texture`).
   - Load the corresponding image files.
2. **Connect Maps to the Principled Shader**
   - Albedo: Connect to **Base Color**.
   - Roughness: Connect to **Roughness**.
   - Normal: Add a **Normal Map** node and connect it to **Normal**.
   - Displacement: Add a **Displacement** node and connect it to the **Material Output's Displacement** input.
3. **UV Mapping**
   - Ensure proper UV mapping for accurate texture placement. Use the **UV Editor** to adjust UV islands.

Example: Applying Multiple Texture Maps

```python
# Assuming a material is already created
material = bpy.context.object.active_material
nodes = material.node_tree.nodes
links = material.node_tree.links


# Add Image Texture for Albedo
albedo = nodes.new(type='ShaderNodeTexImage')
albedo.image = bpy.data.images.load("//textures/albedo.jpg")
albedo.location = (-300, 300)
links.new(albedo.outputs['Color'], nodes['Principled
BSDF'].inputs['Base Color'])


# Add Roughness Map
roughness = nodes.new(type='ShaderNodeTexImage')
roughness.image = bpy.data.images.load("//textures/roughness.jpg")
roughness.location = (-300, 100)
links.new(roughness.outputs['Color'], nodes['Principled
BSDF'].inputs['Roughness'])


# Add Normal Map
normal = nodes.new(type='ShaderNodeTexImage')
normal.image = bpy.data.images.load("//textures/normal.jpg")
normal.location = (-300, -100)

normal_map = nodes.new(type='ShaderNodeNormalMap')
normal_map.location = (-100, -100)
links.new(normal.outputs['Color'], normal_map.inputs['Color'])
```

```
links.new(normal_map.outputs['Normal'], nodes['Principled
BSDF'].inputs['Normal'])
```

Simulating Realistic Materials: Examples

Glass

1. Use the **Glass BSDF** node.
2. Adjust **IOR (Index of Refraction)** to match the material (e.g., 1.5 for standard glass).
3. Add a subtle Roughness for frosted glass effects.

Skin

1. Use **Subsurface Scattering** (SSS) to simulate light penetration.
2. Add a texture map to the Subsurface Color input for skin tone variations.

Metal

1. Set Metallic to 1.
2. Adjust Roughness based on the metal type (e.g., polished chrome vs. rough iron).

Fine-Tuning and Rendering

1. **HDRI Lighting**
   - Use high-quality HDRI images for realistic lighting and reflections. Add an HDRI image in the World Shader node.
2. **Rendering Settings**
   - Use Cycles for physically accurate renders.
   - Enable **Denoising** to reduce noise in the final image.
3. **Post-Processing**
   - Use Blender's Compositor to enhance realism with effects like bloom, color grading, and depth of field.

Conclusion

Creating realistic materials requires a combination of accurate base properties, detailed texture maps, and thoughtful lighting. By leveraging Blender's Principled BSDF shader and PBR workflows, you can achieve materials that mimic real-world surfaces. Experiment with different combinations and techniques to refine your results and push the boundaries of realism in your 3D projects.

Chapter 6: Lighting and Rendering

Understanding Blender's Render Engines: Eevee and Cycles

Lighting and rendering are among the most critical aspects of creating stunning 3D visuals in Blender. Blender offers two primary rendering engines, Eevee and Cycles, each with distinct features and applications. Understanding their differences and how to use them effectively can elevate the quality of your projects and streamline your workflow.

Blender Render Engines: An Overview

Blender includes two powerful render engines:

1. **Eevee**:
    - Eevee is Blender's real-time rendering engine.
    - It is designed for speed, making it ideal for previewing scenes and creating animations where ultra-realistic effects are not a priority.
    - Eevee uses rasterization, the same technique used by most game engines.
2. **Cycles**:
    - Cycles is a physically-based path-tracing engine.
    - It focuses on accuracy, offering realistic lighting, reflections, and shadows.
    - Cycles is better suited for high-quality stills or animations where photorealism is essential.

Choosing the right engine depends on your project's requirements. For example, if you're working on a game prototype or quick animation previews, Eevee might be the better choice. However, for product visualization, architectural renderings, or cinematic projects, Cycles delivers unmatched realism.

Key Features of Eevee and Cycles

Eevee:

- **Real-Time Rendering**: Offers immediate feedback during the design process.
- **Screen Space Reflections (SSR)**: Simulates reflective surfaces efficiently, though not as accurately as Cycles.
- **Ambient Occlusion**: Enhances depth perception by simulating soft shadows in corners.
- **Volumetrics**: Supports effects like fog and smoke with minimal performance impact.
- **Soft Shadows**: Provides visually appealing shadows without excessive rendering time.
- **Shader-to-RGB**: Allows the use of shaders for non-photorealistic effects.

Cycles:

- **Global Illumination**: Accurately calculates how light bounces around a scene.
- **Caustics**: Handles complex light interactions like those seen in glass or water.
- **Physically Accurate Shaders**: Ensures materials behave realistically under different lighting conditions.
- **GPU Acceleration**: Utilizes your graphics card for faster rendering.
- **Denoising**: Reduces noise in the render output, enhancing clarity and quality.

Setting Up Render Engines in Blender

To switch between render engines:

1. Open the **Properties** panel.
2. Navigate to the **Render Properties** tab.
3. Select either **Eevee** or **Cycles** from the drop-down menu.

Tips for Choosing the Right Engine:

- Use Eevee when you need fast results, or your scene relies on artistic rather than photorealistic visuals.
- Opt for Cycles if your goal is lifelike rendering or if you need advanced light simulations.

Lighting Fundamentals

Lighting plays a pivotal role in setting the mood and highlighting the details of a 3D scene. Blender provides various light types to cater to different scenarios:

1. **Point Light**: Emits light uniformly in all directions from a single point.
2. **Sun Light**: Simulates sunlight and provides consistent parallel rays.
3. **Spot Light**: Creates a cone-shaped beam, ideal for focused illumination.
4. **Area Light**: Emits light from a defined surface, producing soft, natural shadows.
5. **Environment Lighting**: Uses an HDRI (High Dynamic Range Image) for realistic ambient lighting.

Adjusting Light Settings:

Each light type has customizable settings:

- **Strength**: Controls the intensity of the light.
- **Color**: Sets the light's hue, allowing for creative color schemes.
- **Shadow**: Enables or disables shadow casting for the light source.

Example of adding a light in Python scripting:

```
import bpy
```

```
# Add a point light
bpy.ops.object.light_add(type='POINT', location=(2, 5, 3))

# Access the light object
light = bpy.context.object.data

# Adjust light properties
light.energy = 500  # Strength of the light
light.color = (1.0, 0.9, 0.7)  # Slightly warm light
```

Using HDRI for Environment Lighting

HDRIs are an excellent way to achieve realistic lighting with minimal effort. Here's how to use them:

1. Go to the **World Properties** tab in the Properties panel.
2. Under the **Surface** section, select **Environment Texture**.
3. Load an HDRI image.
4. Adjust the **Strength** setting to control brightness.

HDRI lighting often results in soft shadows and balanced illumination, ideal for exterior scenes or product shots.

Rendering Optimization Tips

Efficient rendering can save time and resources. Below are tips to optimize your renders:

Eevee:

- Use **baked lighting** for static scenes to reduce computation during renders.
- Minimize the use of high-resolution textures if not necessary.
- Adjust the **Render Samples** in the Render Properties to balance quality and speed.

Cycles:

- Enable **Denoising** to clean up noisy renders without increasing sample counts.
- Use **Adaptive Sampling** to focus computational power on complex areas of the scene.
- Utilize GPU rendering by configuring the settings in the Preferences menu.

Post-Processing with Blender's Compositor

The Compositor is a powerful tool for refining renders:

- Add color grading, blur effects, and overlays directly within Blender.
- Chain together nodes to create complex effects.
- Example: Add a vignette effect for a cinematic touch.

Sample Compositor node setup for color correction:

```python
import bpy

# Ensure the Compositor is enabled
bpy.context.scene.use_nodes = True
nodes = bpy.context.scene.node_tree.nodes

# Add a Color Balance node
color_balance = nodes.new(type='CompositorNodeColorBalance')
color_balance.lift = (1.0, 0.9, 0.9)   # Adjust shadows
color_balance.gamma = (1.0, 1.1, 1.0)   # Adjust midtones
color_balance.gain = (1.2, 1.0, 1.0)   # Adjust highlights
```

Conclusion

Mastering Blender's render engines and lighting tools can dramatically improve the quality of your 3D creations. By understanding the capabilities of Eevee and Cycles, leveraging the right light types, and optimizing render settings, you can bring your scenes to life with stunning detail and efficiency.

Mastering Lighting for 3D Scenes

Lighting is a cornerstone of 3D artistry. It shapes the visual story, defines mood, and brings depth to your compositions. In Blender, mastering the art of lighting requires an understanding of its tools, techniques, and the underlying physics of light. This section delves deep into the various lighting strategies and best practices to help you create captivating scenes.

Types of Lights in Blender

Blender provides several light types, each suited for specific purposes:

1. **Point Light**:
     o Emits light uniformly in all directions from a single point.
     o Ideal for simulating localized light sources like lamps or candles.
2. **Sun Light**:
     o Mimics sunlight by projecting parallel rays.
     o Useful for outdoor scenes with consistent illumination.
3. **Spot Light**:
     o Produces a cone-shaped light beam.
     o Perfect for highlighting specific areas or creating dramatic effects.
4. **Area Light**:
     o Casts light from a defined surface.

       ○ Produces soft shadows, making it excellent for studio setups.
5. **Environment Light**:
       ○ Uses HDRI images to provide realistic ambient lighting.
       ○ Particularly effective for outdoor or highly reflective scenes.

Adding and Configuring Lights

To add a light in Blender:

1. Press `Shift + A` and select **Light** from the menu.
2. Choose the desired light type.

Each light has adjustable properties to control its behavior:

- **Strength**: Sets the intensity of the light.
- **Color**: Defines the light's hue, useful for creative lighting schemes.
- **Shadow**: Enables or disables shadow casting.

For example, to create a dramatic spotlight:

1. Add a **Spot Light**.
2. Increase the **Spot Size** for a wider beam or decrease it for a sharper focus.
3. Adjust the **Blend** value to control edge softness.

Example in Python:

```python
import bpy

# Add a spot light
bpy.ops.object.light_add(type='SPOT', location=(2, 4, 6))

# Access the light object
light = bpy.context.object.data

# Configure the light properties
light.energy = 1000  # Set intensity
light.color = (1.0, 0.8, 0.6)  # Warm light
light.spot_size = 1.0  # Adjust beam angle
light.shadow_soft_size = 0.2  # Soften shadows
```

Layering Lights for Realism

Layering multiple light sources can add depth and realism to your scene. A common setup involves:

1. **Key Light**:

- o   The primary source of illumination.
- o   Positioned to highlight the subject's most important features.

2. **Fill Light**:
    - o   Softens shadows created by the key light.
    - o   Typically placed opposite the key light.
3. **Back Light (Rim Light)**:
    - o   Outlines the subject by lighting its edges.
    - o   Positioned behind and slightly above the subject.

Example Setup:

- Add a **Key Light** (Spot Light) at a 45-degree angle.
- Place a **Fill Light** (Area Light) on the opposite side.
- Use a **Back Light** (Point Light) to create separation from the background.

Using HDRI for Natural Lighting

HDRI (High Dynamic Range Image) lighting is an essential tool for achieving realistic ambient lighting. HDRIs simulate real-world environments, providing natural light and reflections.

Steps to apply HDRI lighting:

1. Switch to the **World Properties** tab in the Properties editor.
2. Change the surface type to **Environment Texture**.
3. Load an HDRI file.
4. Adjust the **Strength** setting to control the brightness.

Example in Python:

```python
import bpy

# Set up HDRI lighting
world = bpy.context.scene.world
world.use_nodes = True

# Access the node tree
nodes - world.node_tree.nodes
links = world.node_tree.links

# Add an Environment Texture node
env_tex = nodes.new(type='ShaderNodeTexEnvironment')
env_tex.image = bpy.data.images.load('/path/to/hdri.hdr')

# Connect the Environment Texture to the Background node
```

```
links.new(env_tex.outputs['Color'],
nodes['Background'].inputs['Color'])

# Adjust strength
nodes['Background'].inputs['Strength'].default_value = 2.0
```

Lighting Techniques for Different Scenarios

Studio Lighting:

- Use **Area Lights** to replicate softbox effects.
- Position lights at angles to reduce harsh shadows.
- Add reflectors (white planes) for subtle light bounces.

Outdoor Scenes:

- Use a **Sun Light** with a slight angle to mimic natural sunlight.
- Combine with HDRI for dynamic skies and realistic reflections.
- Add volumetric effects like fog for atmospheric depth.

Interior Scenes:

- Mix **Point Lights** and **Area Lights** to replicate indoor fixtures.
- Use **IES Textures** for realistic light distribution.
- Add **Bounce Lighting** to simulate light scattering in enclosed spaces.

Volumetric Lighting for Atmosphere

Volumetric lighting can add mood and depth to your scene by simulating the scattering of light in a medium. Blender allows you to create volumetric effects easily.

Steps to create volumetric lighting:

1. Add a cube that encloses your scene.
2. Assign a new material to the cube.
3. In the Shader Editor, use a **Principled Volume** shader.
4. Adjust the **Density** to control the thickness of the effect.

Example in Python:

```
import bpy

# Add a cube for volumetric effects
bpy.ops.mesh.primitive_cube_add(scale=(10, 10, 10))
cube = bpy.context.object
```

```python
# Create a new material
mat = bpy.data.materials.new(name="VolumeMaterial")
mat.use_nodes = True

# Access the node tree
nodes = mat.node_tree.nodes
links = mat.node_tree.links

# Add a Principled Volume shader
volume_shader = nodes.new(type='ShaderNodeVolumePrincipled')
volume_shader.inputs['Density'].default_value = 0.1  # Adjust
density

# Connect the Volume shader to the Material Output
links.new(volume_shader.outputs['Volume'], nodes['Material
Output'].inputs['Volume'])

# Assign the material to the cube
cube.data.materials.append(mat)
```

Shadow Control

Shadows contribute significantly to the realism of a scene. Blender allows fine-tuning of shadows:

1. **Soft Shadows**:
   - Increase the light size to blur shadow edges.
   - Works well with **Area Lights** and **Sun Lights**.
2. **Contact Shadows**:
   - Adds small, detailed shadows where objects meet surfaces.
   - Enable **Contact Shadows** in the light settings.
3. **Shadow Exclusion**:
   - Prevent specific objects from casting shadows.
   - Use the **Object Properties** tab to disable shadow casting.

Conclusion

Lighting is an art that combines technical knowledge and creative intuition. By mastering Blender's lighting tools, experimenting with different setups, and refining your skills, you can elevate your 3D scenes to professional standards. Whether you're creating photorealistic renders or stylized visuals, effective lighting is the key to compelling results.

Optimizing Rendering Settings

Rendering is the final and often most resource-intensive step in the 3D creation pipeline. Blender's robust rendering options allow you to balance quality and speed, but achieving the best results requires a deep understanding of its settings. This section explores strategies and techniques for optimizing rendering in Blender, ensuring you can create high-quality visuals efficiently.

Blender's Render Engines: A Quick Recap

Blender supports two main rendering engines:

- **Eevee**: Real-time, rasterization-based, optimized for speed and interactivity.
- **Cycles**: Path-tracing, physically accurate, optimized for realism.

The optimization process differs slightly between Eevee and Cycles due to their underlying technologies. Understanding their strengths and limitations is essential for making informed decisions during the rendering process.

Setting the Render Resolution and Aspect Ratio

Render resolution directly impacts both the quality of the final image and the rendering time. Higher resolutions yield sharper images but increase computational demands.

To adjust the resolution:

1. Open the **Properties Editor**.
2. Navigate to the **Output Properties** tab.
3. Set the desired resolution under the **Resolution X** and **Resolution Y** fields.
4. Adjust the **Aspect Ratio** if necessary, especially for non-standard formats.

Example Use Case:

- For a cinematic shot, use a resolution of 1920x1080 (HD) or 3840x2160 (4K).
- For social media posts, consider square formats (e.g., 1080x1080).

Sampling: Balancing Quality and Speed

Sampling controls how many rays Blender calculates per pixel. Higher samples improve image quality but increase render times.

Cycles Sampling:

1. Navigate to the **Render Properties** tab.
2. Under **Sampling**, set values for:
   - **Render**: The number of samples for the final render.
   - **Viewport**: The number of samples for real-time previews.

3. Example settings:
   - **Draft render**: 32-64 samples.
   - **High-quality render**: 512-2048 samples.
4. Enable **Adaptive Sampling**:
   - Allows Blender to allocate more samples to complex areas and fewer to simple ones.
   - Improves efficiency while maintaining quality.

Eevee Sampling:

Eevee's sampling settings are simpler:

1. Adjust the **Render Samples** value under the **Render Properties** tab.
2. For interactive performance, keep the value low (e.g., 16-32).

Python Example:

```python
import bpy

# Set sampling for Cycles
bpy.context.scene.cycles.samples = 512
bpy.context.scene.cycles.use_adaptive_sampling = True

# Set sampling for Eevee
bpy.context.scene.eevee.taa_render_samples = 32
```

Denoising: Removing Noise from Renders

Noise is an inherent issue in path-traced renders like Cycles. Blender provides denoising options to clean up noisy images without increasing sample counts.

Using Viewport Denoising:

- Enable **Denoising** in the **Viewport Sampling** settings for real-time previews.

Final Render Denoising:

1. In the **Render Properties** tab, scroll to the **Denoising** section.
2. Enable **Render** denoising.
3. Choose between **OpenImageDenoise** (CPU-based) or **OptiX** (GPU-accelerated, for NVIDIA GPUs).

Node-Based Denoising:

For more control, use the Compositor to apply denoising:

1. Enable the **Use Nodes** option in the **Compositing** tab.
2. Add a **Denoise** node.
3. Connect it to the render layer's **Image** output.

Python Example:

```
import bpy

# Enable denoising in Cycles
bpy.context.scene.cycles.use_denoising = True
```

Optimizing Lighting for Rendering

Lighting has a direct impact on rendering efficiency. Simple lighting setups reduce render times without sacrificing quality.

Eevee Lighting Optimization:

1. Use **Baked Lighting**:
   - In static scenes, bake indirect lighting to save computation during rendering.
   - Navigate to **Render Properties > Indirect Lighting** and click **Bake Indirect Lighting**.
2. Adjust **Shadow Settings**:
   - Enable **Contact Shadows** for detailed shadows without increasing resolution.
   - Reduce **Shadow Map Size** if high precision is unnecessary.

Cycles Lighting Optimization:

1. Limit **Light Bounces**:
   - Navigate to **Render Properties > Light Paths**.
   - Reduce the maximum bounce count:
     - **Diffuse**: 4-6.
     - **Glossy**: 2-4.
     - **Transmission**: 4-6.
2. Use **Simplify** settings:
   - Enable **Simplify** in the Render Properties.
   - Set maximum subdivision levels and culling thresholds to optimize performance.

GPU vs. CPU Rendering

Blender supports both CPU and GPU rendering. GPUs typically render faster, especially for complex scenes.

Configuring GPU Rendering:

1. Open the **Preferences** menu.
2. Go to the **System** tab.
3. Under **Cycles Render Devices**, enable your GPU.
4. In the **Render Properties** tab, select **GPU Compute** as the render device.

Multi-GPU Rendering:

For systems with multiple GPUs, ensure all are enabled under the **Preferences > System** settings.

Python Example:

```python
import bpy

# Enable GPU rendering
bpy.context.scene.cycles.device = 'GPU'

# Ensure all available GPUs are used
bpy.context.preferences.addons['cycles'].preferences.compute_device_type = 'CUDA'
```

Render Layers and Passes

Render layers and passes allow you to separate elements of your scene for efficient post-processing.

1. Use **View Layers** to isolate objects or groups.
2. In the **Render Properties**, enable passes such as **Diffuse**, **Glossy**, **Shadow**, or **Z Depth**.
3. Combine passes in the Compositor to fine-tune the final image.

Example: Isolating Shadows

1. Create a new view layer for the shadow-catching object.
2. Use a **Shadow Catcher** material on the object.
3. Composite the shadow pass over your background image.

Rendering Animation Efficiently

For animations, the following techniques can significantly reduce rendering time:

1. **Output as Image Sequences**:

- ○ Instead of rendering directly to a video file, output frames as PNGs or EXRs.
- ○ This allows you to re-render specific frames without losing progress.

2. **Motion Blur Optimization**:
   - ○ Enable **Motion Blur** in the Render Properties for smoother animations.
   - ○ Adjust shutter values to control the intensity.
3. **Frame Step**:
   - ○ For test renders, increase the **Frame Step** to render every nth frame.

Post-Processing for Final Touches

Post-processing can enhance the visual quality of renders without re-rendering:

1. Use the **Compositor** for color grading, glare, and depth of field.
2. Add subtle vignette or bloom effects for a cinematic look.
3. Chain nodes for advanced effects like chromatic aberration or lens distortion.

Conclusion

Optimizing rendering settings in Blender involves balancing quality, speed, and resources. By understanding and leveraging features such as sampling, denoising, GPU acceleration, and render passes, you can streamline your workflow and produce stunning results efficiently. Experiment with these settings to find the perfect balance for your projects.

Post-Processing with Blender's Compositor

Post-processing is the stage where raw renders are refined into polished visuals. Blender's powerful Compositor offers a node-based workflow to enhance renders, correct colors, add visual effects, and integrate 3D scenes into real-world footage. Mastering the Compositor can elevate your renders from good to professional-quality.

Enabling the Compositor

To start using the Compositor:

1. Navigate to the **Compositing Workspace**.
2. Enable **Use Nodes** at the top of the Node Editor.
3. You'll see two default nodes:
   - ○ **Render Layers**: Connects to the raw render output.
   - ○ **Composite**: The final output node.

You can add and link various nodes between these to process the render output.

Essential Nodes in the Compositor

Blender's Compositor features a wide range of nodes. Below are some key categories and their applications:

Input Nodes

- **Render Layers**: Links the rendered image to the compositor.
- **Image**: Loads external images for compositing.
- **Movie Clip**: Imports video files for integration.

Color Nodes

- **RGB Curves**: Adjusts brightness and contrast across tonal ranges.
- **Color Balance**: Fine-tunes highlights, midtones, and shadows.
- **Hue/Saturation**: Modifies color intensity.

Filter Nodes

- **Blur**: Adds depth of field, motion blur, or soft-focus effects.
- **Glare**: Produces bloom, streaks, or lens flares.
- **Denoise**: Reduces noise in renders.

Converter Nodes

- **Math**: Performs mathematical operations on input values.
- **Alpha Over**: Combines images with transparency.

Output Nodes

- **Composite**: Sends the final output to the image or video file.
- **Viewer**: Displays intermediate results in the Image Editor.

Basic Compositing Workflow

Let's explore a simple compositing workflow to add a vignette and color grading:

1. **Adding a Vignette**:
   - Create a **Circle** mask using the **Mask** node.
   - Scale and soften the edges with a **Blur** node.
   - Multiply the vignette over the image using a **Mix** node.
2. **Color Grading**:
   - Use the **RGB Curves** node to adjust tonal values.
   - Add a **Color Balance** node for fine-tuning hues.

Example Node Setup in Python:

```python
import bpy
```

```python
# Enable nodes
bpy.context.scene.use_nodes = True
nodes = bpy.context.scene.node_tree.nodes
links = bpy.context.scene.node_tree.links

# Add a vignette effect
circle_node = nodes.new('CompositorNodeEllipseMask')
blur_node = nodes.new('CompositorNodeBlur')
mix_node = nodes.new('CompositorNodeMixRGB')

circle_node.width = 0.8
circle_node.height = 0.8
blur_node.size_x = 50
blur_node.size_y = 50
mix_node.blend_type = 'MULTIPLY'

links.new(circle_node.outputs[0], blur_node.inputs[0])
links.new(blur_node.outputs[0], mix_node.inputs[2])
```

Advanced Techniques in Compositing

1. Depth of Field (DoF)

Depth of Field adds realism by simulating camera focus. Use the Z-depth pass to achieve this effect:

1. Enable **Z Pass** in the Render Layers settings.
2. Add a **Defocus** node in the Compositor.
3. Connect the Z output from the Render Layers node to the Defocus node.

Adjust parameters:

- **F-Stop**: Controls the aperture size (lower values increase blur).
- **Z-Scale**: Scales the depth data.

Example Workflow:

- Render a scene with a distant object.
- Use the Defocus node to blur the foreground or background selectively.

2. Motion Blur

Simulate motion blur in post-processing:

1. Enable **Vector Pass** in the Render Layers settings.
2. Add a **Vector Blur** node.
3. Connect the **Image**, **Z**, and **Speed** outputs from the Render Layers node to the Vector Blur node.

Adjust parameters:

- **Samples**: Determines the blur smoothness.
- **Blur Factor**: Controls the intensity.

---

3. Green Screen Keying

Blender's Compositor is excellent for chroma keying:

1. Import the video using the **Movie Clip** node.
2. Add a **Keying** node to remove the green background.
3. Use an **Alpha Over** node to composite the keyed footage onto a background.

Adjust the **Key Color** to match the green screen, and fine-tune settings like **Clip Black** and **Clip White** for cleaner edges.

Compositing for Visual Effects (VFX)

1. Adding Lens Flares

Lens flares can enhance cinematic quality:

1. Use the **Glare** node.
2. Set the type to **Streaks** or **Fog Glow**.
3. Adjust threshold and intensity for subtle or dramatic effects.

2. Color Matching for Integration

When integrating 3D objects into live-action footage:

- Add a **Color Balance** node.
- Adjust highlights, midtones, and shadows to match the scene's lighting.
- Use the **Ambient Occlusion** pass for realistic contact shadows.

Rendering with Passes

Render passes allow you to break a render into individual components (e.g., shadows, reflections, diffuse color). These can be recombined or modified in the Compositor.

Enabling Render Passes:

1. Go to the **View Layers** settings.
2. Enable passes such as **Diffuse Direct**, **Glossy Indirect**, or **Ambient Occlusion**.
3. Connect these passes in the Compositor to customize their contribution.

Example Node Setup for Ambient Occlusion:

- Use an **Ambient Occlusion** pass to add soft shadows.
- Combine it with the base image using a **Mix** node set to Multiply.

Optimizing Compositing Performance

Compositing can be resource-intensive, especially with high-resolution renders. Optimize performance by:

1. **Proxy Nodes**:
   - Use lower-resolution proxies for testing.
   - Enable proxies in the **Render Settings**.
2. **Chunk Size**:
   - Adjust chunk size in the Performance settings to balance speed and memory usage.
3. **Disable Unused Nodes**:
   - Temporarily mute nodes not needed for testing.

Exporting the Final Composite

Once your composite is ready:

1. Connect the last node to the **Composite** node.
2. Set the output format in the **Output Properties** tab.
3. Use the **Render Animation** button for sequences or **Render Image** for stills.

For lossless exports, choose formats like **OpenEXR** or **TIFF**. For final delivery, formats like **PNG** or **MP4** are more practical.

Conclusion

Blender's Compositor is a powerful tool for refining renders and adding creative effects. By combining nodes effectively and exploring advanced techniques, you can create stunning visuals and integrate 3D content seamlessly into real-world footage. Experiment with these workflows to discover the limitless possibilities of post-processing in Blender.

Chapter 7: Animation Essentials

Basics of Keyframe Animation

Keyframe animation is the foundation of creating dynamic and visually engaging content in Blender. At its core, keyframe animation is the process of defining specific points in time (keyframes) and interpolating the transformations, properties, or behaviors of objects between these points. This technique allows you to animate objects, cameras, lights, and nearly every property within Blender.

Understanding Keyframes in Blender

Keyframes mark significant moments in an animation. When you set a keyframe, Blender records the value of an object's property (such as location, rotation, or scale) at a specific frame. Blender then interpolates the values between keyframes to create smooth transitions.

- **Types of Keyframes:**
  - **LocRotScale**: Sets the location, rotation, and scale of an object.
  - **Location**: Only records changes in the object's position.
  - **Rotation**: Records changes in the object's rotation.
  - **Scale**: Tracks changes in the size of the object.
  - **Custom Properties**: Records user-defined attributes.

Setting Up Your Animation Scene

To start animating in Blender, set up your workspace for optimal efficiency:

1. **Switch to the Animation Workspace**: Blender provides a pre-configured Animation workspace. Access it by selecting the `Animation` tab at the top of the interface.
2. **Familiarize Yourself with the Timeline**: The timeline panel is located at the bottom of the workspace and allows you to control the playback and keyframe settings.
3. **Enable Auto Keyframing (Optional)**: By enabling the auto keyframe feature (the red circle in the timeline toolbar), Blender automatically adds keyframes when you change an object's properties.

Creating Your First Keyframe Animation

1. **Select an Object**: Choose an object you want to animate.
2. **Set the First Keyframe**:
   - Place the playhead (the vertical line in the timeline) at the desired starting frame.
   - With the object selected, press `I` to bring up the Insert Keyframe menu.
   - Choose `LocRotScale` to insert a keyframe that records the object's location, rotation, and scale.

3. **Move the Playhead**: Advance the playhead to another frame.
4. **Transform the Object**: Use tools like G (grab), R (rotate), or S (scale) to modify the object's properties.
5. **Insert Another Keyframe**: Press I again and choose the same keyframe type as before.

When you play back the animation (Spacebar), Blender will interpolate the transformations between the two keyframes.

Fine-Tuning Animation with the Graph Editor

The Graph Editor is a powerful tool that lets you refine your animations by editing the interpolation curves:

- Open the Graph Editor from the bottom-left corner of the Animation workspace.
- Select an animated object to view its keyframe curves.
- Adjust the handles of the curves to control the easing (acceleration and deceleration) of the animation.
- Use interpolation modes like Bezier, Linear, or Constant for different effects:
  - **Bezier**: Smooth, natural motion.
  - **Linear**: Uniform motion with no easing.
  - **Constant**: Sudden changes without interpolation.

Working with Dope Sheet

The Dope Sheet is another vital tool for managing keyframes across multiple objects:

- Access it from the Animation workspace.
- View and edit all keyframes in a tabular format.
- Use tools like G (grab) to move keyframes, D to duplicate them, or X to delete unwanted keyframes.

Animating with Constraints

Constraints are an essential aspect of Blender's animation system, allowing you to automate complex behaviors:

- **Example**: Use the "Track To" constraint to make an object (o.g., a camera) follow a target.
  1. Select the object you want to constrain.
  2. Go to the **Constraints** tab in the Properties panel.
  3. Add the **Track To** constraint and set the target object.

Example Python Script for Keyframe Automation

Python scripting allows you to automate keyframe animation in Blender. Here's a simple script to animate an object's location:

```python
import bpy

# Create a cube
bpy.ops.mesh.primitive_cube_add(location=(0, 0, 0))
cube = bpy.context.object

# Add keyframes
cube.location = (0, 0, 0)
cube.keyframe_insert(data_path="location", frame=1)

cube.location = (5, 5, 5)
cube.keyframe_insert(data_path="location", frame=50)

cube.location = (0, 0, 0)
cube.keyframe_insert(data_path="location", frame=100)
```

Advanced Keyframe Techniques

- **Bake Keyframes**: Bake dynamic effects like physics simulations into keyframes for greater control.
- **Driven Keyframes**: Use drivers to control one property based on another.
- **Motion Paths**: Visualize an object's trajectory by enabling motion paths in the Object menu.

Tips for Efficient Keyframe Animation

- Use **Numpad 0** to switch to the camera view and preview your animation.
- Work in **wireframe mode (Z)** for faster performance with complex scenes.
- Save your work frequently and create backups before experimenting with major changes.

Mastering the basics of keyframe animation sets the stage for exploring advanced animation techniques, such as rigging, nonlinear animation, and dynamic simulations. Take your time to practice these foundational skills, as they are crucial for creating compelling animations.

Using the Graph Editor for Smooth Animations

The Graph Editor is a cornerstone of animation refinement in Blender, providing animators with precise control over keyframe interpolation and motion curves. While the timeline handles the broad strokes of animation, the Graph Editor allows you to tweak every detail, ensuring fluid, natural, and professional results.

Understanding the Graph Editor Interface

The Graph Editor displays your animation data as curves, each representing a property of an animated object. The horizontal axis represents time (frames), and the vertical axis corresponds to the value of the property.

- **Keyframes**: Displayed as points along the curves, representing recorded values at specific frames.
- **Interpolation Curves**: The lines connecting keyframes, defining how Blender calculates values between keyframes.
- **Handles**: Small markers attached to keyframes that allow you to adjust the shape and behavior of the curves.

Accessing the Graph Editor

To open the Graph Editor:

1. Select the **Animation** workspace or switch to any workspace where you can access the Graph Editor.
2. Change any viewport into the Graph Editor by selecting it from the editor type dropdown.

Navigating the Graph Editor

- **Pan and Zoom**: Use the middle mouse button (MMB) to pan and scroll to zoom in and out.
- **Frame Selection**: Press A to select all keyframes or B to box-select specific ones.
- **View All**: Press Home to frame all keyframes within the view.

Editing Keyframes in the Graph Editor

Moving Keyframes

To adjust the timing or value of a keyframe:

1. Select a keyframe by clicking on it.
2. Press G to grab and move the keyframe.
   - Move horizontally to change the frame.
   - Move vertically to adjust the property value.

Adding and Deleting Keyframes

- **Adding**: Place the playhead where you want the keyframe, right-click the curve, and choose Insert Keyframe.
- **Deleting**: Select the keyframe and press X or Delete.

Interpolation Modes

Interpolation determines how Blender calculates the motion between keyframes. The Graph Editor provides several interpolation modes:

1. **Bezier (Default)**: Smooth and natural motion.
   - Use the keyframe handles to adjust the curve for fine-tuning.
2. **Linear**: Constant motion between keyframes without easing.
   - Useful for mechanical movements.
3. **Constant**: No motion between keyframes; the value changes abruptly.
   - Ideal for toggling properties like visibility.

To change the interpolation mode:

1. Select keyframes.
2. Press T to open the Interpolation menu.
3. Choose the desired mode.

Customizing Curves with Handles

Keyframe handles allow you to modify the shape of the interpolation curves, giving you precise control over motion dynamics. Types of handles:

1. **Auto**: Smooth transitions between keyframes.
2. **Free**: Fully manual adjustment of each handle.
3. **Aligned**: Keeps handles aligned for symmetrical curves.
4. **Vector**: Creates linear transitions to the next keyframe.

To adjust handles:

- Select a keyframe and press H to toggle handle types.
- Use G to move the handles and reshape the curve.

Advanced Techniques in the Graph Editor

Smoothing Animation

Blender's Graph Editor provides tools to smooth animations:

1. Select the curve or keyframes.
2. Press Shift + O to adjust the keyframe's easing type.
3. Use the **Smooth Keys** operation (Alt + O) to refine the curve further.

Using Modifiers

Modifiers automate repetitive animations:

- Open the **Modifiers** tab in the Graph Editor side panel.
- Add modifiers like **Noise** for random variation or **Cycles** for looping animations.

Example: Applying a Cycles Modifier

```
import bpy
```

```
# Select an object and ensure it has keyframes
obj = bpy.context.object
fcurve = obj.animation_data.action.fcurves[0]

# Add a Cycles modifier
modifier = fcurve.modifiers.new(type='CYCLES')
modifier.mode_before = 'REPEAT'
modifier.mode_after = 'REPEAT'
```

Baking Curves

Baking converts dynamic motion or modifiers into editable keyframes:

1. Select the curve.
2. Use the `Bake Action` tool from the Animation menu.
3. Choose the desired frame range and baking options.

Syncing Animation Across Objects

When animating multiple objects or properties, synchronization is essential. Use the Graph Editor to:

- Copy keyframes (`Ctrl + C`) from one object and paste (`Ctrl + V`) them onto another.
- Use drivers to link properties, automating one based on another.

Example: Linking Properties with Drivers

```
import bpy

# Select the driver object
driver_obj = bpy.data.objects['Cube']

# Add a driver to another object
target_obj = bpy.data.objects['Sphere']
target_obj.location.x = driver_obj.location.x
target_obj.driver_add("location", 0).driver.expression = "var * 2"

# Link driver variable
driver = target_obj.animation_data.drivers[-1]
var = driver.variables.new()
var.name = "var"
var.targets[0].id = driver_obj
```

```
var.targets[0].data_path = "location.x"
```

Tips for Effective Graph Editor Use

1. **Organize Keyframes**: Use the `Channels` panel to group and rename properties for clarity.
2. **Use Shortcuts**: Learn Blender's hotkeys (`A`, `G`, `T`, `H`) for faster workflow.
3. **Enable Auto-Snap**: Activate snapping (`Shift + Tab`) to align keyframes with frames or time markers.
4. **Work in Layers**: Separate animations into layers for modular adjustments.

Refining Animations for Realism

Achieving lifelike animations often requires subtle adjustments:

- **Overshoot and Settle**: Add slight overshoot to mimic natural motion.
- **Anticipation and Follow-Through**: Adjust timing for dramatic effects.
- **Custom Easing**: Manually tweak curves for nuanced motion dynamics.

Conclusion

The Graph Editor is an indispensable tool for refining animations in Blender. By mastering its features, you can elevate the quality of your animations, ensuring they are polished and professional. With practice, you'll develop an intuitive sense for how curves translate to motion, enabling you to bring your creative visions to life.

Rigging and Skinning: Animating Characters

Rigging and skinning are essential processes in character animation that bring static models to life. Rigging involves creating a skeleton for a 3D model, while skinning binds the skeleton to the model, allowing it to deform naturally as the skeleton moves. This section will walk through these processes in Blender, from creating bones to preparing your character for animation.

Understanding Rigging and Skinning

Rigging is the process of building an armature—a structure made of interconnected bones—that acts as the framework for animation. Each bone controls specific parts of the model, enabling lifelike movements such as bending, twisting, or stretching.

Skinning involves attaching the 3D model to the rig, ensuring the mesh follows the armature's movements. Skinning also requires weight painting, where influence areas for each bone are defined.

Preparing the Model for Rigging

Before creating a rig, ensure your model is clean and optimized:

1. **Check for Overlapping Geometry**: Remove duplicate vertices (`M > Merge by Distance`).
2. **Apply Transforms**: Use `Ctrl + A` to apply scale, rotation, and location to ensure consistent behavior.
3. **Place the Model in a Neutral Pose**: Models should typically be in a T-pose or A-pose for easy rigging.

Creating an Armature

An armature is the skeleton of your character, consisting of bones that drive the animation.

1. **Adding an Armature**:
   - Select your character.
   - Press `Shift + A` and choose **Armature > Single Bone**.
2. **Switch to X-Ray View**:
   - In the Object Data Properties tab of the Armature, enable **In Front** to view the armature through the mesh.
3. **Editing the Armature**:
   - Enter Edit Mode (`Tab`) with the armature selected.
   - Use `E` to extrude new bones.
   - Position bones inside the mesh to match the character's structure, such as arms, legs, spine, and head.
4. **Naming Bones**:
   - In Edit Mode, name each bone according to its role (e.g., `upper_arm.L`, `lower_leg.R`).
   - Consistent naming conventions are crucial for symmetry and ease of animation.

Mirroring the Rig

For symmetrical models, you can create one side of the rig and mirror it to the other side:

1. Name bones on one side with `.L` suffix (e.g., `arm.L`).
2. In Edit Mode, select the bones on one side.
3. Press `Shift + D` to duplicate, then `S` and `X` to scale and flip.
4. Use the **Symmetrize** operator (`Ctrl + M > Symmetry`), and Blender will automatically mirror and rename the bones.

Binding the Armature to the Model

Once the armature is created, bind it to the model using an Armature Modifier.

1. **Parenting the Mesh to the Armature**:
   - Select the mesh, then `Shift + Click` the armature.

- ○ Press `Ctrl + P` and choose **With Automatic Weights**.
- ○ Blender will calculate the initial weight painting, binding the mesh to the bones.
2. **Testing the Rig**:
    - ○ Enter Pose Mode (`Ctrl + Tab`) with the armature selected.
    - ○ Select and rotate bones to test if the mesh deforms correctly.
    - ○ If deformation issues arise, refine the weights.

Weight Painting

Weight painting defines how much influence each bone has over the mesh. Areas with high weights move fully with the bone, while areas with low weights move less.

1. **Switch to Weight Paint Mode**:
    - ○ Select the mesh, then choose Weight Paint Mode from the mode dropdown.
2. **Adjusting Weights**:
    - ○ Use the `Brush` tool to paint weights. Red areas represent full influence, while blue represents none.
    - ○ Ensure smooth transitions between weights for natural deformation.
3. **Fine-Tuning**:
    - ○ Use tools like **Normalize All** and **Smooth Weights** to balance the weights automatically.

Adding Inverse Kinematics (IK)

IK simplifies animation by allowing you to control multiple bones with a single target, useful for arms, legs, and other appendages.

1. **Create an IK Target**:
    - ○ Add a new bone outside the mesh (e.g., `foot_target.L`).
2. **Add an IK Constraint**:
    - ○ In Pose Mode, select the lower leg bone.
    - ○ Go to the Bone Constraints tab and add an **IK** constraint.
    - ○ Set the target to the armature and the specific target bone (e.g., `foot_target.L`).
3. **Set the Chain Length**:
    - ○ Define how many bones in the chain are affected by the IK constraint (e.g., 2 for a leg with thigh and calf bones).

Rigging the Face

For advanced characters, rigging the face enables detailed expressions.

1. **Add Facial Bones**:
    - ○ Create bones for the jaw, eyebrows, eyelids, and lips.
2. **Use Shape Keys for Fine Control**:
    - ○ Add shape keys to the mesh for specific facial movements.

       ○ Animate these keys alongside the rig.

Automating with Rigify

Blender's Rigify add-on can automate much of the rigging process:

1. Enable Rigify in the Preferences menu.
2. Add a Rigify Meta-Rig (`Shift + A > Armature > Human Meta-Rig`).
3. Adjust the Meta-Rig to match your character, then generate the rig.

Exporting the Rigged Model

If the rigged model is intended for use in game engines or other software, ensure proper export settings:

1. Apply all transformations (`Ctrl + A`).
2. Export in FBX format with **Armature** and **Mesh** selected.
3. Enable **Bake Animations** if animations are included.

Example Python Script for Rigging

Python scripting can automate the rigging process. Below is an example to create a simple armature:

```python
import bpy

# Create a new armature
bpy.ops.object.armature_add()
armature = bpy.context.object
bpy.ops.object.mode_set(mode='EDIT')

# Add bones
bones = armature.data.edit_bones
root_bone = bones.new('Root')
root_bone.head = (0, 0, 0)
root_bone.tail - (0, 0, 1)

leg_bone = bones.new('Leg')
leg_bone.head = root_bone.tail
leg_bone.tail = (0, 0, 2)
leg_bone.parent = root_bone

# Return to Object Mode
bpy.ops.object.mode_set(mode='OBJECT')
```

Testing and Refining the Rig

Rigging is an iterative process. Test the rig extensively by posing the character and observing how the mesh deforms. Adjust weights, bone placement, or constraints as needed for optimal results.

Conclusion

Rigging and skinning are complex but rewarding processes that form the backbone of character animation. By mastering these techniques, you can create rigs that bring your characters to life with fluid, realistic movements. Practice, attention to detail, and experimentation are key to mastering this art.

Introduction to Physics-Based Animation

Physics-based animation in Blender brings scenes to life by simulating real-world behaviors such as gravity, collisions, and fluid dynamics. Whether you want to create falling objects, cloth simulations, or flowing water, Blender's physics system provides robust tools for achieving realistic results. This section explores the fundamentals of physics-based animation, guiding you through various physics systems and techniques.

Enabling Physics for Objects

Physics properties are applied to objects using the Physics tab in the Properties panel. Blender offers multiple physics types, including rigid bodies, soft bodies, cloth, fluids, and particles. Each system has unique properties and settings to tailor simulations to specific needs.

Accessing the Physics Panel

1. Select an object in the 3D Viewport.
2. Open the **Physics** tab in the Properties panel.
3. Choose a physics type such as **Rigid Body**, **Cloth**, or **Fluid**.

Rigid Body Simulations

Rigid body physics simulate hard, non-deformable objects like rocks, furniture, or machinery. These objects can move, collide, and respond to forces like gravity.

Setting Up a Basic Rigid Body Simulation

1. **Add Objects**:
   - Create a plane as the ground and scale it (S key).
   - Add a cube or sphere above the plane to simulate a falling object.
2. **Enable Rigid Body Physics**:
   - Select the falling object and go to the Physics tab.

- ○ Click **Rigid Body** to enable the simulation.
- ○ Set the type to **Active** (movable object).
- ○ Adjust the mass, friction, and bounciness as needed.

3. **Make the Ground Static**:
   - ○ Select the ground plane, enable **Rigid Body**, and set the type to **Passive** (non-moving).
4. **Simulate**:
   - ○ Press Spacebar to play the animation and observe the object fall and collide with the ground.

Key Settings for Rigid Bodies

- **Mass**: Controls the weight of the object.
- **Friction**: Affects how objects slide across surfaces.
- **Bounciness**: Determines how elastic collisions are.
- **Collision Shape**: Choose between **Box**, **Sphere**, **Convex Hull**, or **Mesh** for precise simulations.

Adding Constraints

Constraints restrict the motion of rigid bodies:

1. **Add a Constraint**:
   - ○ In the Physics tab, select **Rigid Body Constraint**.
2. **Types of Constraints**:
   - ○ **Fixed**: Locks an object in place.
   - ○ **Hinge**: Allows rotation around a single axis.
   - ○ **Slider**: Restricts movement to a linear path.

Cloth Simulation

Cloth physics simulate the behavior of fabrics, allowing you to create realistic clothing, curtains, or flags.

Setting Up a Cloth Simulation

1. **Add a Plane**:
   - ○ Create a plane and subdivide it (Right-click > Subdivide) to increase geometry for better deformation.
2. **Enable Cloth Physics**:
   - ○ Select the plane, go to the Physics tab, and choose **Cloth**.
3. **Adjust Cloth Settings**:
   - ○ Set the **Quality Steps** to improve simulation accuracy.
   - ○ Use presets like **Cotton** or **Silk** for quick material settings.
4. **Pin Cloth Vertices**:
   - ○ Enter Edit Mode and select vertices to pin (e.g., the top edge of a flag).
   - ○ Assign the selection to a vertex group and enable **Pinning** in the cloth settings.
5. **Simulate**:

    ○   Press `Spacebar` to watch the cloth fall and interact with the environment.

Collision Settings for Cloth

To prevent cloth from passing through other objects:

1. Add a **Collision Modifier** to objects the cloth interacts with.
2. Adjust **Friction** and **Distance** values to fine-tune the interaction.

Particle Systems

Particle systems are versatile for creating effects like sparks, rain, or swarms.

Creating a Basic Particle System

1. **Add an Emitter**:
   - Select an object (e.g., a plane) to emit particles.
   - Go to the **Particles** tab in the Properties panel and click **+** to add a new system.
2. **Adjust Settings**:
   - Set the **Number** of particles, their **Lifetime**, and the **Frame Range** for emission.
   - Enable **Gravity** for natural falling behavior.
3. **Visualize Particles**:
   - Choose the **Render As** option to display particles as objects, paths, or collections.
4. **Bake the Simulation**:
   - In the Cache section, click **Bake** to finalize the particle motion.

Combining Particle Systems with Physics

Particle systems can interact with physics for complex effects:

- Add **Force Fields** like Wind or Turbulence to influence particle motion.
- Enable **Collision** to make particles bounce off surfaces.

Fluid Simulation

Fluid physics simulate liquids such as water or lava, offering tools for realistic flows and splashes.

Setting Up a Fluid Simulation

1. **Define Domains and Emitters**:
   - Create a domain (a cube that contains the simulation).
   - Add an object inside the domain and set its physics type to **Fluid > Flow**.
2. **Adjust Domain Settings**:
   - Set the resolution for simulation detail.
   - Choose the **Type** (Gas or Liquid) and enable **Mesh** to generate fluid surfaces.

3. **Bake the Fluid**:
   - Click **Bake** in the domain settings to calculate the simulation.

Soft Body Dynamics

Soft bodies simulate deformable objects like jelly or cushions. They combine elastic deformation with collision detection.

Setting Up Soft Bodies

1. **Enable Soft Body Physics**:
   - Select an object and go to the Physics tab.
   - Click **Soft Body** and adjust the **Goal Strength** to control shape retention.
2. **Adjust Soft Body Settings**:
   - Increase **Stiffness** for less deformation.
   - Enable **Self-Collision** to prevent parts of the mesh from overlapping.

Example Python Script for Physics Setup

Automate physics settings with Python:

```python
import bpy

# Create objects
bpy.ops.mesh.primitive_plane_add(size=10, location=(0, 0, 0))
ground = bpy.context.object
bpy.ops.rigidbody.object_add()
ground.rigid_body.type = 'PASSIVE'

bpy.ops.mesh.primitive_cube_add(size=1, location=(0, 0, 5))
cube = bpy.context.object
bpy.ops.rigidbody.object_add()
cube.rigid_body.mass = 2
```

Tips for Physics-Based Animation

1. **Bake Simulations**: Always bake physics simulations for consistent results.
2. **Use Subdivisions**: Increase mesh detail for realistic deformations.
3. **Optimize Performance**: Lower simulation resolution while testing and increase for final renders.
4. **Combine Systems**: Mix rigid bodies, particles, and fluids for complex scenes.

Conclusion

Physics-based animation in Blender provides endless possibilities for creating realistic and dynamic scenes. With practice and experimentation, you can master these tools to enhance your animations and bring your ideas to life. From simple collisions to intricate fluid simulations, Blender's physics systems are powerful assets in any animator's toolkit.

Chapter 8: Advanced Animation Techniques

Advanced Rigging: IK and FK Systems

Advanced rigging techniques are essential for creating sophisticated and versatile character animations. Two pivotal systems in rigging are Inverse Kinematics (IK) and Forward Kinematics (FK). Understanding how these systems work and how to apply them in Blender will empower animators to create fluid, lifelike movements with precision.

Understanding IK and FK

Forward Kinematics (FK)

FK is the default method for animating a rig. In FK, the animator manually rotates each joint in a hierarchical sequence, starting from the root joint to the end effector. This approach offers fine control but can be tedious for complex animations, especially those requiring contact with external surfaces.

For example, to animate an arm reaching out, you would rotate the shoulder, then the elbow, and finally the wrist.

Inverse Kinematics (IK)

IK automates the movement of joints by allowing the animator to move the end effector (e.g., the hand or foot), and the intermediate joints adjust automatically to maintain a natural pose. This is particularly useful for animations requiring precise positioning, such as walking or interacting with objects.

For instance, when animating a character picking up an object, IK lets you move the hand to the object, and the arm adjusts accordingly.

Setting Up FK and IK in Blender

Preparing the Rig

1. **Create or Import a Rigged Model**: Start by creating or importing a rigged model. Blender's Rigify add-on is a great tool for generating standard rigs quickly.
2. **Switch to Pose Mode**: Select the armature and enter Pose Mode (`Ctrl + Tab`).
3. **Enable IK Bones**: Add IK bones to your rig for easier manipulation.

Adding an IK Constraint

1. **Select the End Effector**: In Pose Mode, select the bone that will act as the end effector (e.g., the hand).
2. **Add the IK Constraint**:
   - Go to the **Bone Constraints** tab in the Properties Editor.
   - Click **Add Bone Constraint** and select **Inverse Kinematics**.
3. **Set the Target**:
   - In the IK constraint, set the armature as the target.
   - Specify the bone that the end effector should influence.
4. **Adjust the Chain Length**:
   - Define the number of bones affected by the IK chain (e.g., 2 for an arm with a shoulder and elbow).

Creating an FK/IK Switch

1. **Add a Custom Property**:
   - Select the root bone of the armature.
   - Go to the **Bone Properties** tab, and under **Custom Properties**, add a new property (e.g., FK_IK_Switch).
2. **Driver Setup**:
   - Add a driver to the IK constraint's influence.
   - Use the FK_IK_Switch property as the driver variable.
   - Set the driver to control the transition between FK and IK.

Advanced IK Features

Pole Targets

Pole Targets are used to control the orientation of the IK chain. Without a pole target, the chain may rotate unpredictably. To set up a Pole Target:

1. Add a helper bone near the joint (e.g., near the elbow for an arm IK chain).
2. In the IK constraint, assign the helper bone as the Pole Target.
3. Adjust the Pole Angle to fine-tune the IK chain's orientation.

Stretchy IK

Stretchy IK allows the bones in the IK chain to stretch, enabling dynamic limb movements. To enable stretchy IK:

1. Add a Stretch To constraint to the bones in the IK chain.
2. Use a helper bone to control the stretch factor.

Animating with FK and IK

Keyframing IK Movements

1. **Pose the IK End Effector**:
   - Position the end effector where you want it.
   - Adjust the Pole Target as necessary to refine the pose.

2. **Set Keyframes**:
   - Press I and choose **Location/Rotation** to keyframe the pose.

Blending FK and IK

Using the FK/IK Switch, you can seamlessly blend between FK and IK animation:

1. Start with an FK pose and keyframe it.
2. Gradually increase the IK influence, allowing a smooth transition.
3. Refine the animation by adjusting the poses in both FK and IK.

Practical Application: Walking Cycle

1. **Set Up the Rig**:
   - Use IK for the legs to ensure they maintain contact with the ground.
   - Use FK for the arms for a natural swinging motion.
2. **Keyframe the Leg Movements**:
   - Move the IK handles for the legs to simulate stepping.
   - Adjust the Pole Targets for proper knee orientation.
3. **Keyframe the Arm Movements**:
   - Rotate the shoulder and elbow joints to create a smooth swinging motion.
4. **Loop the Animation**:
   - Use the Graph Editor to create a cyclic action for the walk.

Troubleshooting Common Issues

Unstable IK Chains

- Ensure the chain length is set correctly.
- Use a Pole Target to stabilize the orientation.

FK/IK Blending Artifacts

- Smooth out transitions by carefully placing keyframes.
- Avoid abrupt changes in the FK/IK Switch property.

Conclusion

Mastering IK and FK systems opens up a world of possibilities for animators, enabling the creation of complex, lifelike movements with ease. By combining these techniques, you can tackle any animation challenge, from simple gestures to intricate character interactions. With practice, these skills will become second nature, enhancing both your workflow and the quality of your animations.

Mastering Blender's Nonlinear Animation Editor

The Nonlinear Animation (NLA) Editor in Blender is a powerful tool for managing and combining animations. It enables animators to layer, blend, and sequence multiple actions, making it ideal for complex projects such as character animations, animated scenes, and reusable motion clips. This section will cover the essential features, workflows, and advanced techniques for mastering the NLA Editor.

Understanding the NLA Editor

The NLA Editor allows you to:

- Organize animations into reusable **actions**.
- Layer animations to create complex behaviors.
- Blend multiple animations seamlessly.
- Control the timing and sequence of animations.

It acts as a higher-level control system for animations, working alongside the Dope Sheet and Graph Editor to provide complete animation management.

Accessing the NLA Editor

1. **Switch to the NLA Editor**:
   - Open a new editor window or switch an existing one.
   - Select **NLA Editor** from the editor type dropdown.
2. **Basic Interface Overview**:
   - The **Channels Region** on the left displays objects and animation tracks.
   - The **Timeline Area** shows strips, which represent actions applied to objects.
   - Use the playback controls at the bottom to test animations.

Creating and Managing Animation Strips

Converting Actions to Strips

1. Animate an object in the Dope Sheet or Graph Editor.
2. In the NLA Editor, click the **Push Down Action** button in the header. This converts the current action into a strip.

Adding New Strips

1. Select the object or armature in the NLA Editor.
2. Press Shift + A to add a new action strip.
3. Choose an existing action from the list or create a new one.

Moving and Scaling Strips

- To move a strip, select it and press G. Move it along the timeline to adjust its position.
- Scale a strip by pressing S, which changes its duration without affecting playback speed.

Layering Animations

Layering allows you to build complex animations by combining multiple strips. For instance, you can layer a walking cycle with a waving motion.

Adding a Layer

1. In the NLA Editor, select the object or armature.
2. Click the **Add Track** button or press `Shift + A` to create a new track.
3. Add a new strip to the track.

Adjusting Influence

- Each strip has an **Influence** slider in the Properties panel, allowing you to control how much it affects the final animation.
- Use the **Blending Mode** option to define how the strip interacts with others:
  - **Replace**: Overrides the underlying animation.
  - **Add**: Adds the animation to the previous layer.
  - **Multiply**: Multiplies the animation values.

Sequencing Animations

Sequencing involves arranging strips on the timeline to play one after another.

Chaining Strips

1. Place multiple strips on a single track or separate tracks.
2. Ensure the strips are positioned sequentially.
3. Adjust the transitions to ensure a smooth flow.

Using Hold and Hold Forward

- Enable **Hold Forward** on a strip to extend its influence until the next strip begins.
- Use **Hold** to maintain the last keyframe of a strip until it is explicitly replaced.

Advanced Techniques

Blending Animations

Blending lets you create smooth transitions between animations, such as moving from a walk cycle to a run.

1. Overlap two strips on separate tracks.
2. Select the overlapping strip and adjust its **Blend In** and **Blend Out** properties in the Properties panel.
3. Fine-tune the influence and blending mode for a seamless transition.

Using Action Clips

Action clips are reusable animations that can be applied to multiple objects or characters.

1. Save an animation as an action in the Action Editor.

2. Import the action as a strip in the NLA Editor.
3. Apply the action to different objects for consistent animations.

Syncing Audio with Animations

1. Add audio to your scene by importing it into the Video Sequencer or syncing it with the timeline.
2. Use the NLA Editor to align animation strips with the audio cues.

Using Meta Strips

Meta strips consolidate multiple strips into a single unit, making the timeline easier to manage.

1. Select the strips you want to combine.
2. Press Ctrl + G to group them into a meta strip.
3. To edit the meta strip, press Tab. Exit edit mode with Tab again.

Python Scripting in the NLA Editor

Python scripting can automate tasks and enhance your control over the NLA Editor.

Example: Creating a New Strip Programmatically

```python
import bpy

# Select the object
obj = bpy.context.object

# Create a new action
action = bpy.data.actions.new("NewAction")

# Assign the action to the object
track = obj.animation_data.nla_tracks.new()
strip = track.strips.new(action.name, start=1, action=action)

# Adjust strip properties
strip.blend_type = 'ADD'
strip.influence = 0.8
```

Example: Batch Renaming Tracks

```python
import bpy

for obj in bpy.data.objects:
```

```
if obj.animation_data:
    for i, track in enumerate(obj.animation_data.nla_tracks):
        track.name = f"Track_{i + 1}"
```

Troubleshooting Common Issues

Strips Not Playing

- Ensure the **Muted** checkbox is not enabled for the strip.
- Verify that the timeline playback range includes the strips.

Transition Artifacts

- Check the blending mode and ensure it matches the desired effect.
- Adjust keyframes in overlapping strips to avoid conflicts.

Unintended Influences

- Use the Influence slider to isolate specific strips.
- Disable **Auto-Blending** if manual control is needed.

Conclusion

The NLA Editor is an indispensable tool for animators working on complex projects. By mastering its features, you can streamline your workflow, create layered animations, and manage reusable motion clips. Experimenting with these techniques will elevate the quality and efficiency of your animation projects.

Particle Systems and Dynamic Simulations

Particle systems and dynamic simulations are powerful tools in Blender that bring scenes to life by simulating real-world phenomena like fire, smoke, rain, hair, and other effects. Understanding how to create, control, and customize these systems will allow you to create visually stunning and highly dynamic animations.

Overview of Particle Systems

Blender's particle system enables you to generate and animate a collection of particles that can represent objects, hair, fluids, or even abstract visual effects. Particle systems are tied to a specific object called the **emitter**.

Types of Particle Systems

1. **Emitter**: Generates particles that move based on physics, commonly used for fire, smoke, sparks, and explosions.
2. **Hair**: Creates static or dynamic strands that can be styled, animated, or converted into mesh objects. Often used for hair, fur, or grass.

Creating a Particle System

Setting Up the Scene

1. Add an object to act as the emitter (e.g., a plane or sphere).
2. Select the object, go to the **Particle Properties** tab, and click **+** to add a new particle system.

Configuring the Particle System

- **Emission Settings**:
  - **Number**: Controls how many particles are emitted.
  - **Frame Start/End**: Defines when particles are generated.
  - **Lifetime**: Determines how long particles remain active.
- **Physics**:
  - **Mass** and **Damping** control particle motion.
  - **Gravity** affects the trajectory based on the scene's gravity setting.
- **Render Settings**:
  - Choose how particles are displayed, such as as halos, objects, or groups.
  - Assign an object (e.g., a sphere) to the particle system for rendering.

Example: Simple Emitter

```python
import bpy

# Create a plane to act as the emitter
bpy.ops.mesh.primitive_plane_add(size=2, location=(0, 0, 0))
emitter = bpy.context.object

# Add a particle system
particle_system = emitter.modifiers.new(name="ParticleSystem",
type='PARTICLE_SYSTEM')
particle_system_settings = particle_system.particle_system.settings

# Configure the particle system
particle_system_settings.type = 'EMITTER'
particle_system_settings.count = 1000
particle_system_settings.frame_start = 1
particle_system_settings.frame_end = 100
particle_system_settings.lifetime = 50
particle_system_settings.gravity = 0.98
```

Advanced Emitter Particle Settings

Forces and Fields

Blender allows you to apply external forces like wind, turbulence, and vortexes to control particle behavior.

1. **Adding a Force Field**:
   - Add a force field from the **Add > Force Field** menu.
   - Configure its strength, flow, and falloff in the **Physics Properties** tab.
2. **Combining Forces**:
   - Use multiple force fields to create complex motion, like particles swirling in a vortex while being pushed by wind.

Collision with Other Objects

To make particles interact with other objects:

1. Select the object you want particles to collide with.
2. Enable the **Collision** property in the **Physics Properties** tab.
3. Adjust settings like **Friction** and **Damping** for realistic effects.

Hair Particles

Hair particles are ideal for creating fur, grass, or stylized hair. They can be combed, styled, and rendered with high levels of detail.

Setting Up Hair Particles

1. Select the emitter object.
2. Add a new particle system and set the type to **Hair**.
3. Adjust settings like **Hair Length**, **Segments**, and **Children** for detailed results.

Styling Hair

1. Switch to **Particle Edit Mode**.
2. Use tools like **Comb**, **Cut**, and **Smooth** to shape the hair.
3. Apply textures to control the distribution and density of hair.

Converting Hair to Geometry

1. In the **Modifiers** tab, convert the particle system to a mesh.
2. Edit the resulting mesh to add custom details.

Dynamic Simulations

Smoke and Fire

Blender's smoke simulation system creates realistic smoke and fire effects.

1. Add a **Smoke Domain**:
   - Create a cube and set its physics type to **Domain**.
   - Configure the domain for either gas (smoke) or fire.
2. Add a Smoke Emitter:

- ○ Select an object and set its physics type to **Flow**.
- ○ Choose **Smoke** or **Fire + Smoke** as the flow type.
- ○ Animate the flow to control emission over time.

3. Bake the Simulation:
   - ○ In the Smoke Domain settings, bake the simulation for real-time playback.

Example: Smoke Simulation

```
import bpy

# Create the smoke domain
bpy.ops.mesh.primitive_cube_add(size=5, location=(0, 0, 2))
domain = bpy.context.object
bpy.ops.object.modifier_add(type='FLUID')
domain.modifiers["Fluid"].fluid_type = 'DOMAIN'

# Create the emitter
bpy.ops.mesh.primitive_ico_sphere_add(location=(0, 0, 0))
emitter = bpy.context.object
bpy.ops.object.modifier_add(type='FLUID')
emitter.modifiers["Fluid"].fluid_type = 'FLOW'
emitter.modifiers["Fluid"].flow_settings.flow_type = 'SMOKE'
```

Fluid Simulation

Blender's fluid simulation system enables the creation of realistic liquid effects like water splashes, pouring, and flooding.

1. **Domain**: Define the simulation space with a domain object.
2. **Emitter**: Create an object as the fluid source.
3. **Obstacle**: Add objects with collision properties to interact with the fluid.

Particle System Tips and Tricks

- **Caching Simulations**: Always bake your simulations to ensure consistent results during rendering.
- **Using Textures**: Apply textures to control particle distribution and behavior, such as creating areas with higher particle density.
- **Combining Systems**: Combine multiple particle systems and dynamic simulations to create intricate effects.

Troubleshooting Particle Systems

1. **Particles Not Rendering**:
   - ○ Ensure the render type is set correctly (e.g., **Object** or **Group**).

      ○ Verify that the particle system is active in the timeline.
2. **Simulation Artifacts**:
      ○ Increase simulation resolution for better detail.
      ○ Adjust collision or damping settings to prevent particles from intersecting.
3. **Performance Issues**:
      ○ Reduce the number of particles or simulation resolution during testing.
      ○ Use the **Simplify** option in the Render Properties to optimize viewport playback.

Conclusion

Particle systems and dynamic simulations are essential tools for creating rich, immersive animations in Blender. By mastering their features and combining them creatively, you can simulate everything from natural phenomena to fantastical effects. Practice and experimentation are key to unlocking the full potential of these systems.

Creating Cinematic Animations

Cinematic animations in Blender elevate storytelling by incorporating advanced techniques like camera choreography, environment interaction, and dynamic lighting. These animations blend artistic vision with technical execution to produce visually compelling scenes for film, games, or presentations. This section explores how to create cinematic animations step-by-step, covering everything from pre-visualization to rendering.

Pre-visualization: Planning the Animation

Cinematic animations begin with a clear plan. Pre-visualization, or "previs," involves sketching or drafting the sequence to define key scenes, camera angles, and movements.

Storyboarding

1. Use simple sketches or diagrams to outline the key moments in your animation.
2. Identify the focus of each shot—whether it's a character, object, or environment.

Scene Layout

1. **Blocking**:
      ○ Position rough models of characters, objects, and props in the scene.
      ○ Use basic shapes (cubes, spheres, planes) to represent assets before detailing them.
2. **Defining the Camera Path**:
      ○ Set up one or more cameras in your scene.
      ○ Plan camera movements for each shot, such as tracking, dolly, or panning.

Setting Up Cameras

Cameras play a central role in cinematic animations. Understanding their setup and capabilities is crucial for storytelling.

Adding and Configuring a Camera

1. Add a camera (`Shift + A > Camera`).
2. Position and rotate the camera using the `G` (grab) and `R` (rotate) keys.
3. In the **Camera Properties** tab, adjust settings like:
   - **Focal Length**: Controls the zoom level.
   - **Depth of Field**: Blurs the background to focus attention.

Animating the Camera

1. **Keyframing Camera Movement**:
   - Move the camera to the starting position and press `I > Location/Rotation` to set a keyframe.
   - Move the timeline to another frame, adjust the camera position, and set another keyframe.
2. **Using Follow Paths**:
   - Create a curve object (`Shift + A > Curve`).
   - Select the camera, add a **Follow Path** constraint, and target the curve.
   - Animate the camera along the curve by keyframing the **Offset** value.

Example: Camera Flythrough

```python
import bpy

# Add a camera
bpy.ops.object.camera_add(location=(0, 0, 5))
camera = bpy.context.object

# Add a path
bpy.ops.curve.primitive_bezier_circle_add(radius=10, location=(0, 0, 0))
path = bpy.context.object

# Add a follow path constraint
camera.constraints.new(type='FOLLOW_PATH')
camera.constraints["Follow Path"].target = path
camera.constraints["Follow Path"].use_curve_follow = True

# Animate the camera along the path
bpy.context.scene.frame_start = 1
bpy.context.scene.frame_end = 100
camera.constraints["Follow Path"].offset = 0
camera.keyframe_insert(data_path='constraints["Follow Path"].offset', frame=1)
```

```
camera.constraints["Follow Path"].offset = 100
camera.keyframe_insert(data_path='constraints["Follow
Path"].offset', frame=100)
```

Creating Realistic Character Animation

Character animation is a core component of cinematic scenes. Blender's tools like keyframing, rigging, and the Nonlinear Animation (NLA) Editor help create lifelike motion.

Animating with Keyframes

1. **Pose the Character**:
   - Select the armature and enter Pose Mode.
   - Use the manipulator tools (G, R, S) to adjust bones.
2. **Set Keyframes**:
   - Position the character in the starting pose.
   - Press I and choose **Location/Rotation/Scale** to set a keyframe.
   - Move to the next frame, create a new pose, and set another keyframe.

Refining Animation in the Graph Editor

1. Open the **Graph Editor** to adjust the interpolation between keyframes.
2. Use handles to create smooth transitions or dramatic movements.
3. Add noise modifiers to introduce subtle variations for realism.

Environmental Animation

The environment in cinematic animations enhances the story's atmosphere and mood.

Animating Props and Background Elements

1. Animate props like doors, vehicles, or falling objects using keyframes.
2. Parent props to characters or moving elements to synchronize motion.
3. Use particle systems for effects like falling leaves, rain, or debris.

Dynamic Lighting

1. Add lights (Shift + A > Light).
2. Keyframe light intensity and color to reflect mood changes.
3. Use **Eevee** or **Cycles** render engines for realistic lighting effects.

Example: Animating Weather

```
import bpy


# Add a plane for the rain emitter
bpy.ops.mesh.primitive_plane_add(size=10, location=(0, 0, 10))
```

```
emitter = bpy.context.object

# Add a particle system for rain
bpy.ops.object.particle_system_add()
particle_system = emitter.particle_systems[0]
particle_system.settings.type = 'EMITTER'
particle_system.settings.count = 5000
particle_system.settings.lifetime = 100
particle_system.settings.frame_start = 1
particle_system.settings.frame_end = 200

# Configure gravity and velocity
particle_system.settings.normal_factor = 0
particle_system.settings.effector_weights.gravity = 1.0
```

Scene Transitions and Effects

Smooth transitions and effects like fades and overlays create professional-grade animations.

Using Scene Strips

1. Switch to the **Video Sequencer**.
2. Add scene strips (Shift + A > Scene) for each shot.
3. Add transitions like crossfades by overlapping strips.

Post-Processing

1. Open the **Compositor** and enable **Use Nodes**.
2. Add effects like motion blur, depth of field, and color grading.
3. Render each layer separately for flexibility.

Rendering Cinematic Animations

Rendering is the final step where all elements come together.

Render Settings

1. Choose the render engine:
   - Use **Eevee** for fast previews.
   - Use **Cycles** for high-quality, ray-traced results.
2. Adjust settings:
   - **Resolution**: Set output dimensions (e.g., 1920x1080 for HD).
   - **Frame Rate**: Use standard cinematic rates like 24 fps.
   - **Samples**: Increase for smoother results.

Exporting the Animation

1. Set the file format to **FFmpeg Video** for videos or **PNG** for image sequences.
2. Choose the encoding format (e.g., H.264) and specify the output directory.
3. Press **Render Animation** to export.

Troubleshooting Common Issues

1. **Camera Jitters**:
   - Check keyframe interpolation for smooth transitions.
   - Use constraints to align the camera with its path.
2. **Lighting Artifacts**:
   - Adjust sample counts and light clipping settings.
   - Use light probes for accurate reflections.
3. **Performance Lag**:
   - Reduce render samples during previews.
   - Use proxies or simplify modifiers for faster viewport playback.

Conclusion

Creating cinematic animations in Blender requires careful planning, technical expertise, and artistic flair. By mastering cameras, character animation, dynamic lighting, and environmental effects, you can craft visually engaging stories that captivate your audience. Experimentation and refinement are essential to achieving professional-quality results.

Chapter 9: Scripting with Python

Why Learn Python in Blender?

Python scripting in Blender offers a powerful way to extend and automate its functionality, making it an indispensable tool for users who want to enhance their workflows. Whether you are creating custom tools, automating repetitive tasks, or developing plugins, Python scripting opens up endless possibilities in Blender.

Blender's Python API allows access to almost every part of the software, enabling the creation of highly tailored workflows and tools. In this section, we will explore the fundamental reasons why learning Python in Blender is a game-changer and how it can take your skills to the next level.

Unlocking Customization and Efficiency

Blender's flexibility is one of its strongest features, but manually performing certain actions repeatedly can become tedious and time-consuming. Python scripting provides a solution by allowing you to:

- Automate repetitive tasks such as setting up scenes, applying modifiers, or managing assets.
- Create custom operators and panels for streamlined workflows.
- Develop scripts that adjust settings or generate content dynamically.

For example, a script to apply a specific set of modifiers to selected objects can save hours of manual effort in large projects. Here's a simple example:

```python
import bpy

# Apply a subdivision surface modifier to all selected objects
for obj in bpy.context.selected_objects:
    if obj.type == 'MESH':
        mod = obj.modifiers.new(name="Subdivision", type='SUBSURF')
        mod.levels = 2
        mod.render_levels = 2
```

Enhancing Collaboration and Reusability

In collaborative projects, consistency and reusability are critical. Python scripts allow you to create tools and workflows that can be shared across teams, ensuring everyone follows the same standards and best practices. For instance:

- Generate templates for scene setup that match project requirements.
- Create scripts to export assets with specific naming conventions or settings.
- Automate rendering tasks with predefined configurations.

Here's an example script to automate exporting objects to a specific format:

```python
import bpy

# Export all objects as FBX files to a specified directory
export_path = "/path/to/export/directory/"

for obj in bpy.data.objects:
    if obj.type == 'MESH':

bpy.ops.export_scene.fbx(filepath=f"{export_path}{obj.name}.fbx",
use_selection=True)
```

Expanding Blender's Capabilities

Blender's default tools are robust, but Python scripting allows you to go beyond the default capabilities by:

- Creating custom add-ons to integrate third-party tools or workflows.
- Developing interactive tools such as real-time property controls or dynamic UI elements.
- Accessing low-level data to create unique effects or functionality.

For example, you could create a script to procedurally generate an entire environment:

```python
import bpy
import random

def create_random_tree(location):
    bpy.ops.mesh.primitive_cylinder_add(radius=0.1, depth=3,
location=location)
    trunk = bpy.context.object
    bpy.ops.mesh.primitive_uv_sphere_add(location=(location[0],
location[1], location[2] + 2))
    leaves = bpy.context.object
    trunk.name = "Tree_Trunk"
    leaves.name = "Tree_Leaves"
```

```
    leaves.scale = (random.uniform(1, 2), random.uniform(1, 2),
random.uniform(1, 2))

# Generate a forest
for i in range(20):
    create_random_tree((random.uniform(-10, 10), random.uniform(-10,
10), 0))
```

Learning Resources for Blender Python Scripting

To become proficient in Blender Python scripting, the following resources and practices are recommended:

- **Blender API Documentation**: The official documentation provides a comprehensive guide to Blender's Python API.
- **Community Forums**: Blender's community forums and Stack Exchange are excellent for troubleshooting and discovering creative solutions.
- **Open Source Projects**: Explore the source code of popular Blender add-ons to understand advanced scripting techniques.
- **Experimentation**: Build small projects to practice scripting concepts and gradually expand your skills.

Practical Applications of Python in Blender

Python scripting can be applied in numerous scenarios, including:

1. **Automating Scene Management**: Scripts can be used to organize and clean up scenes, such as automatically grouping objects or assigning materials.
2. **Custom Tools for Artists**: Provide non-technical team members with easy-to-use tools by creating custom operators and UI panels.
3. **Game Development Pipelines**: Automate asset preparation and export processes for integration with game engines like Unity or Unreal Engine.
4. **Dynamic Content Generation**: Use procedural algorithms to generate models, textures, and animations dynamically.

For instance, here's a script to create a dynamic panel in Blender's UI:

```
import bpy

class SimplePanel(bpy.types.Panel):
    bl_label = "My Custom Panel"
    bl_idname = "VIEW3D_PT_custom_panel"
    bl_space_type = 'VIEW_3D'
    bl_region_type = 'UI'
```

```
    bl_category = "Tool"

    def draw(self, context):
        layout = self.layout
        row = layout.row()
        row.operator("object.simple_operator")

class SimpleOperator(bpy.types.Operator):
    bl_idname = "object.simple_operator"
    bl_label = "Click Me"

    def execute(self, context):
        self.report({'INFO'}, "Hello from Python!")
        return {'FINISHED'}

# Register the classes
def register():
    bpy.utils.register_class(SimplePanel)
    bpy.utils.register_class(SimpleOperator)

def unregister():
    bpy.utils.unregister_class(SimplePanel)
    bpy.utils.unregister_class(SimpleOperator)

if __name__ == "__main__":
    register()
```

This code adds a new panel to the 3D Viewport's UI with a simple button that triggers an operator.

Conclusion

Learning Python scripting in Blender empowers you to customize and optimize your workflows, develop advanced tools, and expand Blender's capabilities. By leveraging Python, you can bridge the gap between Blender's existing tools and the unique needs of your projects, whether you're an artist, game developer, or technical director. Begin by experimenting with small scripts and gradually work your way toward building complex tools and add-ons. The possibilities are limitless!

Basics of Python Scripting in Blender

Python scripting in Blender is a powerful way to interact with and manipulate every aspect of the software. By understanding the basics, you can create scripts to automate tasks, build tools, and extend Blender's capabilities to suit your specific needs. This section covers foundational concepts that will prepare you to start scripting confidently.

Getting Started with Blender's Python Console

Blender includes a built-in Python console that allows you to test and execute Python commands in real time. This is an excellent way to explore Blender's Python API and learn how different commands affect your scene.

1. Open the Python Console:
   ○ Navigate to the **Scripting** workspace in Blender.
   ○ Switch one of the editor areas to the **Python Console**.
2. Execute Simple Commands:

For example, you can print Blender's version by typing:
python

```
print(bpy.app.version)
```

   ○
3. Access Scene Data:

You can access and manipulate objects in your scene. For instance:
python

```
for obj in bpy.data.objects:
    print(obj.name)
```

   ○

Understanding the bpy Module

The bpy module is the heart of Blender's Python API. It allows you to interact with Blender's data, operators, and settings.

Key Concepts in bpy:

1. **Data Access**:
   ○ Access Blender's data structure, such as meshes, materials, and cameras, through bpy.data.

Example:
python

```
print(bpy.data.objects["Cube"].location)
```

○

2. **Context**:
    ○ Use `bpy.context` to get information about the current state, such as the selected object or active tool.

Example:
python

```
active_object = bpy.context.active_object
print(active_object.name)
```

○

3. **Operators**:
    ○ Perform actions like adding objects, applying transformations, or rendering using `bpy.ops`.

Example:
python

```
bpy.ops.mesh.primitive_cube_add(size=2, location=(0, 0, 0))
```

○

Creating and Executing Scripts

Scripts in Blender can be written and executed in the **Text Editor**. To create a script:

1. Open the **Scripting** workspace.
2. Use the **Text Editor** to write your script.
3. Click **Run Script** to execute it.

Here's a simple script to add a sphere to the scene:

```
import bpy

# Add a UV Sphere
bpy.ops.mesh.primitive_uv_sphere_add(radius=1, location=(2, 2, 0))
```

Manipulating Objects

Blender allows you to manipulate objects using Python, such as changing their position, rotation, and scale.

Example: Move and Scale Objects

```
import bpy

# Select an object by name
obj = bpy.data.objects["Cube"]

# Change location
obj.location = (5, 5, 5)

# Scale the object
obj.scale = (2, 2, 2)
```

You can also apply transformations to multiple objects:

```
for obj in bpy.context.selected_objects:
    obj.location.x += 2
    obj.scale *= 1.5
```

Working with Mesh Data

The bpy module provides access to mesh data, allowing you to create and modify geometry programmatically.

Example: Create a Custom Mesh

```
import bpy
import bmesh

# Create a new mesh and object
mesh = bpy.data.meshes.new("CustomMesh")
obj = bpy.data.objects.new("CustomObject", mesh)

# Link the object to the scene
bpy.context.collection.objects.link(obj)

# Create geometry using bmesh
bm = bmesh.new()
bmesh.ops.create_cube(bm, size=2.0)

# Write the bmesh data to the mesh
bm.to_mesh(mesh)
```

```
bm.free()
```

Adding Materials and Textures

Materials and textures can also be created and assigned using Python.

Example: Add a Material

```python
import bpy

# Create a new material
material = bpy.data.materials.new(name="MyMaterial")
material.use_nodes = True

# Assign the material to an object
obj = bpy.context.active_object
if obj.type == 'MESH':
    obj.data.materials.append(material)
```

Example: Modify Shader Nodes

```python
# Access the material's node tree
nodes = material.node_tree.nodes
principled = nodes.get("Principled BSDF")

# Change the base color
principled.inputs["Base Color"].default_value = (1, 0, 0, 1)  # Red
```

Automating Common Tasks

Python is perfect for automating repetitive tasks. For example, you can rename all objects in a scene:

```python
for i, obj in enumerate(bpy.data.objects):
    obj.name = f"Object_{i}"
```

Or create a grid of objects:

```python
import bpy
```

```
for x in range(-5, 6, 2):
    for y in range(-5, 6, 2):
        bpy.ops.mesh.primitive_cube_add(location=(x, y, 0))
```

Debugging and Error Handling

When writing scripts, debugging is an essential skill. Use `print()` statements and Blender's system console to track your script's progress.

Example: Catch Errors Gracefully

```
try:
    obj = bpy.data.objects["NonExistentObject"]
    print(obj.name)
except KeyError:
    print("Object not found!")
```

Best Practices for Python Scripting in Blender

1. **Comment Your Code**: Provide clear comments to explain your scripts.
2. **Use Meaningful Variable Names**: Choose names that reflect the purpose of your variables.
3. **Test Incrementally**: Run parts of your script step by step to identify issues early.
4. **Leverage the API Documentation**: Blender's API documentation is an invaluable resource.

Conclusion

By understanding the basics of Python scripting in Blender, you can begin automating tasks, creating custom tools, and manipulating data programmatically. Practice is key, so start with small scripts and gradually tackle more complex projects. As you grow more comfortable, you'll find that Python becomes an indispensable part of your Blender workflow.

Automating Tasks with Scripts

Automating tasks in Blender using Python scripting is a game-changer for efficiency, especially in large projects or repetitive workflows. With a fundamental understanding of the Blender Python API, you can build scripts that handle complex or tedious operations with minimal user input.

The Philosophy of Automation

Before diving into automation, it's important to identify tasks that benefit from scripting. Common use cases include:

1. **Scene Setup**: Automating the creation and arrangement of objects, cameras, and lights.
2. **Batch Processing**: Applying operations to multiple objects or files, such as renaming, modifying geometry, or exporting.
3. **Data Management**: Organizing and standardizing assets within a scene or across projects.
4. **Rendering Pipelines**: Automating rendering tasks with specific settings.

Blender's Python API provides tools to interact with nearly every aspect of the application, making automation flexible and powerful.

Example 1: Automating Scene Setup

A common task in Blender is setting up a scene with predefined objects, lighting, and camera configurations. Automating this process ensures consistency and saves time.

Script: Scene Setup with Default Objects

```python
import bpy

def setup_scene():
    # Clear existing objects
    bpy.ops.object.select_all(action='SELECT')
    bpy.ops.object.delete(use_global=False)

    # Add a camera
    bpy.ops.object.camera_add(location=(0, -5, 5), rotation=(1.2, 0, 0))
    camera = bpy.context.object
    bpy.context.scene.camera = camera

    # Add a light source
    bpy.ops.object.light_add(type='SUN', location=(10, 10, 10))

    # Add a default cube
    bpy.ops.mesh.primitive_cube_add(size=2, location=(0, 0, 1))

setup_scene()
```

Running this script sets up a basic scene with a camera, light, and cube, ready for further customization.

Example 2: Batch Renaming Objects

Managing object names in large scenes can be tedious. A script can automate the renaming process, ensuring objects follow a consistent naming convention.

Script: Renaming All Objects

```python
import bpy

def rename_objects():
    for i, obj in enumerate(bpy.data.objects):
        obj.name = f"Object_{i+1}"

rename_objects()
```

After running the script, all objects in the scene will be renamed sequentially as Object_1, Object_2, and so on.

Example 3: Automating Modifier Application

Blender's modifiers are powerful tools, but applying them manually to multiple objects can be time-consuming. A script can simplify this process.

Script: Applying a Subdivision Modifier to All Selected Objects

```python
import bpy

def apply_subdivision_modifier(levels=2):
    for obj in bpy.context.selected_objects:
        if obj.type == 'MESH':
            mod = obj.modifiers.new(name="Subdivision",
type='SUBSURF')
            mod.levels = levels
            bpy.ops.object.modifier_apply(modifier="Subdivision")

apply_subdivision_modifier()
```

This script applies a subdivision surface modifier with the specified level to all selected objects.

Example 4: Exporting Objects in Batch

Exporting multiple objects to separate files is a repetitive task that can be automated. The following script exports all selected objects as individual FBX files.

Script: Batch Export to FBX

```python
import bpy
import os

def batch_export_fbx(export_dir):
    if not os.path.exists(export_dir):
        os.makedirs(export_dir)

    for obj in bpy.context.selected_objects:
        if obj.type == 'MESH':
            filepath = os.path.join(export_dir, f"{obj.name}.fbx")
            bpy.ops.object.select_all(action='DESELECT')
            obj.select_set(True)
            bpy.ops.export_scene.fbx(filepath=filepath,
use_selection=True)

batch_export_fbx("C:/BlenderExports")
```

This script ensures each object is exported as a separate FBX file to the specified directory.

Example 5: Automating Material Assignment

Assigning materials to multiple objects can be automated to ensure consistency in scenes with many assets.

Script: Assigning a Material to All Objects

```python
import bpy

def assign_material_to_all(material_name):
    # Create or get the material
```

```python
    if material_name in bpy.data.materials:
        mat = bpy.data.materials[material_name]
    else:
        mat = bpy.data.materials.new(name=material_name)
        mat.use_nodes = True

    # Assign material to all objects
    for obj in bpy.data.objects:
        if obj.type == 'MESH':
            if mat not in obj.data.materials:
                obj.data.materials.append(mat)

assign_material_to_all("DefaultMaterial")
```

This script creates a new material if it doesn't exist and assigns it to all mesh objects in the scene.

Example 6: Automating Rendering Pipelines

Rendering tasks can also be automated to save time and ensure consistent settings.

Script: Rendering Multiple Views of an Object

```python
import bpy

def render_views(output_path, angles=(0, 90, 180, 270)):
    # Set up rendering
    scene = bpy.context.scene
    camera = scene.camera

    for angle in angles:
        camera.rotation_euler[2] = angle * (3.14159 / 180)  #
Convert to radians
        scene.render.filepath = f"{output_path}/render_{angle}.png"
        bpy.ops.render.render(write_still=True)

render_views("C:/Renders")
```

This script renders an object from multiple angles and saves each render as an image.

Best Practices for Automating Tasks

1. **Plan Your Workflow**: Identify repetitive tasks and define clear goals for automation.
2. **Use Descriptive Names**: Name your scripts, variables, and functions meaningfully to make the code easier to understand and maintain.
3. **Test Incrementally**: Test your scripts on a small subset of data before scaling up to the entire scene or project.
4. **Leverage the API Documentation**: The Blender Python API documentation is an invaluable resource for understanding available functions and classes.
5. **Keep It Modular**: Break complex automation scripts into smaller, reusable functions.

Conclusion

Automating tasks with Python scripting in Blender transforms how you interact with the software, enhancing productivity and creativity. From setting up scenes to batch processing and rendering pipelines, scripts provide a level of precision and efficiency that manual workflows cannot match. Mastering automation ensures you can handle projects of any scale with confidence and ease.

Building Custom Add-ons

Blender's Python API allows you to create custom add-ons to extend the software's capabilities, integrate new tools, and streamline workflows. Add-ons are Python scripts that register new functionality within Blender, such as operators, menus, panels, or entire workflows. This section explains how to build custom add-ons, step by step, providing code examples and best practices.

Why Build Custom Add-ons?

1. **Streamline Workflows**: Add-ons allow you to combine repetitive actions into single-click tools.
2. **Enhance User Experience**: Custom panels and operators make complex functionality accessible to artists and non-technical users.
3. **Extend Blender**: Add-ons can introduce new features that are not part of Blender's default toolkit.
4. **Collaborative Tools**: Share custom solutions with teams or the Blender community.

Structure of a Blender Add-on

A Blender add-on is a Python script containing specific components to register and unregister itself. At a minimum, an add-on includes:

1. **Metadata Block**: Provides information about the add-on, such as its name, version, author, and description.
2. **Registration Functions**: Register and unregister the functionality provided by the add-on.
3. **Classes**: Define operators, panels, and other custom features.

Example: Minimal Add-on Structure

```python
bl_info = {
    "name": "My First Add-on",
    "blender": (3, 0, 0),
    "category": "Object",
    "author": "Your Name",
    "version": (1, 0, 0),
    "description": "A simple example add-on",
}

import bpy

# Define a simple operator
class SimpleOperator(bpy.types.Operator):
    bl_idname = "object.simple_operator"
    bl_label = "Simple Operator"
    bl_description = "This is a simple operator example"

    def execute(self, context):
        self.report({'INFO'}, "Hello from My First Add-on!")
        return {'FINISHED'}

# Register and unregister classes
def register():
    bpy.utils.register_class(SimpleOperator)

def unregister():
    bpy.utils.unregister_class(SimpleOperator)

if __name__ == "__main__":
    register()
```

Save this script as a `.py` file and install it in Blender via **Edit > Preferences > Add-ons > Install**. Once enabled, the operator will appear in the **Search Menu** (F3) as "Simple Operator."

Adding Panels to the User Interface

Custom panels are used to integrate tools directly into Blender's UI. Panels can be added to any editor, such as the 3D Viewport or Properties Editor.

Example: Adding a Panel in the 3D Viewport

```python
class SimplePanel(bpy.types.Panel):
    bl_label = "My Simple Panel"
    bl_idname = "VIEW3D_PT_simple_panel"
    bl_space_type = 'VIEW_3D'
    bl_region_type = 'UI'
    bl_category = "Tool"

    def draw(self, context):
        layout = self.layout
        layout.label(text="Hello from the Panel!")
        layout.operator("object.simple_operator")

def register():
    bpy.utils.register_class(SimpleOperator)
    bpy.utils.register_class(SimplePanel)

def unregister():
    bpy.utils.unregister_class(SimplePanel)
    bpy.utils.unregister_class(SimpleOperator)

if __name__ == "__main__":
    register()
```

This panel, added to the **Tool** tab in the 3D Viewport, includes a button to execute the `SimpleOperator` defined earlier.

Advanced Operators and User Input

Operators can include properties for user input, making tools more flexible and interactive.

Example: Operator with User Input

```python
class AdvancedOperator(bpy.types.Operator):
    bl_idname = "object.advanced_operator"
    bl_label = "Advanced Operator"

    my_float: bpy.props.FloatProperty(name="Scale", default=1.0,
min=0.1, max=10.0)
    my_string: bpy.props.StringProperty(name="Object Name",
default="NewObject")

    def execute(self, context):
        # Create a cube and scale it
        bpy.ops.mesh.primitive_cube_add(size=self.my_float,
location=(0, 0, 0))
        obj = bpy.context.object
        obj.name = self.my_string
        self.report({'INFO'}, f"Created {obj.name} with scale
{self.my_float}")
        return {'FINISHED'}

class AdvancedPanel(bpy.types.Panel):
    bl_label = "Advanced Panel"
    bl_idname = "VIEW3D_PT_advanced_panel"
    bl_space_type = 'VIEW_3D'
    bl_region_type = 'UI'
    bl_category = "Tool"

    def draw(self, context):
        layout = self.layout
        layout.operator("object.advanced_operator")

def register():
    bpy.utils.register_class(AdvancedOperator)
    bpy.utils.register_class(AdvancedPanel)

def unregister():
    bpy.utils.unregister_class(AdvancedPanel)
    bpy.utils.unregister_class(AdvancedOperator)

if __name__ == "__main__":
    register()
```

This operator creates a cube with a user-defined scale and name, and the panel provides an interface for input.

Organizing Complex Add-ons

For larger add-ons, organizing code into multiple files or modules improves maintainability. Use Python packages by creating a folder with an `__init__.py` file as the main entry point.

Example: Add-on Folder Structure

```
my_addon/
├── __init__.py
├── operators.py
├── panels.py
```

- `__init__.py`: Registers the add-on and imports functionality.
- `operators.py`: Contains operator classes.
- `panels.py`: Contains panel definitions.

Example: Importing from Modules

```python
# __init__.py
bl_info = {
    "name": "Modular Add-on",
    "blender": (3, 0, 0),
    "category": "Object",
}

import bpy
from . import operators, panels

def register():
    operators.register()
    panels.register()

def unregister():
    panels.unregister()
```

```
    operators.unregister()

if __name__ == "__main__":
    register()
```

Distributing Add-ons

Once an add-on is complete, you can distribute it as a `.zip` file for others to install:

1. Compress the add-on folder.
2. Ensure it includes all necessary scripts and assets.
3. Provide clear installation and usage instructions.

Best Practices for Add-on Development

1. **Follow Naming Conventions**: Use clear and descriptive names for classes, properties, and functions.
2. **Comment Your Code**: Add meaningful comments to explain functionality.
3. **Test Thoroughly**: Ensure compatibility with different Blender versions and operating systems.
4. **Use Version Control**: Track changes using Git or other version control systems.
5. **Engage with the Community**: Share your add-ons on platforms like Blender Artists or GitHub for feedback and improvement.

Conclusion

Building custom add-ons unlocks the full potential of Blender's Python API, allowing you to create powerful tools tailored to your needs. By mastering the basics of add-on development, you can streamline workflows, enhance usability, and contribute to the vibrant Blender community. Whether you're automating simple tasks or introducing groundbreaking features, add-ons are a vital step toward becoming a proficient Blender developer.

Chapter 10: Special Effects and Simulation

Working with Blender's Physics Simulations

Physics simulations in Blender offer a powerful way to create realistic effects, enabling artists to simulate everything from falling objects to complex fluid dynamics. Understanding the core concepts of Blender's physics simulation tools is essential for adding a touch of realism to your projects.

Getting Started with Blender Physics

Blender provides a dedicated physics tab in the Properties panel. This tab contains several simulation types, such as:

- **Cloth**
- **Fluid**
- **Smoke**
- **Rigid Body**
- **Soft Body**
- **Particles**

Each type has unique properties and use cases. Before diving into individual simulations, familiarize yourself with Blender's approach to physics:

1. **Scene Scale**: Physics simulations are sensitive to the scale of your scene. Ensure your objects are scaled appropriately to real-world dimensions.
2. **Subdivisions**: For high-quality simulations, increase the resolution of your objects. Use modifiers like Subdivision Surface to refine meshes.
3. **Caching**: Most simulations require caching for playback. Caches store pre-calculated data, allowing smooth playback and rendering.

Setting Up Basic Physics Simulations

Adding a Physics Type

1. Select the object in your scene.
2. Navigate to the **Physics Properties** tab.
3. Choose a simulation type (e.g., Rigid Body, Cloth).

Example: Creating a Simple Rigid Body Simulation

Rigid Body simulations are used for simulating hard objects like boxes, balls, or walls. Follow these steps to create a simple falling object:

1. Add a plane to serve as the ground (Shift + A > Mesh > Plane).
2. Scale the plane to a suitable size (S key, followed by dragging the mouse).
3. Add a cube above the plane (Shift + A > Mesh > Cube).
4. With the cube selected, go to the **Physics Properties** tab and enable **Rigid Body**.
5. Set the **Type** to Active (for movable objects).
6. Select the plane, enable **Rigid Body**, and set the **Type** to Passive (for static objects).
7. Press Spacebar or Play to simulate.

The cube will fall and collide with the plane due to gravity.

Advanced Physics Simulations

Cloth Simulation

Cloth simulations are ideal for creating dynamic, flowing fabrics. For example, you can simulate a curtain or a flag:

1. Add a plane (Shift + A > Mesh > Plane) and scale it to the desired size.
2. Subdivide the plane for better results (Right-click > Subdivide).
3. Select the plane and enable **Cloth** under the Physics tab.
4. Adjust parameters:
   - **Mass**: Determines the weight of the cloth.
   - **Stiffness**: Controls how rigid or flexible the cloth appears.
5. Add collision to nearby objects to interact with the cloth:
   - Select the object, enable **Collision** in the Physics tab.
6. Simulate by pressing Play.

Smoke Simulation

Smoke simulations are excellent for creating effects like explosions, fire, or fog. Here's how to set up a basic smoke effect:

1. Add a cube to act as the smoke domain (Shift + A > Mesh > Cube).
2. Scale the cube to encompass the area where the smoke will appear.
3. Select the cube and enable **Fluid > Domain** in the Physics tab. Set the **Domain Type** to Gas.
4. Add an emitter object (e.g., a sphere). Select the sphere and enable **Fluid > Flow**. Set the **Flow Type** to Smoke.
5. Play the simulation to generate smoke within the domain.

Particle Systems

Particles are versatile for effects like rain, sparks, or debris:

1. Select an object to emit particles (e.g., a plane or sphere).

2. Go to the **Particle Properties** tab and click **+** to add a new system.
3. Adjust key settings:
    ○ **Number**: Total particles emitted.
    ○ **Lifetime**: How long each particle exists.
    ○ **Physics Type**: Choose between Newtonian, Fluid, etc.
4. Add a material to the particles for customization.

Tips for Optimizing Physics Simulations

- **Simplify Meshes**: Use low-poly objects for simulation and replace them with high-poly models during rendering.
- **Bake Simulations**: Baking caches the simulation, reducing calculation times during playback.
- **Use Substeps**: Increase substeps in the simulation settings to prevent jittery or unrealistic motion.
- **GPU Acceleration**: Enable GPU compute in Preferences to speed up simulations.

Python for Automating Physics

Automating physics setups with Python scripting can streamline workflows. Below is an example script for setting up a Rigid Body simulation:

```python
import bpy

# Add a ground plane
bpy.ops.mesh.primitive_plane_add(size=10, location=(0, 0, 0))
ground = bpy.context.object
bpy.ops.rigidbody.object_add()
ground.rigid_body.type = 'PASSIVE'

# Add a falling cube
bpy.ops.mesh.primitive_cube_add(size=1, location=(0, 0, 5))
cube = bpy.context.object
bpy.ops.rigidbody.object_add()
cube.rigid_body.type = 'ACTIVE'
```

Run this script in Blender's scripting workspace to quickly create a basic Rigid Body setup.

Common Challenges and Solutions

1. **Objects Passing Through**:
   - Increase collision margin in the Physics settings.
   - Use higher-quality mesh settings.
2. **Slow Simulations**:
   - Lower the resolution during testing and increase it for final renders.
   - Use simplified domains for fluid or smoke.
3. **Inconsistent Results**:
   - Clear caches when changing parameters to avoid conflicts.

Physics simulations in Blender provide a wealth of tools to bring your scenes to life. Whether you're crafting flowing fabrics or explosive action, mastering these techniques can elevate your projects to new heights.

Creating Explosions, Fire, and Smoke

Explosions, fire, and smoke are among the most dramatic effects you can create in Blender, adding visual interest and realism to animations and renders. Blender's physics and simulation tools, especially its Fluid simulation system, make it possible to simulate these phenomena with precision and creativity.

Understanding the Basics of Fire and Smoke Simulation

Blender uses a **Fluid Domain** system to simulate fire and smoke. The simulation is based on computational fluid dynamics (CFD) principles, which allow for the realistic representation of gaseous phenomena. The key components of a fire or smoke simulation are:

- **Domain**: The area where the simulation occurs.
- **Flow Object**: The emitter of fire or smoke.
- **Collision Objects**: Objects that interact with the simulation.
- **Force Fields**: Optional elements like wind or turbulence that influence the flow of smoke or fire.

Setting Up a Simple Smoke Simulation

Follow these steps to create a basic smoke effect:

1. **Add the Domain**:
   - In the 3D Viewport, press `Shift + A > Mesh > Cube` to add a cube.
   - Scale the cube to define the bounds of the simulation (`S` key, followed by dragging the mouse).
   - With the cube selected, go to the **Physics Properties** tab and enable **Fluid**. Set the **Type** to `Domain`.
   - In the **Domain Settings**, set the **Domain Type** to `Gas`.

2. **Add the Flow Object**:
    ○ Add a mesh (e.g., a sphere or plane) to act as the smoke emitter (`Shift + A > Mesh > Sphere`).
    ○ Position it inside the domain.
    ○ Select the flow object and enable **Fluid** in the Physics Properties. Set the **Type** to `Flow`.
    ○ Under the **Flow Type**, choose `Smoke`.
3. **Play the Simulation**:
    ○ Press `Spacebar` or `Play` in the Timeline to simulate.
    ○ Smoke will begin to appear, filling the domain.

Adding Fire to the Smoke Simulation

Fire can be added to a smoke simulation by modifying the Flow settings:

1. **Adjust the Flow Object**:
    ○ Select the smoke emitter.
    ○ In the **Flow Type**, set it to `Fire + Smoke`.
    ○ Adjust the **Temperature** setting under **Flow Source** to control the intensity of the fire.
2. **Modify the Domain Settings**:
    ○ Select the domain.
    ○ In the **Physics Properties**, enable the **Noise** option to add high-resolution detail to the fire and smoke.
    ○ Adjust the **Flame** settings, such as **Reaction Speed** and **Vorticity**, to refine the fire's appearance.
3. **Material Setup**:
    ○ In the Shader Editor, create a material for the domain.
    ○ Use the **Principled Volume** shader to render fire and smoke.
    ○ Connect the **Density** and **Flame** attributes from the simulation to the material inputs to achieve realistic results.

Advanced Techniques for Explosions

Explosions involve combining fire, smoke, and debris for a dynamic effect. Here's how to create an explosion:

1. **Setup the Domain and Flow Object**:
    ○ Create a domain and flow object as described earlier.
    ○ For the flow object, set **Flow Type** to `Fire + Smoke`.
2. **Add a Quick Explosion**:
    ○ Select the flow object, then go to the **Object Properties** menu.

- o Use `Object > Quick Effects > Quick Explosion` to automatically configure an explosion setup.
3. **Enhance with Particles**:
    - o Add a particle system to the flow object in the **Particle Properties** tab.
    - o Emit particles from the object during the explosion, using settings like **Velocity** to scatter particles realistically.
    - o Use the particles as debris or secondary emitters for the explosion.
4. **Lighting and Camera**:
    - o Use area lights or point lights to illuminate the fire and smoke. Adjust the light's intensity and color to match the explosion's tone.
    - o Position the camera to capture the explosion dramatically, using depth of field for added focus.

Python Automation for Explosions

Blender's Python API can be used to automate the creation of fire and smoke effects. Here is an example script to set up a basic fire simulation:

```python
import bpy

# Create the domain
bpy.ops.mesh.primitive_cube_add(location=(0, 0, 0), scale=(3, 3, 3))
domain = bpy.context.object
bpy.ops.object.modifier_add(type='FLUID')
domain.modifiers['Fluid'].fluid_type = 'DOMAIN'
domain.modifiers['Fluid'].domain_settings.domain_type = 'GAS'

# Create the emitter
bpy.ops.mesh.primitive_uv_sphere_add(location=(0, 0, 1))
emitter = bpy.context.object
bpy.ops.object.modifier_add(type='FLUID')
emitter.modifiers['Fluid'].fluid_type = 'FLOW'
emitter.modifiers['Fluid'].flow_settings.flow_type =
'FIRE_AND_SMOKE'
emitter.modifiers['Fluid'].flow_settings.flow_behavior = 'INFLOW'

# Play the simulation
bpy.context.scene.frame_start = 1
bpy.context.scene.frame_end = 100
bpy.ops.ptcache.bake_all()
```

Run this script in Blender's scripting workspace to create a fire and smoke simulation.

Optimizing Fire and Smoke Simulations

- **Resolution**: Increase the domain resolution for detailed simulations. Use **Adaptive Domain** to focus detail only where needed.
- **Cache Settings**: Always bake simulations before rendering to avoid playback inconsistencies.
- **Lighting and Shadows**: Use volumetric lighting to enhance the realism of fire and smoke. Enable shadows for added depth.

Common Challenges and Solutions

1. **Flickering Smoke**:
   - Increase the simulation resolution.
   - Enable **Dissolve** in the Flow settings to remove old smoke.
2. **Unrealistic Fire**:
   - Adjust the **Reaction Speed** and **Flame Intensity** in the domain settings.
   - Refine the material shader.
3. **Slow Simulations**:
   - Use lower resolution for testing.
   - Optimize the domain size to encompass only the required area.

Creating explosions, fire, and smoke in Blender involves a balance of artistic vision and technical precision. By mastering the tools and techniques available, you can bring dynamic and realistic effects to your projects, enhancing both their visual and emotional impact.

Fluid Simulations for Realistic Effects

Fluid simulations in Blender allow creators to simulate realistic liquid behaviors such as pouring water, splashing, and flowing streams. Blender's Fluid system leverages the Mantaflow engine, providing artists with a powerful and flexible toolset for creating natural and visually engaging effects.

Understanding the Basics of Fluid Simulations

A fluid simulation in Blender is composed of several key elements:

1. **Domain**: Defines the boundaries of the simulation and contains all fluid behavior.
2. **Flow Object**: The emitter or source of the fluid.
3. **Effector**: Objects that interact with the fluid, such as obstacles or collision surfaces.

4. **Force Fields**: Optional elements, like wind or gravity modifiers, to influence fluid behavior.

Setting Up a Basic Fluid Simulation

Follow these steps to create a simple fluid simulation:

1. **Add the Domain**:
   - Press Shift + A > Mesh > Cube to create a cube.
   - Scale the cube to define the fluid simulation boundaries (S key, then drag to resize).
   - With the cube selected, navigate to the **Physics Properties** tab and enable **Fluid**. Set the **Type** to Domain.
   - In the **Domain Type** dropdown, choose Liquid.
2. **Add a Flow Object**:
   - Add a sphere or another mesh shape to act as the fluid emitter (Shift + A > Mesh > UV Sphere).
   - Position the sphere inside the domain.
   - Select the sphere, go to **Physics Properties**, and enable **Fluid**. Set the **Type** to Flow.
   - Under **Flow Type**, select Liquid.
   - Set the **Flow Behavior** to Inflow to continuously emit liquid.
3. **Add an Effector Object**:
   - Add a plane or another mesh object to act as an obstacle or container (Shift + A > Mesh > Plane).
   - Position the plane below the flow object.
   - Select the plane, go to **Physics Properties**, and enable **Fluid**. Set the **Type** to Effector.
   - Under the **Effector Type**, choose Collision.
4. **Bake the Simulation**:
   - Select the domain.
   - Scroll down to the **Cache** settings in the Physics tab.
   - Set the frame range and choose a folder for the cache files.
   - Click **Bake** to calculate the simulation.
5. **Play the Simulation**:
   - Press Spacebar to preview the simulation.

Refining the Simulation

Fluid simulations often require adjustments to achieve realistic effects. Blender provides several parameters to fine-tune the behavior and appearance of liquids.

Domain Settings

- **Resolution Divisions**: Increase this value to improve simulation detail.
- **Time Scale**: Adjust this to slow down or speed up the simulation.
- **Boundary Type**: Set how the fluid interacts with domain walls (e.g., `Free` or `No-Slip`).

Flow Settings

- **Flow Rate**: Controls how much fluid is emitted.
- **Initial Velocity**: Sets the starting speed and direction of the fluid.
- **Use Mesh**: Enables conversion of fluid particles into a renderable surface.

Effector Settings

- **Friction**: Adjusts how the fluid slides over the effector surface.
- **Thickness**: Sets the perceived size of the effector for interactions.

Advanced Techniques for Realistic Fluid Effects

Adding Obstacles and Interactions

To create dynamic scenes, add multiple effector objects:

1. Create additional obstacles, like cubes or walls, to interact with the fluid.
2. Assign each obstacle the **Effector** type under the Physics tab.
3. Adjust the **Friction** and **Stickiness** values for unique interactions.

Using Force Fields

Force fields can be used to guide the fluid's motion:

1. Add a force field (`Shift + A > Force Field > Wind`).
2. Position the force field near the domain.
3. Adjust the force strength and direction to influence the fluid.

Simulating Pouring and Splashing

1. Position the flow object above an effector (e.g., a glass or bowl).
2. Set the flow object to **Inflow** with a moderate **Flow Rate**.
3. Add a high-resolution domain and bake the simulation.

Python Automation for Fluid Setups

Python scripting can simplify repetitive fluid setups. Here's a script to create a basic fluid simulation:

```python
import bpy

# Create the domain
bpy.ops.mesh.primitive_cube_add(location=(0, 0, 0), scale=(3, 3, 3))
domain = bpy.context.object
bpy.ops.object.modifier_add(type='FLUID')
domain.modifiers['Fluid'].fluid_type = 'DOMAIN'
domain.modifiers['Fluid'].domain_settings.domain_type = 'LIQUID'

# Create the flow object
bpy.ops.mesh.primitive_uv_sphere_add(location=(0, 0, 2))
flow = bpy.context.object
bpy.ops.object.modifier_add(type='FLUID')
flow.modifiers['Fluid'].fluid_type = 'FLOW'
flow.modifiers['Fluid'].flow_settings.flow_type = 'LIQUID'
flow.modifiers['Fluid'].flow_settings.flow_behavior = 'INFLOW'

# Add an effector
bpy.ops.mesh.primitive_plane_add(location=(0, 0, -1), scale=(4, 4, 1))
effector = bpy.context.object
bpy.ops.object.modifier_add(type='FLUID')
effector.modifiers['Fluid'].fluid_type = 'EFFECTOR'
```

Run this script in Blender's scripting workspace to quickly generate a fluid simulation.

Tips for High-Quality Fluid Simulations

1. **Increase Resolution**:
   - For detailed splashes and interactions, increase the **Resolution Divisions** in the domain settings.
2. **Refine Materials**:
   - Use the **Principled BSDF** shader with a water texture for realistic rendering.
3. **Add Motion Blur**:
   - Enable motion blur in the render settings to capture dynamic movements.
4. **Bake at High Resolution**:
   - Always test at lower resolutions before baking high-quality simulations to save time.

Common Challenges and Solutions

1. **Slow Simulations**:
   - Use lower resolution for testing.
   - Limit the domain size to the necessary area.
2. **Unrealistic Fluid Behavior**:
   - Check the scale of your objects; ensure they match real-world dimensions.
   - Increase the resolution for finer details.
3. **Artifacts or Flickering**:
   - Enable **Adaptive Domain** to optimize simulation boundaries.
   - Increase the **Substeps** in the domain settings.

Fluid simulations are a cornerstone of creating lifelike effects in Blender. By mastering the tools and settings, you can create everything from gentle streams to chaotic torrents, elevating your projects to new levels of realism and artistry.

Visual Effects (VFX) Workflow

Creating stunning visual effects (VFX) in Blender involves combining simulation, compositing, and rendering techniques to seamlessly integrate digital elements into live-action footage or standalone CG scenes. Blender's all-in-one suite offers tools for modeling, animating, simulating, and compositing, making it a powerful choice for VFX workflows.

Understanding the VFX Workflow in Blender

A typical VFX workflow includes the following stages:

1. **Pre-production**: Preparing reference footage, storyboarding, and planning shots.
2. **Matchmoving**: Tracking the camera and objects in the scene.
3. **Scene Integration**: Adding CG elements to match the tracked footage.
4. **Simulations**: Applying physics-based effects like explosions, fluids, or debris.
5. **Compositing**: Merging CG and live-action elements seamlessly.
6. **Rendering**: Producing the final output with high-quality settings.

Each stage requires a blend of technical skill and artistic vision to achieve realistic results.

Preparing for VFX Work in Blender

Setting Up Your Workspace

1. Open Blender and switch to the **Motion Tracking** workspace from the top menu.
2. Arrange the layout to include:
   - The **Video Sequencer** for footage reference.
   - The **3D Viewport** for adding objects.

○ The **Graph Editor** for refining keyframes and tracks.

Importing Reference Footage

1. Navigate to the **Motion Tracking** tab.
2. Click **Open** and load your footage.
3. Ensure your footage is compatible (preferably image sequences for precision).
4. Adjust the playback settings under the **Footage Settings** panel to match the frame rate and resolution of your video.

Matchmoving: Tracking the Camera and Objects

Matchmoving ensures your 3D elements align perfectly with the live-action footage. Follow these steps for camera tracking:

Camera Tracking

1. **Detect Features**:
   ○ Click **Detect Features** in the **Track Panel**. Blender will automatically identify trackable points in your footage.
2. **Track Features**:
   ○ Press `Ctrl + T` to track the detected features frame by frame.
   ○ Review the tracks in the **Graph Editor** for anomalies.
3. **Solve the Camera Motion**:
   ○ Navigate to the **Solve Panel** and click **Solve Camera Motion**.
   ○ Ensure the error value is below 1.0 for accurate tracking. Refine if necessary by manually adjusting the tracks.

Object Tracking

For moving objects in the footage:

1. Add an **Empty** object to represent the tracked item.
2. Use manual or automatic tracking tools to follow the object's motion.
3. Parent the Empty to CG objects for seamless integration.

Scene Integration: Adding CG Elements

Adding 3D Objects

1. Position the 3D cursor in the **3D Viewport**.
2. Add objects such as meshes, lights, or cameras using `Shift + A`.
3. Align objects with the tracked scene using the tracked camera as a reference.

Setting up Materials

1. Go to the **Shader Editor** and create materials for your objects.
2. Use the **Principled BSDF** shader for realism, adjusting properties like:
   - Base Color
   - Roughness
   - Metallic
3. Add textures or environment maps to enhance realism.

Adding Simulations

Simulations like debris or smoke can add depth to the scene:

1. Use **Rigid Body** physics for falling debris.
2. Apply **Fluid** or **Smoke** simulation for environmental effects.
3. Parent simulations to tracked objects to ensure proper alignment.

Compositing: Blending CG and Live-Action Elements

Blender's **Compositor** is essential for merging CG elements into the final scene.

Setting Up the Compositor

1. Switch to the **Compositing** workspace and enable **Use Nodes**.
2. Add the following nodes:
   - **Movie Clip**: Load your footage.
   - **Render Layers**: Add CG elements.
   - **Alpha Over**: Combine CG and footage.
3. Connect the nodes:
   - Input your live-action footage into the **Alpha Over** node.
   - Input your rendered CG elements into the second input of the **Alpha Over** node.

Color Grading and Corrections

1. Add a **Color Balance** or **RGB Curves** node to match the CG lighting to the footage.
2. Use the **Glare** node for effects like lens flares or blooming lights.
3. Apply **Masking** to isolate specific areas for adjustments.

Adding Depth of Field

1. In the **Render Settings**, enable **Depth of Field** under the camera properties.
2. Use the **Z Pass** from your render layers to create realistic focus effects in the Compositor.

Rendering the Final Output

1. Switch to the **Render Properties** tab and select the appropriate **Render Engine**:

- o Use **Eevee** for fast previews.
  - o Use **Cycles** for photorealistic rendering.
2. Set the resolution and frame rate to match your footage.
3. Enable **Denoising** for smoother results, especially in low-light scenes.
4. Render the animation using `Ctrl + F12` and save it as a video file.

Python Automation for VFX Workflows

Python scripting can simplify repetitive tasks in VFX workflows. Below is a script to automate camera tracking setup:

```python
import bpy

# Load footage
clip = bpy.data.movieclips.load("path_to_footage.mp4")

# Set up tracking scene
tracking = bpy.context.scene
tracking.use_nodes = True

# Add tracking markers
track = clip.tracking.objects.new("Camera")
for i in range(10):  # Add 10 markers for example
    marker = track.tracks.new()
    marker.name = f"Track_{i}"
    marker.select = True

# Solve camera motion
tracking.tracking.reconstruction.solve_camera()
```

Modify the script to fit your project needs and run it in Blender's scripting workspace.

Tips for High-Quality VFX

1. **Ensure Lighting Matches**:
   - o Match the lighting of your 3D scene to the real-world footage by analyzing shadows and light angles.
2. **Use HDRI**:
   - o Add HDRI images as environment maps for accurate reflections and lighting.
3. **Render in Passes**:

- Render elements like shadows, reflections, and highlights separately for greater control in compositing.
4. **Test in Low Resolution**:
   - Use lower resolution and sample rates during testing to save time.

Common Challenges and Solutions

1. **Misaligned CG Elements**:
   - Refine camera tracking points and solve errors below 0.5.
2. **Footage and Render Quality Mismatch**:
   - Match motion blur and depth of field settings between the live-action footage and CG elements.
3. **Slow Renders**:
   - Use render farms or optimize scene complexity by hiding unnecessary objects.

By mastering Blender's VFX tools, you can create seamless integrations of CG and live-action elements, crafting scenes that captivate and immerse viewers. This workflow enables you to handle complex projects with efficiency and precision.

Chapter 11: Game Asset Creation

Preparing Assets for Game Engines

Creating assets for game engines requires a unique approach compared to traditional 3D modeling. Unlike assets designed for static renders, game assets must be optimized for real-time performance while maintaining visual fidelity. This involves understanding the constraints of game engines, such as polygon limits, texture memory, and rendering pipelines.

Understanding Game Engine Requirements

Before creating assets, it's essential to know the requirements and limitations of the target game engine. Game engines like Unity and Unreal Engine have specific guidelines for asset creation:

1. **Polygon Count**: Keep the polygon count as low as possible without compromising quality. High-polygon models can strain the game engine, causing performance issues.
2. **Texture Resolution**: Use textures that balance quality and performance. While 4K textures look great, they might not be suitable for all platforms, especially mobile devices.
3. **Naming Conventions**: Use consistent and descriptive naming for meshes, materials, and textures to ensure compatibility with the game engine's asset management system.
4. **Scale and Units**: Match your asset's scale to the game engine's standard units. For example, in Unity, 1 unit typically equals 1 meter.
5. **Pivot Points**: Set pivot points appropriately to make asset placement and animation easier.

Creating Low-Poly Models

A good game asset starts with a low-poly base model. Here are steps to create one:

1. **Start with Basic Shapes**: Use primitives like cubes, spheres, and cylinders to outline the general form of your model.
2. **Optimize Topology**: Avoid unnecessary vertices, edges, and faces. Use tools like Blender's Decimate modifier to reduce polygon count if needed.
3. **Use Quads Over Triangles**: While game engines convert quads to triangles during rendering, working with quads ensures better edge flow and easier editing.
4. **Simplify Details**: Focus on silhouette and essential features. Complex details can be added later using normal maps.

UV Unwrapping for Game Assets

Efficient UV unwrapping is crucial for game assets. Follow these best practices:

1. **Avoid Overlapping UVs**: Overlapping UVs can cause texture issues in game engines, especially when using lightmaps.
2. **Maximize UV Space**: Use as much UV space as possible to increase texture resolution.
3. **Use a Consistent Scale**: Maintain consistent texel density across all UV islands to ensure uniform texture quality.
4. **Separate Different Materials**: Assign different materials to distinct parts of the asset and keep their UV islands separate.

Baking High-Poly Details to Low-Poly Models

To achieve a high-quality appearance without increasing polygon count, bake high-poly details onto the low-poly model using normal maps. Here's how:

1. **Create a High-Poly Model**: Add fine details using sculpting or subdivision.
2. **Match Low-Poly and High-Poly Models**: Ensure the two models overlap perfectly in the same 3D space.
3. **Bake the Normal Map**:
   - Select the low-poly model.
   - In Blender, go to the Render Properties tab and choose "Cycles" as the engine.
   - Under the Bake settings, select "Normal."
   - Assign a blank image texture to the low-poly model and bake the details.
4. **Apply the Normal Map**: Use the baked normal map in the material settings to simulate the high-poly details.

Texturing Game Assets

Game-ready textures should balance quality and performance:

1. **Use PBR Workflow**: Most game engines support Physically Based Rendering (PBR), which uses maps like Base Color, Metallic, Roughness, and Normal.
2. **Optimize Texture Sizes**: Use appropriate resolutions (e.g., 1024x1024 for small objects, 2048x2048 for larger ones).
3. **Compress Textures**: Use game-engine-specific compression formats like DDS (DirectDraw Surface) for Unity or PNG for Unreal.

Exporting to Game Engines

When your model is ready, export it for use in a game engine:

1. **Choose the Right Format**: Common formats include FBX, OBJ, and glTF. FBX is widely supported and includes animations and materials.
2. **Check Export Settings**:
   - Apply transformations (location, rotation, scale).
   - Export only the necessary objects.

- ○ Include UVs and normals.
3. **Test in the Game Engine**:
    - ○ Import the asset and check for issues like incorrect scaling or missing textures.
    - ○ Adjust settings as needed to ensure the asset behaves as expected.

Workflow Tips for Game Asset Creation

1. **Iterate Frequently**: Test your asset in the game engine at different stages of development to identify and fix issues early.
2. **Use Modular Design**: Create assets that can be reused in different scenes to save time and resources.
3. **Leverage Add-Ons**: Blender has add-ons like "Blender-to-Unreal" or "Unity Tools" that streamline the export process.
4. **Automate Repetitive Tasks**: Use Python scripts to automate tasks like UV unwrapping or exporting.
5. **Seek Feedback**: Collaborate with team members or share your work with the community to gain insights and improve your assets.

By following these guidelines, you can create optimized, visually stunning assets that integrate seamlessly into modern game engines, ensuring a smooth workflow from modeling to real-time rendering.

Optimizing Models for Real-Time Use

Optimizing models for real-time use is essential for achieving high performance in game engines while maintaining visual quality. Real-time optimization involves reducing resource usage without sacrificing detail, ensuring that your game assets run smoothly across various platforms. This section explores techniques and tools to help you create efficient, game-ready assets.

Understanding Optimization Goals

Before diving into techniques, it's crucial to identify your optimization goals. These goals may vary depending on the platform and game type:

1. **Performance**: Reduce the impact on processing power, GPU, and memory.
2. **Compatibility**: Ensure assets run efficiently on multiple platforms, from PCs to mobile devices.
3. **Visual Fidelity**: Balance quality and performance, retaining the details critical to gameplay.

Reducing Polygon Count

One of the primary ways to optimize models is to reduce polygon count:

1. **Simplify Geometry**:
    - ○ Remove unnecessary faces, edges, and vertices.

      ○   Combine multiple objects into a single mesh where applicable.

Use the Decimate modifier in Blender to reduce polygons while preserving shape:
python

```
import bpy

# Select the object
bpy.context.view_layer.objects.active =
bpy.data.objects['YourObjectName']
obj = bpy.context.active_object

# Add Decimate modifier
decimate = obj.modifiers.new(name='Decimate', type='DECIMATE')
decimate.ratio = 0.5  # Adjust this value for desired reduction
bpy.ops.object.modifier_apply(modifier='Decimate')
```

      ○

2. **Retopology**:
    - ○ For detailed models, use retopology to create a low-poly version.
    - ○ Blender's Quad Remesher or Retopology tools can automate this process.
3. **Level of Detail (LOD)**:
    - ○ Create multiple versions of your model with varying levels of detail.
    - ○ Use the LOD system in your game engine to dynamically switch between models based on the camera distance.

Optimizing Textures

Textures often consume a significant amount of memory. Optimize them using these methods:

1. **Texture Resolution**:
    - ○ Use appropriate resolutions based on the object's size and importance. For example, a small object might only need a 512x512 texture, while a main character may use a 2048x2048 texture.
2. **Compress Textures**:
    - ○ Compress textures to reduce memory usage. Most game engines support formats like JPEG, PNG, or DDS.

In Blender, export textures with optimal compression:
python

```
import bpy

# Export selected object's texture
bpy.ops.image.save_as(
```

```
    filepath='optimized_texture.png',
    compress=True,
    quality=80
)
```

     ○

3. **Reuse Textures**:
   - ○ Where possible, use the same texture maps for multiple objects to save memory.
4. **Texture Atlases**:
   - ○ Combine multiple textures into a single atlas to reduce draw calls in the game engine.
5. **Optimize UV Maps**:
   - ○ Minimize wasted space in UV maps.
   - ○ Ensure consistent texel density across the asset.

Baking Lighting and Details

To offload rendering tasks, bake lighting and detailed textures:

1. **Baking Ambient Occlusion**:
   - ○ Ambient Occlusion (AO) adds realistic shadows without increasing real-time rendering costs.

Use Blender's bake function to generate AO maps:
python

```
bpy.context.scene.render.bake_type = 'AO'
bpy.ops.object.bake(type='AO')
```

     ○

2. **Normal Maps**:
   - ○ Replace high-poly geometry with normal maps to simulate surface details.
3. **Specular and Roughness Maps**:
   - ○ Bake these maps to control the reflective and rough properties of your materials.

Optimizing Materials

Efficient material management reduces computational overhead:

1. **Simplify Shaders**:
   - ○ Use simple shaders with fewer nodes.
   - ○ Avoid complex procedural textures unless necessary.
2. **Combine Materials**:
   - ○ Use a single material for multiple objects when possible.
3. **Optimize Transparency**:

- o Minimize the use of transparent materials, as they require additional rendering effort.
4. **PBR Workflow**:
   - o Adopt Physically Based Rendering (PBR) for compatibility and efficiency in modern game engines.

Reducing Draw Calls

Each object, material, and texture in your scene can increase draw calls, which affect performance. Reduce draw calls using these techniques:

1. **Batching**:
   - o Combine multiple static meshes into a single object.
2. **Texture Atlases**:
   - o As mentioned earlier, combine textures into atlases.
3. **Material Instancing**:
   - o Use instanced materials to reduce the number of unique shaders.

Optimizing Rigged Models

For animated models, reduce the complexity of the rig:

1. **Simplify Bone Count**:
   - o Use only the bones necessary for animation.
2. **Limit Weight Influences**:
   - o Ensure each vertex is influenced by a maximum of 4 bones.
3. **Bake Animations**:
   - o Bake complex animations into simple keyframes to reduce runtime computation.

Testing and Validation

Once optimization is complete, test your assets in the game engine:

1. **Performance Testing**:
   - o Use the game engine's profiling tools to monitor frame rates, memory usage, and draw calls.
2. **Visual Comparison**:
   - o Compare the optimized asset with the original to ensure the visual quality remains acceptable.
3. **Stress Testing**:
   - o Place multiple instances of the asset in a scene to check for performance bottlenecks.

Automation and Scripting for Efficiency

Automating repetitive tasks can save time and improve consistency. Here's an example script to automate LOD creation in Blender:

```python
import bpy

def create_lod(obj, levels=3):
    for i in range(1, levels + 1):
        lod = obj.copy()
        lod.name = f"{obj.name}_LOD{i}"
        bpy.context.collection.objects.link(lod)
        decimate = lod.modifiers.new(name="Decimate",
type="DECIMATE")
        decimate.ratio = 1 / (i + 1)
        bpy.ops.object.modifier_apply(modifier="Decimate")

# Select the object to create LODs for
create_lod(bpy.context.active_object)
```

Conclusion

Optimizing models for real-time use is a critical step in game asset creation. By reducing polygon count, optimizing textures and materials, and leveraging game engine features like LODs, you can create assets that perform well across platforms while maintaining high visual quality. Consistent testing and refinement ensure that your assets meet the demands of modern game development.

Exporting to Unity and Unreal Engine

Exporting assets to game engines like Unity and Unreal Engine is a crucial step in game development. Proper export ensures that models, textures, animations, and other elements are correctly integrated and function seamlessly. This section covers the processes, best practices, and tools for exporting assets from Blender to Unity and Unreal Engine.

Preparing Assets for Export

Before exporting, ensure your assets meet the requirements of the target engine. This preparation includes:

1. **Apply Transformations**:
   - Reset the location, rotation, and scale of your objects.
   - In Blender, use Ctrl+A to apply transformations.
   - Ensure the object's origin point aligns with its intended pivot point in the game engine.
2. **Triangulate Meshes**:
   - Most game engines render models as triangles. Convert all quads and n-gons to triangles.

Use the Triangulate modifier in Blender or apply it before exporting:
python

```
import bpy

obj = bpy.context.active_object
bpy.ops.object.mode_set(mode='EDIT')
bpy.ops.mesh.quads_convert_to_tris()
bpy.ops.object.mode_set(mode='OBJECT')
```

   o
3. **Check Naming Conventions**:
     o Use clear and consistent naming for objects, textures, and materials. Avoid spaces and special characters.
     o Example: Use names like `character_body`, `building_wall`, or `weapon_sword`.
4. **Optimize Texture Paths**:
     o Ensure all textures are packed or have relative paths set in Blender.
     o Use Blender's File menu: `External Data > Make Paths Relative`.
5. **UV Unwrapping**:
     o Verify that all objects have clean UV maps. Ensure no overlapping UVs unless required for specific materials.

Exporting for Unity

Unity primarily uses the FBX format for 3D models. Follow these steps to export from Blender to Unity:

1. **Set Export Settings**:
     o In Blender, go to `File > Export > FBX (.fbx)`.
     o Use the following settings:
        ▪ **Scale**: Set to 1.0.
        ▪ **Apply Transform**: Enabled.
        ▪ **Object Types**: Mesh, Armature (if rigged models are included).
        ▪ **Path Mode**: Copy (ensure textures are embedded).
        ▪ **Axis Conversion**: Set to Unity's coordinate system (Y Forward, Z Up).
2. **Export Workflow**:
     o Select the objects to export.
     o Open the export menu (`File > Export > FBX`).
     o Adjust settings based on your needs.
     o Export the file to a folder accessible by Unity.
3. **Import into Unity**:
     o Place the exported FBX file into Unity's `Assets` folder.
     o Unity automatically imports the model and associated materials.
     o Check the Inspector for import settings:

- **Scale Factor**: Ensure it matches the intended size.
- **Material**: Assign materials if they don't import correctly.

4. **Adjust Materials**:
   - If textures don't link automatically, drag the texture files onto the material slots in Unity.
   - Use Unity's Standard Shader for PBR workflows.

5. **Testing in Unity**:
   - Create a scene and place the asset in the environment.
   - Test animations, collisions, and other properties.

Exporting for Unreal Engine

Unreal Engine also supports the FBX format, but there are specific settings and considerations for optimal integration.

1. **Set Export Settings**:
   - In Blender, go to `File > Export > FBX (.fbx)`.
   - Use these settings:
     - **Scale**: Set to 1.0.
     - **Apply Transform**: Enabled.
     - **Object Types**: Mesh, Armature (if applicable).
     - **Path Mode**: Copy.
     - **Axis Conversion**: Set to Unreal's coordinate system (X Forward, Z Up).

2. **Export Workflow**:
   - Select the objects to export.
   - Open the export menu (`File > Export > FBX`).
   - Name the file descriptively.
   - Export the file to your Unreal project directory.

3. **Import into Unreal Engine**:
   - Open Unreal Engine and navigate to the Content Browser.
   - Click `Import` and select the FBX file.
   - Adjust import options:
     - **Skeletal Mesh**: Enable if the model is rigged.
     - **Material Import**: Enable to import materials automatically.
     - **Scale**: Ensure the correct scale is set.

4. **Adjust Materials**:
   - Unreal Engine uses a different shader system compared to Blender.
   - Check imported materials and link textures to the appropriate slots (Base Color, Normal, Roughness, etc.).
   - For complex materials, recreate the node setup in Unreal's Material Editor.

5. **Testing in Unreal**:
   - Place the model in a test level.
   - Check collisions, animations, and lighting.
   - Test performance in Play mode.

Best Practices for Cross-Engine Exports

1. **Consistent Units**:
    - Use metric units in Blender and ensure 1 unit equals 1 meter in the game engine.
2. **Check Compatibility**:
    - Regularly test exports in the target engine during development to catch issues early.
3. **Texture Formats**:
    - Use game-engine-friendly formats like PNG, TGA, or DDS for textures.
4. **LOD Preparation**:
    - Prepare Level of Detail (LOD) meshes and export them alongside the base model.
5. **Collision Meshes**:
    - Create simplified collision meshes for physical interactions in the game engine.
6. **Automating Exports**:

Use Python scripting to automate repetitive export tasks in Blender:
python

```
import bpy

def export_to_fbx(filepath):
    bpy.ops.export_scene.fbx(
        filepath=filepath,
        use_selection=True,
        apply_scale_options='FBX_SCALE_UNITS',
        axis_forward='-Z',
        axis_up='Y'
    )

# Set export path
export_path = "/path/to/your/exported_model.fbx"
export_to_fbx(export_path)
```

    -

Troubleshooting Export Issues

1. **Scaling Problems**:
    - If the model appears too large or small in the game engine, check the scale settings in both Blender and the engine.
2. **Missing Textures**:
    - Ensure textures are either packed or stored in the same directory as the FBX file.
3. **Incorrect Orientation**:

- ○ Adjust axis settings during export to match the game engine's coordinate system.
  4. **Animation Issues**:
     - ○ Verify that animations are baked into the FBX file during export.

Conclusion

Exporting to Unity and Unreal Engine involves understanding the specific requirements and workflows of each platform. By following these steps and adhering to best practices, you can ensure a seamless transition from Blender to your target engine, enabling efficient asset integration and enhanced game performance. Regular testing and validation are key to a smooth export process.

Creating Game-Ready Animations

Creating game-ready animations involves optimizing animations for real-time playback while maintaining fluidity and responsiveness. These animations must be efficient and compatible with game engine requirements to ensure smooth integration and performance. This section delves into the processes, tools, and techniques for producing high-quality animations suitable for modern games.

Understanding Game-Ready Animation Requirements

Before creating animations, it's important to understand the specific requirements of game engines:

1. **Real-Time Optimization**:
   - ○ Animations must play smoothly at consistent frame rates.
   - ○ Reduce unnecessary keyframes and use interpolation efficiently.
2. **Looping and Transitioning**:
   - ○ Design animations to loop seamlessly where necessary (e.g., walking, running).
   - ○ Create transition animations to blend between states (e.g., idle to run).
3. **Frame Rate Consistency**:
   - ○ Most game engines use 30, 60, or higher frames per second. Ensure animations match these frame rates.
4. **Root Motion**:
   - ○ For certain animations, movement is controlled via the root bone. This must be properly configured for the engine.

Rigging and Skinning for Animation

Animation starts with a well-prepared rig. Rigging involves creating a skeleton (armature) for the model, while skinning binds the skeleton to the mesh.

Creating a Basic Rig in Blender

1. **Add an Armature**:

- o In Blender, go to `Add > Armature > Single Bone`.
- o Position the bone within the model.
2. **Build the Skeleton**:
    - o Enter Edit Mode (`Tab`) and add more bones (`E` to extrude).
    - o Structure the bones logically, e.g., pelvis, spine, arms, legs.
3. **Set Bone Hierarchy**:
    - o Parent child bones to their respective parent bones (e.g., fingers to the hand, hand to the arm).
4. **Name Bones**:
    - o Use clear, consistent naming conventions like `arm.L`, `leg.R`.

Skinning the Mesh

1. **Bind Mesh to Armature**:
    - o Select the mesh, then the armature.
    - o Press `Ctrl+P` and choose "With Automatic Weights" to bind.
2. **Refine Weight Painting**:
    - o Enter Weight Paint mode and adjust vertex weights to ensure proper deformation.
3. **Test Deformations**:
    - o Pose the rig in Pose Mode to test how the mesh deforms with movement.

Animating in Blender

With the rig set up, create animations in Blender using the timeline and keyframes.

Keyframe Animation Basics

1. **Set Keyframes**:
    - o In Pose Mode, move bones to the desired position.
    - o Press `I` and choose the type of keyframe (e.g., Location, Rotation).
2. **Use the Timeline**:
    - o Navigate through the timeline to set keyframes at different frames for each motion.
3. **Interpolation**:
    - o Blender interpolates motion between keyframes. Adjust interpolation curves in the Graph Editor for smooth or dynamic movements.
4. **Looping Animations**:
    - o Ensure the first and last frames of the animation match for seamless loops.
    - o Use the Dope Sheet to duplicate or adjust keyframes for consistent timing.

Common Game Animations

1. **Idle Animation**:
    - o Create subtle movements (e.g., breathing, shifting weight).
    - o Use minor rotations and translations to avoid a static look.
2. **Walk Cycle**:
    - o Start with a standard walk cycle:

- Frame 1: Left foot forward, right arm forward.
- Frame 15: Feet meet in the middle.
- Frame 30: Right foot forward, left arm forward.
    - Loop the animation by matching the first and last frames.
3. **Jump Animation**:
    - Divide into three phases: takeoff, airborne, and landing.
    - Use exaggerated movements to convey weight and momentum.
4. **Attack Animation**:
    - Include anticipation (e.g., winding up for a punch).
    - Add follow-through for realism (e.g., arm continues moving after impact).
5. **Run Cycle**:
    - Similar to the walk cycle but with faster timing and more dynamic poses.

Baking Animations for Export

Game engines often require animations to be baked, meaning all movements are consolidated into keyframes.

1. **Bake Action**:
    - In Blender, select the armature and go to `Object > Animation > Bake Action`.
    - Enable options like "Visual Keying" and "Clear Constraints" to ensure all movements are captured.
2. **Exporting Baked Animations**:
    - Use the FBX format for export.
    - In the FBX export settings, ensure "Bake Animation" is enabled and set the correct frame range.

Importing Animations into Game Engines

Unity Workflow

1. **Import FBX File**:
    - Drag and drop the FBX file into Unity's `Assets` folder.
2. **Animation Settings**:
    - Select the imported file and go to the Inspector.
    - Under the Animation tab, set:
        - **Loop Time**: Enable for looping animations like walking.
        - **Root Motion**: Enable if the animation controls character movement.
3. **Animator Controller**:
    - Create an Animator Controller and assign animations to states (e.g., Idle, Walk, Run).
    - Use transitions to blend between animations.
4. **Testing in Unity**:
    - Assign the Animator Controller to a character.
    - Play the game and test the animation transitions.

Unreal Engine Workflow

1. **Import FBX File**:
   - Use the Import option in the Content Browser to add the FBX file.
2. **Animation Settings**:
   - During import, ensure the Skeleton is properly assigned.
   - Enable options like "Import Animations" and "Use Default Sample Rate."
3. **Animation Blueprint**:
   - Create an Animation Blueprint to manage animation states.
   - Add state transitions (e.g., Idle to Run) and define conditions.
4. **Testing in Unreal**:
   - Assign the Animation Blueprint to a character.
   - Test transitions and playback in the game.

Advanced Techniques

Blend Shapes

Blend shapes (or shape keys) allow for facial expressions and other deformations without rigging.

1. **Create Shape Keys in Blender**:
   - Add a basis shape key.
   - Modify the mesh and add new shape keys for each expression or deformation.
2. **Exporting Shape Keys**:
   - Ensure the FBX exporter has "Shape Keys" enabled.
3. **Using in Game Engines**:
   - In Unity or Unreal, map the shape keys to animations or player controls.

Physics-Based Animations

Physics can enhance animations by adding realism:

1. **Simulating Cloth or Hair**:
   - Use Blender's physics simulations to animate cloth or hair.
   - Bake the simulation to keyframes before export.
2. **Ragdoll Physics**:
   - In game engines, combine animations with physics for realistic character interactions.

Conclusion

Creating game-ready animations requires a balance of artistry and technical precision. By understanding rigging, skinning, keyframing, and exporting workflows, you can produce animations that enhance the player's experience while ensuring optimal performance. Regular testing in game engines and iterative improvements are crucial for achieving high-quality results.

Chapter 12: Collaborative Projects and Workflow Optimization

Managing Large Projects with Collections

When working on large-scale projects in Blender, organizing and managing assets effectively is crucial for maintaining efficiency and clarity throughout the production process. One of Blender's most powerful organizational tools for this purpose is **Collections**. Collections allow you to group objects together logically, enabling better control over visibility, selection, and rendering. This section will explore best practices for using Collections, tips for optimizing workflow in complex projects, and strategies for seamless collaboration with team members.

Understanding Collections: A Primer

Collections in Blender function as containers for organizing objects. They replace the old Layer system, providing more flexibility and hierarchical structuring capabilities. Collections can include any type of object, including meshes, lights, cameras, and even other collections.

Key features of Collections include:

- **Hierarchical Organization**: Nest Collections within each other to create logical groupings.
- **Visibility Control**: Toggle the visibility of Collections in the viewport or for rendering.
- **Selective Rendering**: Include or exclude entire Collections in render outputs.
- **Easy Selection**: Quickly select all objects within a Collection.

Setting Up Collections for Large Projects

When starting a large project, it's essential to define an organizational structure from the beginning. A well-structured Collection hierarchy ensures that all team members can locate assets quickly and avoid unnecessary duplication.

Example Workflow: Setting Up a Scene

Imagine you are working on an animated short film. Your Collections hierarchy might look like this:

```
Scene
├── Characters
│   ├── MainCharacter
```

```
|   ├── SupportingCharacter1
|   └── SupportingCharacter2
├── Environment
|   ├── Buildings
|   ├── Trees
|   └── Props
├── Lighting
├── Cameras
└── SpecialEffects
```

This structure provides clarity and separation of concerns. Each Collection can be managed independently, and you can focus on specific parts of the project without cluttering the viewport.

Practical Tips for Working with Collections

1. **Use Descriptive Names**: Always give Collections meaningful names. Avoid generic names like "Collection 1" or "Stuff."
2. **Leverage Nested Collections**: Organize objects hierarchically. For example, within an "Environment" Collection, create sub-Collections for buildings, foliage, and props.
3. **Enable/Disable for Rendering**: Use the camera icon in the Outliner to exclude Collections from the final render. This is particularly useful for placeholder or reference objects.
4. **Color Code with View Layers**: Combine Collections with View Layers to isolate specific parts of your scene for rendering or compositing.

Collaborative Workflow with Collections

In a collaborative environment, Collections can streamline team workflows. Here are some strategies:

Sharing Specific Collections

When multiple team members are working on different aspects of a project, sharing specific Collections ensures everyone works on their respective parts without interfering with others.

- **Exporting Collections**: Use Blender's `.blend` file format to export and share specific Collections. To do this:
    1. Select the Collection in the Outliner.
    2. Right-click and choose **"Select Objects"**.
    3. Go to **File > Export** and choose an appropriate format, such as `.fbx` or `.obj`.

Linking Collections Between Files

Blender allows you to link Collections from one file to another, which is ideal for collaborative projects. Linked Collections remain synchronized, so updates in the source file automatically reflect in the linked file.

- **Steps to Link a Collection**:
    1. In the target file, go to **File > Link**.
    2. Navigate to the source .blend file.
    3. Open the file and select the desired Collection from the "Collections" folder.
    4. Click **Link** to add the Collection to your scene.
- **Converting Linked Collections to Local**: If you need to modify a linked Collection locally, select the Collection and use **Object > Relations > Make Local**.

Enhancing Productivity with View Layers

View Layers complement Collections by allowing you to define different configurations for rendering and viewport visibility. This is particularly useful for large projects where different layers (e.g., foreground, background, characters) require separate passes for compositing.

- **Creating View Layers**:
    1. In the top-right corner of the Outliner, switch to **View Layer** mode.
    2. Create a new View Layer and assign specific Collections to it by toggling their visibility.

Automating Workflow with Python

Blender's Python API allows you to automate repetitive tasks involving Collections. Here's a script to create and organize Collections automatically:

```python
import bpy

# Create a new Collection
def create_collection(name, parent=None):
    collection = bpy.data.collections.new(name)
    if parent:
        parent.children.link(collection)
    else:
        bpy.context.scene.collection.children.link(collection)
    return collection

# Example: Setting up a project structure
def setup_project_structure():
    main_collection = create_collection("Scene")
```

```
characters = create_collection("Characters", main_collection)
create_collection("MainCharacter", characters)
create_collection("SupportingCharacter1", characters)
create_collection("SupportingCharacter2", characters)

environment = create_collection("Environment", main_collection)
create_collection("Buildings", environment)
create_collection("Trees", environment)
create_collection("Props", environment)

create_collection("Lighting", main_collection)
create_collection("Cameras", main_collection)
create_collection("SpecialEffects", main_collection)

setup_project_structure()
```

Best Practices for Collaborative Projects

1. **Version Control**: Use a version control system like Git with Blender files. Tools like **BlendGit** or Git LFS help manage large binary files effectively.
2. **Centralized Asset Management**: Store assets in a centralized location (e.g., a shared drive or cloud storage) to avoid inconsistencies.
3. **Regular File Reviews**: Schedule regular reviews to ensure that everyone adheres to naming conventions and organizational standards.
4. **Backups**: Always create backups of critical project files to safeguard against data loss.

Conclusion

Collections are a foundational tool in Blender for managing large and complex projects. By adopting best practices for organizing Collections and integrating them into collaborative workflows, you can significantly enhance efficiency and reduce friction in team-based projects. With careful planning and the use of additional tools like Python and version control systems, Collections become a cornerstone for delivering professional results in any Blender production.

Using Version Control Systems with Blender

In collaborative projects, ensuring that everyone on the team works on the correct versions of files, assets, and scripts is vital. Version control systems (VCS) provide an efficient way to track changes, collaborate effectively, and prevent data loss or conflicts. While version control is commonly associated with text-based code, it can also be used for binary files like Blender projects.

This section explores how to integrate version control into your Blender workflow, from setting up systems like Git to best practices for managing files and resolving conflicts.

Introduction to Version Control Systems

A version control system is a tool that helps manage changes to files over time. It allows multiple users to work on the same files, track changes, and revert to previous versions if needed.

Key benefits of using version control in Blender projects:

- **Change History**: Track who made changes, when, and why.
- **Collaboration**: Merge changes from multiple contributors without overwriting each other's work.
- **Backup and Recovery**: Safeguard against accidental file loss or corruption.
- **Branching**: Experiment with changes in isolated branches without affecting the main project.

Choosing a Version Control System for Blender

The most widely used version control system is Git. However, for Blender files, additional considerations are required because `.blend` files are binary, making them less transparent to Git's default mechanisms. To overcome this, tools like **Git Large File Storage (LFS)** or specialized versioning solutions for binary files can be employed.

Git Basics for Blender Projects

Git is a distributed version control system that tracks changes locally and remotely. Here's how to set up Git for a Blender project.

1. **Install Git**:
   - Download and install Git from git-scm.com.
2. **Initialize a Repository**:

Navigate to your project folder and initialize a Git repository:
bash

```
git init
```

   -
3. **Create a** `.gitignore` **File**:

Prevent Git from tracking temporary or unnecessary files by creating a `.gitignore` file:
markdown

```
*.blend1
*.blend2
*.temp
```

```
__pycache__/
```

- o
  - o   Save this file in your project root.
4. **Add and Commit Files**:

Stage your files for version control:
bash

```
git add .
```

- o

Commit the changes:
bash

```
git commit -m "Initial commit of Blender project"
```

- o
5. **Set Up a Remote Repository**:
    - o   Use platforms like GitHub, GitLab, or Bitbucket to create a remote repository.

Link your local repository to the remote:
bash

```
git remote add origin <repository_url>
git push -u origin main
```

- o

Managing Large Binary Files with Git LFS

Blender's .blend files can be large, making them inefficient for standard Git repositories. Git Large File Storage (LFS) addresses this by handling binary files more effectively.

1. **Install Git LFS**:
    - o   Download and install Git LFS from git-lfs.github.com.
2. **Track Blender Files**:

Configure Git LFS to manage .blend files:
bash

```
git lfs track "*.blend"
```

- o

Commit the changes to your repository:
bash

```
git add .gitattributes
git commit -m "Configure Git LFS for Blender files"
```

   ○

3. **Push to Remote**:
   ○ Push your files to the remote repository. Git LFS ensures that large files are stored efficiently.

Setting Up a Collaborative Workflow

A structured workflow is essential for teams working on Blender projects. Here's a recommended setup:

Branching Strategy

Use a branching strategy to isolate changes and manage contributions:

- **Main Branch**: The stable version of the project.
- **Feature Branches**: Separate branches for new features or tasks.
- **Hotfix Branches**: For urgent fixes to the main branch.

Example Workflow:

Create a branch for a new feature:
bash

```
git checkout -b feature-character-modeling
```

   1.

Work on the branch and commit changes:
bash

```
git add .
git commit -m "Add base mesh for character"
```

   2.

Merge the feature branch into the main branch after review:
bash

```
git checkout main
git merge feature-character-modeling
```

   3.

Resolving Merge Conflicts in Blender Files

Merge conflicts in binary files like `.blend` are inevitable in collaborative workflows. While manual resolution is challenging, the following practices can help minimize conflicts:

1. **Divide Work Clearly**:
    o   Use Blender's Collections to split tasks. For example, one person works on characters, another on the environment.
2. **Lock Files**:
    o   Some version control platforms allow file locking to prevent multiple users from editing the same file simultaneously.
3. **Use Append or Link Features**:
    o   Instead of modifying a shared file, work on separate `.blend` files and use Blender's **Append** or **Link** features to combine work.

Example: Linking Objects Between Files

1. Create a new `.blend` file for a character model and save it in the "Assets" folder.
2. In the main scene file, link the character:
    o   Go to **File > Link**.
    o   Select the character file and link the desired object or Collection.
3. Updates to the character file automatically reflect in the main scene.

Automating with Scripts

Version control workflows can be further optimized using Python scripts. Here's an example script to automate file backups and version tracking:

```python
import os
import shutil
import datetime

# Define paths
project_dir = "/path/to/project"
backup_dir = "/path/to/backups"

# Create a backup
def create_backup():
    timestamp = datetime.datetime.now().strftime("%Y%m%d_%H%M%S")
    backup_name = f"backup_{timestamp}"
    shutil.copytree(project_dir, os.path.join(backup_dir,
backup_name))
    print(f"Backup created: {backup_name}")

# Run the backup
create_backup()
```

This script creates timestamped backups of your project directory, ensuring that no work is lost.

Best Practices for Version Control in Blender

1. **Commit Frequently**:
   - Save your progress regularly with descriptive commit messages.
2. **Document Changes**:
   - Use the commit history to document what each team member has done.
3. **Test Before Committing**:
   - Always test major changes in a local environment before pushing to the main branch.
4. **Review Pull Requests**:
   - Use pull requests to review changes and ensure quality control.

Conclusion

Integrating version control systems into Blender projects enhances collaboration, minimizes conflicts, and provides a safety net for your work. By leveraging tools like Git and Git LFS, adopting structured workflows, and following best practices, teams can streamline their workflows and focus on creating high-quality 3D assets and animations.

Rendering on a Network: Blender's Render Farm Setup

When working on large-scale projects in Blender, rendering can be a time-consuming process. Complex scenes with high-resolution textures, intricate lighting setups, or physics simulations often require hours—or even days—of computational effort to produce final outputs. Network rendering, or setting up a render farm, is a solution that distributes the rendering workload across multiple machines, significantly reducing rendering time and improving efficiency.

This section delves into setting up a render farm using Blender, exploring hardware requirements, software configurations, and best practices to ensure seamless distributed rendering.

What is a Render Farm?

A render farm is a cluster of computers working together to render frames of an animation or still images. Each machine in the render farm, referred to as a "node," processes a portion of the rendering task. By dividing the workload, rendering becomes faster and more efficient.

Key benefits of using a render farm include:

- **Speed**: Faster rendering by utilizing the combined power of multiple machines.
- **Scalability**: Add more machines to increase rendering capacity.

- **Cost-Effectiveness**: Optimize rendering time without needing to invest in a single high-end workstation.

Hardware Requirements for a Render Farm

Before setting up a render farm, ensure you have the necessary hardware components:

1. **Master Node**:
   - A central computer to manage and distribute rendering tasks.
   - Moderate specifications (CPU, RAM, and storage) are sufficient.
2. **Render Nodes**:
   - Machines dedicated to rendering tasks.
   - Focus on high CPU/GPU performance and sufficient RAM (at least 16GB for complex scenes).
3. **Networking**:
   - A stable, high-speed local network (Gigabit Ethernet or higher) is essential to transfer large `.blend` files and output data efficiently.
4. **Storage**:
   - A shared storage system or network-attached storage (NAS) for easy access to assets across nodes.
5. **Blender Installation**:
   - Install the same version of Blender on all machines to ensure compatibility.

Software Options for Network Rendering

Blender supports several methods for network rendering, including native solutions and third-party tools. Here are some common options:

1. **Blender's Network Render Add-On**:
   - Built-in functionality for distributed rendering.
   - Suitable for small-scale render farms.
2. **Flamenco**:
   - An open-source render management system developed by Blender Studio.
   - Ideal for medium to large render farms.
3. **Third-Party Solutions**:
   - Tools like **Deadline**, **Qube!**, and **RenderPal** offer robust render farm management features.

This section focuses on setting up Blender's native network render add-on.

Setting Up Blender's Network Render Add-On

Blender's network render add-on allows you to set up a master-slave architecture for distributed rendering. The master node manages the rendering tasks, while slave nodes process frames.

Step 1: Enable the Add-On

1. Open Blender on all machines.
2. Navigate to **Edit > Preferences > Add-ons**.
3. Search for "Network Render" and enable it.

Step 2: Configure the Master Node

1. **Set Up the Master**:
   - In Blender, go to **Render > Network Render > Master**.
   - Click **Start Service** to activate the master node.
2. **Specify Shared Directory**:
   - Choose a shared folder accessible to all nodes.
   - This folder will store `.blend` files, textures, and rendered frames.
3. **Start a Render Job**:
   - Open the project in Blender.
   - Under **Render Settings**, select **Network Render**.
   - Specify the render engine (Eevee or Cycles) and output settings.
   - Start the render job to send tasks to slave nodes.

Step 3: Configure Slave Nodes

1. **Set Up Each Slave**:
   - On each render node, go to **Render > Network Render > Slave**.
   - Specify the IP address of the master node and the shared directory.
2. **Start the Slave**:
   - Click **Start Service** to activate the slave.
   - The slave will now listen for tasks from the master node.

Step 4: Monitor the Render Farm

The master node provides a dashboard to monitor the status of each task and node. You can check:

- Frame progress.
- Nodes currently processing.
- Errors or warnings.

Advanced Configuration for Larger Farms

For more extensive setups, consider these optimizations:

1. **Load Balancing**:
   - Ensure tasks are evenly distributed among nodes. Blender's network render add-on handles this automatically to some extent, but fine-tuning may be needed for nodes with differing hardware capabilities.
2. **Custom Python Scripts**:
   - Use Blender's Python API to create custom scripts for task automation and error handling. For example:

```
import bpy
import os

# Distribute frames across nodes
def distribute_frames(start_frame, end_frame, nodes):
    frames_per_node = (end_frame - start_frame + 1) // len(nodes)
    for i, node in enumerate(nodes):
        frame_start = start_frame + i * frames_per_node
        frame_end = frame_start + frames_per_node - 1
        print(f"Assigning frames {frame_start}-{frame_end} to node
{node['name']}")
        # Logic to assign frames to nodes

# Example usage
nodes = [{"name": "Node1"}, {"name": "Node2"}]
distribute_frames(1, 100, nodes)
```

3. **Render Layer Optimization**:
   o Split the scene into render layers (e.g., background, characters, effects) to reduce complexity on each node.
4. **Automated File Syncing**:
   o Use file syncing tools like **rsync** or **Syncthing** to ensure all nodes have up-to-date assets.

Troubleshooting Common Issues

1. **Slow Network Speeds**:
   o Ensure all nodes are connected via Ethernet instead of Wi-Fi for faster data transfer.
2. **Inconsistent Results**:
   o Check for mismatched Blender versions or missing assets on nodes.
3. **Node Crashes**:
   o Monitor system logs for hardware issues (e.g., insufficient RAM or overheating).

Best Practices for Network Rendering

1. **Pre-Test Scenes**:
   o Test render a few frames locally before deploying to the render farm.
2. **Asset Consolidation**:
   o Pack all textures and external assets into the .blend file to avoid missing files on render nodes.
3. **Energy Efficiency**:

- ○ Schedule rendering during off-peak hours to save energy and utilize spare computational power.
4. **Documentation**:
    - ○ Maintain clear documentation of your render farm setup, including IP addresses, software versions, and folder structures.

Conclusion

Setting up a render farm for Blender can dramatically improve rendering efficiency, making it a vital tool for professionals working on complex projects. By leveraging Blender's network rendering capabilities, following best practices, and optimizing hardware and software configurations, you can streamline the rendering process and focus more on creating stunning visuals.

Streamlining Workflow with Shortcuts and Add-ons

Efficiency is critical in large-scale projects, and Blender offers numerous tools to help streamline your workflow. Two of the most effective ways to save time and reduce repetitive tasks are mastering keyboard shortcuts and leveraging the power of add-ons. This section explores how you can optimize your workflow, from creating custom shortcuts to integrating essential add-ons that cater to specific project needs.

The Power of Shortcuts in Blender

Blender's user interface is designed with shortcuts in mind. While navigating menus can help beginners, advanced users can significantly boost productivity by learning and customizing shortcuts. By eliminating the need to search through menus, shortcuts provide immediate access to frequently used functions.

Essential Shortcuts for Everyday Use

Here is a list of some fundamental shortcuts every Blender user should know:

Action	Shortcut Key
Grab/Move	G
Rotate	R
Scale	S
Extrude	E
Duplicate	Shift + D

Snap to Grid	`Ctrl` (Hold)
Search for Commands	`F3`
Toggle Wireframe View	`Z` (Hold)
Object/Edit Mode Switch	`Tab`
Render Active Frame	`F12`

These shortcuts are only the beginning. Blender provides customizable hotkeys, which allow users to adapt workflows to their preferences.

Customizing Shortcuts

Custom shortcuts can address project-specific needs, improving speed and consistency. Here's how to customize shortcuts in Blender:

1. Go to **Edit > Preferences > Keymap**.
2. Search for the action you want to assign a shortcut to (e.g., "Add Cube").
3. Click on the existing shortcut (if any) or click **Add New** to assign a custom key combination.
4. Test the shortcut in your workflow.

Example: Assigning a shortcut to "Align to View."

1. In **Keymap**, search for "Align to View."
2. Click **Add New** and set the shortcut to `Ctrl + Alt + V`.
3. Save the preferences and test by aligning objects in your scene.

Macros: Automating Repeated Tasks

Blender allows users to chain multiple actions into macros, enabling automation of repetitive workflows.

1. Go to **Scripting** workspace.
2. Enable the **Developer Extras** in **Preferences > Interface**.
3. Record your actions into a Python script using the **Info Editor** to view executed commands.
4. Assign the script to a custom key or button for quick access.

```
import bpy
```

```
# Example macro: Align selected objects to the origin and apply
scale
def align_and_apply_scale():
    for obj in bpy.context.selected_objects:
        obj.location = (0, 0, 0)
        bpy.ops.object.transform_apply(location=True, scale=True,
rotation=True)

align_and_apply_scale()
```

Add-ons: Enhancing Blender's Functionality

Blender's modular design allows users to install add-ons that extend its functionality. Add-ons can range from improving modeling tools to introducing entirely new workflows.

Enabling Built-In Add-ons

Blender comes with a suite of built-in add-ons that can be enabled as needed. Here's how to enable them:

1. Go to **Edit > Preferences > Add-ons**.
2. Search for the add-on you want to enable.
3. Check the box to activate it.

Recommended Built-In Add-ons:

- **Node Wrangler**: Simplifies working with material and compositing nodes.
- **LoopTools**: Enhances modeling with tools for aligning vertices, creating circles, and more.
- **Archimesh**: Assists in architectural modeling by providing pre-made elements like walls and doors.
- **Cell Fracture**: Creates dynamic fractures for simulation work.

Popular Third-Party Add-ons

Third-party add-ons can drastically improve efficiency. Here are a few essential ones:

1. **HardOps**:
    - Focuses on hard-surface modeling, providing tools for boolean operations and mesh cleanup.
    - Perfect for creating mechanical or industrial designs.
2. **Auto-Rig Pro**:
    - Speeds up character rigging with automated workflows and advanced rigging options.
    - Ideal for animators and game developers.
3. **BlenderKit**:
    - Provides a massive library of ready-made assets and materials.

- ○ Saves time during asset creation.
4. **UV Packmaster**:
  - ○ A powerful UV packing tool for optimizing texture space.
  - ○ Useful in projects requiring detailed texturing.
5. **Fluent**:
  - ○ Simplifies the creation of complex shapes, panels, and other design elements with intuitive tools.

Installing Third-Party Add-ons

To install an add-on, follow these steps:

1. Download the add-on as a `.zip` file.
2. In Blender, go to **Edit > Preferences > Add-ons > Install**.
3. Select the downloaded `.zip` file and click **Install Add-on**.
4. Enable the add-on by checking its box in the list.

Combining Shortcuts and Add-ons for Maximum Efficiency

By pairing shortcuts with add-ons, you can create highly efficient workflows. For instance:

- Use **Node Wrangler** shortcuts to quickly manipulate shader nodes (`Ctrl + T` for Texture Mapping setup).
- Combine the **HardOps** add-on with custom shortcuts for faster hard-surface modeling.
- Assign specific keys to toggle frequently used add-ons (e.g., a shortcut for enabling **BoolTool** operations).

Streamlining Scene Management with Add-ons

Add-ons like **Scene Manager** or **Collection Manager** simplify handling complex scenes by providing advanced options for organizing objects, Collections, and view layers. These tools allow:

- Sorting objects into Collections with a single click.
- Toggling visibility, selection, and rendering settings efficiently.

Example: Using the Collection Manager

1. Enable **Collection Manager** in the Add-ons menu.
2. Access its tools from the sidebar or the top of the Outliner.
3. Quickly manage large hierarchies in multi-asset scenes.

Automating Workflows with Custom Add-ons

If existing add-ons don't meet your needs, you can create custom add-ons using Blender's Python API. Here's a simple example of an add-on that automates setting up a basic lighting rig:

```python
bl_info = {
    "name": "Auto Lighting Setup",
    "blender": (3, 0, 0),
    "category": "Object",
}

import bpy

def create_lighting_rig():
    # Add a sun lamp
    bpy.ops.object.light_add(type='SUN', location=(10, 10, 10))
    # Add a point lamp
    bpy.ops.object.light_add(type='POINT', location=(-10, -10, 5))
    print("Lighting rig created!")

class AUTO_OT_LightingSetup(bpy.types.Operator):
    bl_idname = "object.auto_lighting_setup"
    bl_label = "Auto Lighting Setup"
    bl_options = {'REGISTER', 'UNDO'}

    def execute(self, context):
        create_lighting_rig()
        return {'FINISHED'}

def menu_func(self, context):
    self.layout.operator(AUTO_OT_LightingSetup.bl_idname)

def register():
    bpy.utils.register_class(AUTO_OT_LightingSetup)
    bpy.types.VIEW3D_MT_object.append(menu_func)

def unregister():
    bpy.utils.unregister_class(AUTO_OT_LightingSetup)
    bpy.types.VIEW3D_MT_object.remove(menu_func)

if __name__ == "__main__":
    register()
```

Save this script as a `.py` file, install it as an add-on, and use it to quickly set up lighting for scenes.

Best Practices for Workflow Optimization

1. **Plan Your Workflow**:
   - Define which tools and shortcuts are essential for your project and prioritize learning them.
2. **Regularly Update Add-ons**:
   - Ensure add-ons are compatible with the latest Blender version to avoid errors.
3. **Document Your Customizations**:
   - Maintain a record of custom shortcuts and add-ons to ensure consistency across projects.
4. **Learn Incrementally**:
   - Focus on mastering a few shortcuts or add-ons at a time to avoid overwhelm.

Conclusion

Streamlining your workflow in Blender requires a combination of mastering shortcuts and integrating the right add-ons. By investing time in customization, learning, and automation, you can drastically reduce the time spent on repetitive tasks and focus on creativity and productivity. With Blender's flexibility, the possibilities for optimization are virtually limitless.

Chapter 13: Expert Tips and Tricks

Common Mistakes and How to Avoid Them

Blender is an incredibly powerful tool, but its complexity can be intimidating, especially for beginners. Even experienced users encounter pitfalls that hinder productivity and creativity. This section identifies common mistakes users make and provides practical advice for avoiding them, ensuring a smoother and more efficient workflow.

1. Overlooking Scene Organization

The Mistake:
Many users dive into modeling or animating without organizing their scene, leading to confusion as projects grow in complexity. Layers, object names, and collections are often ignored, making navigation cumbersome.

How to Avoid It:

- **Name Your Objects:** Always name your objects and materials descriptively. Avoid default names like "Cube.001" or "Material.002."
- **Use Collections:** Group related objects into collections. For instance, in a scene with a car, create collections for "Body," "Wheels," and "Interior."
- **Layer Management:** Leverage Blender's outliner to manage visibility, selectability, and renderability efficiently.

Pro Tip: Use Blender's shortcuts like M to quickly move objects between collections.

2. Ignoring Proper Scaling

The Mistake:
Scaling objects arbitrarily without applying transformations can lead to incorrect physics simulations, UV mapping distortions, and issues when exporting to game engines.

How to Avoid It:

- Always apply scale (Ctrl + A > Apply Scale) after resizing objects.
- Stick to real-world measurements, especially for game assets or architectural projects. Blender's unit system can be set to metric or imperial under the Scene Properties tab.

Pro Tip: For consistency, set the scale of your objects early in the project to match the requirements of your final output.

3. Forgetting to Save Incrementally

The Mistake:
Relying on a single save file increases the risk of losing work due to crashes or irreversible mistakes.

How to Avoid It:

- Use Blender's built-in incremental save feature (`Ctrl + Shift + S`).
- Activate autosave and adjust the frequency under Preferences > Save & Load.
- Consider version control tools like Git for collaborative projects.

Pro Tip: Regularly create backups of your `.blend` files, especially before performing complex operations.

4. Overcomplicating Geometry

The Mistake:
Using unnecessarily high-resolution meshes can slow down performance and complicate edits.

How to Avoid It:

- Start with simple shapes and build detail incrementally.
- Use modifiers like Subdivision Surface or Multiresolution to add detail without increasing base geometry.
- Optimize models by removing unused vertices, edges, and faces (`Alt + M` for merging vertices or `X` > Dissolve).

Pro Tip: Regularly use the "Decimate" modifier to reduce the poly count of models not requiring high detail.

5. Neglecting UV Mapping

The Mistake:
Skipping proper UV mapping results in poorly applied textures, stretching, or visible seams.

How to Avoid It:

- Learn the basics of UV unwrapping (`U` in Edit Mode).

- Use Smart UV Project for simple objects or manually create seams for more control.
- Use the UV editor to adjust and test texture placement.

Pro Tip: Blender's texture painting mode allows you to identify and fix problematic UV areas directly on the model.

6. Mismanaging Render Settings

The Mistake:
Rendering with incorrect settings can result in poor quality, long render times, or unintended visual effects.

How to Avoid It:

- Familiarize yourself with Blender's render engines (Eevee for speed, Cycles for realism).
- Adjust sampling settings to balance quality and performance.
- Optimize light paths and reduce bounces for faster Cycles renders.

Pro Tip: Use denoising options in the render settings to improve image quality without significantly increasing render time.

7. Ignoring Blender Shortcuts

The Mistake:
Relying solely on menus slows down workflow and increases frustration.

How to Avoid It:

- Memorize key shortcuts for frequently used operations, such as:
  - G for Grab
  - R for Rotate
  - S for Scale
  - Tab for toggling Edit Mode
- Customize shortcuts under Preferences > Keymap to suit your workflow.

Pro Tip: Use the search function (F3) to find operations quickly and learn their associated shortcuts.

8. Failing to Leverage Modifiers

The Mistake:
Underutilizing Blender's modifier stack leads to unnecessary manual work.

How to Avoid It:

- Explore modifiers like Array, Mirror, and Bevel for procedural modeling.
- Use non-destructive workflows by keeping modifiers adjustable until the final stages.
- Apply modifiers only when absolutely necessary (`Ctrl + A` > Apply Modifier).

Pro Tip: Combine modifiers for complex effects, like using Mirror with Subdivision Surface for symmetrical high-detail models.

9. Overloading Scenes with Textures

The Mistake:
Using excessively high-resolution textures for every object increases file size and slows down rendering.

How to Avoid It:

- Match texture resolution to the object's visibility in the final render.
- Use texture atlases to combine multiple textures into one for efficiency.
- Compress image textures without losing noticeable quality.

Pro Tip: For game assets, follow the texture resolution guidelines of your target engine (e.g., Unity or Unreal).

10. Forgetting About Updates and Add-ons

The Mistake:
Using outdated versions of Blender or ignoring its rich add-on ecosystem limits functionality and performance.

How to Avoid It:

- Regularly update Blender to access the latest features and improvements.
- Explore Blender's add-ons under Preferences > Add-ons, such as Node Wrangler for shader creation and LoopTools for modeling.

Pro Tip: Enable experimental features in newer versions, but always back up your work before testing them.

Final Words

Avoiding these common mistakes requires consistent practice and attention to detail. By integrating these tips into your workflow, you'll unlock Blender's full potential and significantly enhance your productivity and output quality. Remember, mastery comes with time, and every mistake is an opportunity to learn and grow.

Speeding Up Your Workflow

Blender is a versatile and feature-packed 3D creation suite, but its breadth can lead to inefficiencies if users aren't familiar with time-saving techniques. This section explores practical strategies, tips, and tools to optimize your workflow, whether you're modeling, animating, texturing, or rendering. Adopting these practices will not only make your work faster but also more enjoyable.

1. Mastering Blender's Shortcut System

Keyboard shortcuts are the cornerstone of an efficient workflow in Blender. By reducing reliance on menus, shortcuts can significantly speed up common tasks.

Essential Shortcuts:

- G, R, S for Grab, Rotate, and Scale respectively.
- Shift + A to quickly add objects to the scene.
- Ctrl + B to create a render border, focusing render efforts on specific areas.
- Shift + R to repeat the last action.

Customizing Shortcuts: If a frequently used action doesn't have a shortcut, create one:

1. Navigate to Preferences > Keymap.
2. Search for the desired operation.
3. Assign a custom key combination.

Pro Tip: Use the Quick Favorites menu (Q) to gather frequently used operations in one place.

2. Efficient Object Manipulation

Blender offers several tools and features to simplify object manipulation and editing.

Snapping and Alignment: Enable snapping (Shift + Tab) for precise positioning. Adjust snapping settings in the toolbar to snap to:

- Vertex
- Edge
- Face
- Increment (grid-based)

Pro Tip: Use the `Shift + S` menu to align objects or the cursor precisely.

Pivot Points: Understanding pivot points can streamline transformations:

- `Comma (,)` to set the pivot point to the active object.
- `Period (.)` to toggle between individual origins and other options.

---

3. Streamlining Scene Management

A well-organized scene is crucial for maintaining efficiency in complex projects.

Using the Outliner:

- Rename objects descriptively (`F2`).
- Use collections to group related objects. For example, a building might have collections for "Walls," "Windows," and "Furniture."

Visibility Controls:

- Use the viewport filters to hide non-essential items temporarily.
- Leverage the `H` and `Alt + H` shortcuts to hide and unhide objects quickly.

Batch Renaming: For projects with many objects, use the Batch Rename tool in the Outliner (`Ctrl + F2`) to apply naming conventions efficiently.

---

4. Leveraging the Power of Modifiers

Modifiers allow for non-destructive editing, enabling rapid iteration and adjustment.

Common Modifiers for Speed:

- **Array Modifier:** Quickly duplicate objects in a linear or circular pattern.
- **Mirror Modifier:** Model symmetrical objects with half the effort.
- **Bevel Modifier:** Add realistic bevels to edges without manual adjustments.

Applying Modifiers: Once satisfied, apply modifiers (`Ctrl + A > Apply Modifier`). Use caution, as this converts procedural changes into permanent edits.

Pro Tip: Combine multiple modifiers for advanced effects, such as using Array with Curve to create complex patterns.

---

5. Optimizing Texturing and Shading

Texturing and shading can become time-intensive without proper techniques.

Node Groups: Simplify shader creation by grouping commonly used nodes:

1. Select nodes in the Shader Editor.
2. Press `Ctrl + G` to group them.
3. Save and reuse node groups across projects.

Texture Painting Tips:

- Use symmetry options when painting textures for symmetrical objects.
- Leverage stencils and masks for detailed work.

Pro Tip: Enable Node Wrangler (`Preferences > Add-ons`) to speed up shader editing. For instance, `Ctrl + T` creates a complete texture mapping setup automatically.

---

6. Rendering Efficiency

Rendering is often a bottleneck in Blender workflows. Optimizing settings and techniques can drastically reduce render times.

Using Render Engines Effectively:

- Use **Eevee** for quick previews or stylized renders.
- Opt for **Cycles** for realistic lighting and materials.

Sampling Settings: Reduce noise while keeping render times manageable:

- Use lower samples for test renders.
- Enable denoising (OptiX or OpenImageDenoise).

Adaptive Sampling: Activate adaptive sampling in Cycles to focus computational power on complex areas of the image.

Pro Tip: Render heavy scenes in smaller chunks using `Ctrl + B` to define a render border.

---

7. Automating Tasks with Python

Scripting can eliminate repetitive tasks and introduce new capabilities to Blender.

Basics of Python Scripting:

- Access the scripting workspace to create and run scripts.
- Use bpy (Blender's Python API) for operations. For example, this script renames all objects in the scene:

```python
import bpy

for obj in bpy.data.objects:
    obj.name = "Object_" + obj.name
```

Creating Custom Operators: Build operators for frequently used tasks. For instance, to create a custom object:

```python
import bpy

def create_custom_cube():
    bpy.ops.mesh.primitive_cube_add(size=2)
    cube = bpy.context.object
    cube.name = "CustomCube"

create_custom_cube()
```

Pro Tip: Automate render farm submissions or batch processing with scripts for large-scale projects.

---

8. Utilizing Add-ons

Add-ons extend Blender's capabilities and often save time on complex workflows.

Built-in Add-ons:

- **Node Wrangler:** Simplifies shader creation.
- **LoopTools:** Enhances modeling with features like circular loops.
- **Archimesh:** Speeds up architectural modeling.

Third-Party Add-ons: Explore BlenderMarket or GitHub for specialized tools. Install them via Preferences > Add-ons > Install.

Pro Tip: Regularly check for add-on updates to ensure compatibility with the latest Blender versions.

---

9. Customizing the Interface

Blender's interface can be tailored to match your preferences and workflow.

Workspaces:

- Create custom workspaces for specific tasks like modeling, shading, or compositing.
- Save workspace layouts for reuse in future projects.

Themes: Adjust interface colors and styles under Preferences > Themes for a comfortable working environment.

Pro Tip: Use `Ctrl + Alt + Space` to maximize the current editor, focusing solely on the active task.

10. Staying Updated

Blender is under active development, with frequent updates and new features.

Regular Updates:

- Download the latest version from the Blender website.
- Use experimental builds to explore upcoming features.

Learning Resources:

- Follow Blender's official documentation.
- Engage with the Blender community through forums, Discord servers, and YouTube tutorials.

Pro Tip: Subscribe to Blender's release notes for insights into new tools and optimizations.

Final Thoughts

Speeding up your Blender workflow requires a combination of technical skills, organization, and familiarity with the software's tools. By incorporating these strategies into your routine, you'll accomplish more in less time while maintaining high-quality results. The key to mastery is consistent practice and the willingness to explore new methods and tools.

Industry Secrets for Professional Results

Achieving professional-quality results in Blender requires not just technical proficiency but also an understanding of the subtle nuances that elevate a project. This section uncovers industry secrets and advanced techniques that professionals use to produce stunning visuals, efficient workflows, and flawless animations.

1. Leveraging Reference Materials

The Secret:
Professional 3D artists rarely work without reference materials. Whether modeling, texturing, or lighting, using references ensures accuracy and realism.

How to Use References Effectively:

- **Image Planes:** Import reference images into the viewport (`Shift + A > Image > Reference`). Align them to the X, Y, or Z axes to guide your modeling.
- **Camera Matching:** Use Blender's camera settings to match perspective in reference photos, aiding in realistic scene composition.

Pro Tip: Create a mood board with color palettes, textures, and styles to maintain consistency across your project.

2. Non-Destructive Workflows

The Secret:
Professionals minimize destructive edits to maintain flexibility throughout the creation process.

Non-Destructive Techniques:

- **Modifiers:** Use Blender's modifiers like Mirror, Bevel, and Subdivision Surface. Avoid applying them until the final stages.
- **Node-Based Materials:** Instead of baking textures prematurely, work with procedural materials to allow real-time adjustments.
- **Linked Objects:** Duplicate objects as instances (`Alt + D`) rather than full copies. Changes to one instance reflect across all duplicates.

Pro Tip: Use the Multi-Resolution modifier to sculpt high-detail models while retaining a low-resolution base mesh for editing.

3. Precision in Lighting

The Secret:
Lighting is one of the most critical aspects of a 3D scene. Professionals spend significant time perfecting it.

Advanced Lighting Techniques:

- **Three-Point Lighting:** Use a combination of key, fill, and rim lights to highlight your subject. Adjust the intensity and color for dramatic effects.
- **Light Groups (Cycles):** Assign specific objects to light groups for precise control.
- **HDRI Environments:** Incorporate HDRI images for realistic environmental lighting. Add an HDRI under the World tab in the Shader Editor.

Pro Tip: Combine area lights and emissive materials for natural-looking indoor scenes.

---

4. Achieving Realism in Materials

The Secret:
Creating realistic materials involves understanding their physical properties and blending procedural and image textures.

Steps to Professional Materials:

1. **Use PBR Textures:** Source or create Physically Based Rendering (PBR) texture sets (albedo, normal, roughness, metallic). Connect them to the Principled BSDF shader.
2. **Node Layers:** Combine multiple textures with MixRGB nodes for added complexity.
3. **Micro-Details:** Add imperfections like smudges, scratches, and dirt using grunge maps.

Example Shader:

```python
# Example Node Setup for a Realistic Metal Material
import bpy

# Add a Principled BSDF shader
bpy.ops.object.material_slot_add()
material = bpy.data.materials.new(name="MetalMaterial")
material.use_nodes = True

# Access nodes
nodes = material.node_tree.nodes
bsdf = nodes["Principled BSDF"]

# Set metallic and roughness properties
bsdf.inputs["Metallic"].default_value = 1.0
bsdf.inputs["Roughness"].default_value = 0.2

# Add texture nodes
texture_node = nodes.new("ShaderNodeTexImage")
texture_node.image = bpy.data.images.load("path_to_texture.jpg")

# Link texture to the Base Color input
material.node_tree.links.new(bsdf.inputs["Base Color"],
texture_node.outputs["Color"])
```

Pro Tip: Use procedural shaders for scalable projects where high-resolution image textures are impractical.

---

5. Advanced Animation Techniques

The Secret:
Fluid and realistic animations often result from meticulous attention to timing, weight, and follow-through.

Key Techniques:

- **Graph Editor:** Fine-tune keyframe interpolation for smoother transitions.
- **Constraints:** Use constraints like "Track To" and "Copy Location" for accurate object interaction.
- **Animation Layers:** Blend multiple animation layers for complex motion.

Example of Smooth Animation in Python:

```python
# Automate Keyframe Animation for a Rotating Object
import bpy

obj = bpy.context.object

# Set initial keyframe
obj.rotation_euler = (0, 0, 0)
obj.keyframe_insert(data_path="rotation_euler", frame=1)

# Set final keyframe
obj.rotation_euler = (0, 0, 3.14)
obj.keyframe_insert(data_path="rotation_euler", frame=50)

# Adjust interpolation to Bezier for smooth motion
action = obj.animation_data.action
for fcurve in action.fcurves:
    for keyframe in fcurve.keyframe_points:
        keyframe.interpolation = 'BEZIER'
```

Pro Tip: Use Blender's Nonlinear Animation (NLA) Editor to combine and layer animations for characters or objects.

6. Camera Composition Like a Cinematographer

The Secret:
Professional-grade visuals often result from careful camera placement and composition.

Cinematic Composition Techniques:

- **Rule of Thirds:** Align key elements along the thirds of the frame.
- **Depth of Field:** Use depth of field settings in the camera properties to focus attention on the subject.
- **Camera Motion:** Use the Timeline and Graph Editor to create smooth camera movements, simulating real-world rigs.

Pro Tip: Parent your camera to an empty object to control complex movements more easily.

7. Efficient Scene Optimization

The Secret:
Even visually stunning scenes must be optimized for performance, especially in animation or game asset production.

Optimization Strategies:

- **Use Proxies:** Replace high-detail objects with low-poly proxies for viewport performance.
- **Cull Hidden Faces:** Remove unseen faces using the Limited Dissolve tool (`X > Limited Dissolve`).
- **Simplify Physics Simulations:** Reduce the resolution of fluid or cloth simulations during testing.

Pro Tip: For rendering, enable adaptive subdivision in Cycles for detailed displacement maps without high base mesh density.

8. Industry Insights on Collaboration

The Secret:
Large-scale productions rely on teamwork, requiring standardized workflows and tools.

Collaborative Techniques:

- **File Naming Conventions:** Maintain consistent and descriptive file names.
- **Version Control:** Use software like Git or Perforce for managing changes in shared projects.

- **Asset Libraries:** Store reusable assets in Blender's Asset Browser for easy access.

Pro Tip: Use Blender's USD or Alembic export formats for seamless integration with other industry-standard tools like Maya or Houdini.

9. Constant Iteration and Feedback

The Secret:
Professional results come from iterative refinement and accepting constructive criticism.

Iterative Workflow Tips:

- **Render Previews:** Render low-resolution previews frequently to identify issues early.
- **Feedback Sessions:** Share work with peers or mentors for fresh perspectives.
- **A/B Testing:** Compare variations of shaders, lighting, or compositions to determine the most effective approach.

Pro Tip: Keep a change log to document major adjustments and their impact on the project.

Final Words

Blender professionals achieve exceptional results by combining technical expertise with artistic vision and a disciplined approach to workflow. The secrets revealed in this section serve as a foundation for taking your projects to the next level. Practice, refine, and push the boundaries of your creativity to unlock Blender's full potential.

Staying Updated: Learning Resources and Communities

Blender is a constantly evolving software with new tools, features, and techniques being introduced frequently. Staying updated with these changes and leveraging the wealth of learning resources and community engagement can elevate your skills and ensure you remain competitive in the industry. This section outlines strategies, resources, and communities that can help you stay ahead of the curve.

1. Keeping Up with Blender Updates

Why It Matters:
Blender's developers frequently release updates that include bug fixes, performance improvements, and new features. Missing out on these updates can result in inefficiencies and an inability to utilize cutting-edge tools.

How to Stay Updated:

- Visit Blender's official website for release notes and download links.
- Follow Blender on social media platforms and subscribe to their newsletter for announcements.
- Regularly read the release logs for in-depth insights into new features.

Pro Tip: Use the Blender Launcher, a community-developed tool, to manage multiple Blender versions seamlessly, including experimental builds.

2. Exploring Blender's Official Documentation

The Resource:
Blender's official documentation is an exhaustive resource that provides detailed explanations of every feature.

How to Use It Effectively:

- Search for specific features or tools using the search bar.
- Bookmark sections relevant to your workflow for quick access.
- Read through the "What's New" section after updates to learn about recent changes.

Pro Tip: For scripting and automation, use the Python API documentation provided alongside the main documentation.

3. Learning from Tutorials and Courses

Why Tutorials are Essential:
Even advanced users can learn new techniques or approaches from tutorials. The variety of available content ensures there's always something to learn.

Top Tutorial Platforms:

- **YouTube:** Channels like Blender Guru, CG Cookie, and Ducky 3D offer free tutorials ranging from beginner to advanced levels.
- **Udemy and Skillshare:** Paid platforms with structured courses on modeling, animation, VFX, and game asset creation.
- **Blender Cloud:** A subscription-based resource from the Blender Foundation, offering high-quality courses and production files.

Pro Tip: Don't just watch tutorials—apply what you learn immediately in your projects to reinforce concepts.

4. Joining Online Communities

The Benefit of Communities:
Blender's vibrant online communities are invaluable for problem-solving, networking, and staying inspired.

Popular Communities:

- **Blender Artists:** A forum where professionals and enthusiasts share their work, ask questions, and provide feedback.
- **Reddit:** Subreddits like r/blender and r/3Dmodeling host discussions on techniques, workflows, and industry trends.
- **Discord Servers:** Join Blender-related servers for real-time discussions and support from peers.

Pro Tip: Actively participate in these communities by sharing your work and helping others. This fosters connections and enhances your reputation.

5. Attending Events and Conferences

Why Attend?
Blender-related events offer opportunities to network with professionals, learn directly from experts, and get inspired by cutting-edge projects.

Key Events:

- **Blender Conference:** Held annually in Amsterdam, this event features talks, workshops, and networking opportunities.
- **SIGGRAPH and GDC:** Broader industry events often showcase Blender in professional use cases.
- **Meetups:** Many cities have local Blender user groups that hold regular meetups.

Pro Tip: If you can't attend in person, many events provide livestreams or recorded sessions online.

6. Following Industry Trends

Why It's Important:
The 3D industry evolves rapidly. Keeping an eye on trends ensures your skills remain relevant and in demand.

Ways to Stay Informed:

- Subscribe to industry publications like CGSociety, 3DTotal, and ArtStation Magazine.
- Watch case studies and making-of videos from studios using Blender in production.

- Explore trending projects on platforms like Behance and ArtStation.

Pro Tip: Analyze trending work and incorporate similar techniques into your personal projects to stay ahead of the curve.

7. Engaging with Open Projects

What Are Open Projects?
Blender's open movie projects (like *Big Buck Bunny*, *Sintel*, and *Spring*) are initiatives where the Blender team produces short films using the software.

How to Benefit:

- Download production files to study professional workflows.
- Follow development blogs to learn about challenges and solutions.
- Experiment with materials and assets from these projects to practice.

Pro Tip: Use these projects as benchmarks to evaluate your progress and identify areas for improvement.

8. Leveraging Social Media and Content Platforms

The Role of Social Media:
Platforms like Twitter, Instagram, and LinkedIn host active Blender communities and provide access to work by professionals.

How to Use Social Media:

- Follow artists, studios, and Blender developers to stay updated.
- Engage with posts by commenting and asking questions.
- Share your own work to receive feedback and recognition.

Pro Tip: Use hashtags like #Blender3D and #3Dmodeling to discover content and connect with other users.

9. Practicing Consistently

Why Practice Matters:
Mastery of Blender, like any skill, requires consistent effort. Regular practice ensures you stay sharp and ready to adapt to new techniques.

Strategies for Effective Practice:

- Participate in challenges like "Inktober" for 3D or weekly modeling challenges hosted on forums.
- Recreate real-world objects or scenes to improve your skills in realism and detail.
- Experiment with new tools and features from recent Blender updates.

Pro Tip: Set aside dedicated time each week to practice specific skills, such as sculpting, rigging, or texturing.

10. Building Your Network

The Value of Networking:
Connecting with other artists and professionals opens up opportunities for collaboration, mentorship, and career growth.

Networking Strategies:

- Attend workshops and meetups (in-person or online).
- Join professional networks like LinkedIn to connect with industry veterans.
- Collaborate on open-source projects to showcase your skills and build relationships.

Pro Tip: Reach out to professionals whose work you admire and ask for advice. Many are happy to share insights and guidance.

Final Thoughts

Blender's rapid evolution and vibrant community provide endless opportunities for growth and learning. By staying updated with software developments, leveraging learning resources, and engaging with the community, you can continuously improve your skills and remain at the forefront of the 3D industry. The journey to mastery is ongoing, but with the right resources and connections, you'll always be prepared for what's next.

Chapter 14: Conclusion

Reflecting on Your Blender Journey

Blender is more than just a piece of software—it is a gateway to a world of limitless creative potential. By reaching this chapter, you've not only explored the depths of Blender's tools and techniques but also embarked on a journey of personal and professional growth. This section will delve into the broader implications of learning Blender, reflect on the progress you've made, and outline how you can continue to build upon your accomplishments.

Celebrating Your Progress

As you look back on your Blender journey, take a moment to appreciate how far you've come. From understanding the basics of the interface to crafting complex animations and simulations, you've achieved a milestone that many never reach. Mastery of Blender involves patience, creativity, and dedication. Each project you've completed, no matter how small, represents a step forward in your skillset.

Reflect on the chapters that challenged you the most. Did you struggle with the intricacies of rigging or the nuances of material nodes? These challenges are the cornerstone of growth. By confronting and overcoming them, you've demonstrated resilience and adaptability—key traits of any successful 3D artist.

Recognizing the Value of a Diverse Skill Set

Blender is a multifaceted tool that offers a broad spectrum of possibilities. Whether your focus is on modeling, texturing, animation, or scripting, each skill you've developed plays a critical role in the larger creative process. This versatility is one of Blender's greatest strengths. Unlike specialized software, Blender equips you to handle every aspect of a 3D pipeline.

Your ability to transition between different areas, such as shifting from creating a character to animating it or preparing it for a game engine, is invaluable. It not only enhances your marketability as a professional but also fosters a deeper understanding of how various components of a project interconnect.

Reflecting on Personal Growth

Beyond technical skills, working with Blender fosters personal growth. It teaches problem-solving, patience, and attention to detail. For example, debugging an animation rig or fine-tuning a material shader requires critical thinking and perseverance. These qualities extend beyond Blender, influencing your approach to challenges in other areas of your life and work.

Moreover, Blender encourages creativity and experimentation. It provides a safe space to test new ideas without fear of failure. Each iteration, no matter the outcome, is an opportunity to learn. This mindset is a powerful tool that can drive innovation in both personal and professional endeavors.

The Importance of Community

One of Blender's most remarkable aspects is its vibrant community. From online forums to local meetups, the Blender ecosystem is a rich source of inspiration, guidance, and camaraderie. Engaging with this community can significantly enhance your learning experience. Whether you're seeking advice on a tricky project or showcasing your latest creation, there's always a network of like-minded individuals ready to support you.

Consider joining Blender-specific groups on platforms like Discord, Reddit, or Facebook. Participate in challenges, attend workshops, or contribute to open-source projects. These activities not only help you grow as an artist but also allow you to give back to the community that has supported you.

Reflecting on Your Creative Identity

Every artist's journey with Blender is unique. The techniques you gravitate towards, the projects you choose to undertake, and the style you develop are all reflections of your creative identity. Take time to analyze your body of work. What themes or patterns emerge? Do you prefer creating architectural visualizations, designing characters, or crafting animations?

Understanding your preferences and strengths can help you define your niche. It can also guide your future learning efforts, ensuring that you focus on areas that align with your goals and passions.

Setting Goals for the Future

As this chapter marks the conclusion of one journey, it also signifies the beginning of another. Set specific, measurable goals for your next steps. These might include mastering an advanced feature of Blender, building a portfolio, or even creating a short film or game.

Write down these goals and break them into actionable steps. For example, if your goal is to create a short film, your steps might include writing a script, designing characters, modeling environments, and animating scenes. Having a clear plan will help you stay focused and motivated.

Overcoming Plateaus

As with any learning journey, you may encounter plateaus where progress feels slow or nonexistent. During these times, revisit your earlier projects to see how much you've improved. Seek out new challenges, such as participating in online contests or learning a complementary skill like drawing or photography.

Remember, growth often happens in cycles. Periods of rapid progress are often followed by phases of consolidation where you internalize what you've learned. Embrace these cycles and trust the process.

Embracing Lifelong Learning

Blender, like any creative tool, is constantly evolving. New features, updates, and techniques emerge regularly, offering endless opportunities for learning and exploration. Commit to staying curious and open to change. Subscribe to Blender release notes, follow industry trends, and continue experimenting with new workflows.

Beyond Blender, consider expanding your knowledge in related fields. Understanding the principles of traditional art, storytelling, or programming can enrich your 3D creations and make you a more well-rounded artist.

Final Thoughts

Your journey with Blender is a testament to your dedication, creativity, and willingness to learn. As you move forward, carry these qualities with you. Remember that mastery is a journey, not a destination. Celebrate your achievements, embrace challenges, and never stop exploring the possibilities that Blender offers. Your potential as an artist is limited only by your imagination and determination.

Next Steps for Continuous Learning

The completion of this book is not the end of your journey with Blender but rather the beginning of a lifelong process of growth, exploration, and creativity. Blender's vast potential means there's always more to learn, new tools to master, and fresh techniques to explore. This section will provide a roadmap for your continued learning, helping you to build upon the foundation you've established and evolve into an even more skilled and versatile 3D artist.

Exploring Advanced Blender Features

Blender is a powerful tool with advanced capabilities that go beyond the scope of this book. Now that you have a strong understanding of the fundamentals, consider diving deeper into areas like:

- **Geometry Nodes**: Blender's node-based procedural system for creating complex geometries opens the door to incredible creative possibilities. Experiment with creating procedural landscapes, dynamic effects, or intricate patterns.
- **Grease Pencil**: This feature is a game-changer for 2D and 2.5D animation. Learn how to integrate Grease Pencil drawings with your 3D scenes to create unique visuals.
- **Video Editing**: Blender's Video Sequence Editor (VSE) allows you to edit and compose videos. Explore how to combine your 3D animations with real-world footage or produce entire videos using only Blender.

Use Blender's official documentation and tutorials to explore these features. The community also offers extensive resources, including YouTube channels, blogs, and forums.

Joining Blender Challenges and Competitions

Participating in challenges is a great way to push your boundaries, learn new techniques, and stay motivated. Platforms like Blender Artists, CGBoost, and ArtStation frequently host contests with themes that encourage you to explore creative ideas.

Challenges often include constraints such as specific themes, time limits, or technical requirements. These limitations encourage problem-solving and foster innovation. Whether you win or not, the experience of participating is immensely valuable.

Building a Professional Portfolio

If you aspire to turn your Blender skills into a career, a strong portfolio is essential. Your portfolio should showcase your best work, highlight your range of skills, and reflect your unique style. Here are some tips:

1. **Quality Over Quantity**: Focus on presenting a few exceptional projects rather than a large number of mediocre ones.
2. **Diverse Skills**: Include a variety of works, such as character modeling, environmental design, animations, and special effects, to demonstrate your versatility.
3. **Document Your Process**: Showcasing your workflow can help potential employers or collaborators understand your technical and creative approaches.

Platforms like ArtStation, Behance, or your personal website are excellent spaces to display your portfolio.

Learning from Industry Professionals

The 3D art and animation industry is filled with talented professionals who share their knowledge through tutorials, courses, and workshops. Seek out resources created by these experts to gain insights into advanced techniques and industry workflows. Popular platforms include:

- **YouTube Channels**: Many Blender experts share free tutorials on YouTube. Channels like Blender Guru, CG Geek, and Default Cube are highly recommended.
- **Online Learning Platforms**: Websites like Udemy, Skillshare, and CG Cookie offer structured courses that can help you deepen your expertise.
- **Webinars and Masterclasses**: Attend live sessions or recorded webinars hosted by professionals to stay updated on the latest trends.

Experimenting with Complementary Tools

While Blender is a versatile tool, integrating it with other software can expand your creative horizons. Consider experimenting with tools like:

- **Substance Painter**: For advanced texturing and material creation.
- **ZBrush**: For high-detail sculpting.
- **Unity or Unreal Engine**: To bring your 3D creations into interactive applications like games or virtual reality.

Blender's compatibility with these tools allows for seamless workflows, enabling you to enhance your projects in ways that Blender alone might not achieve.

Engaging with the Blender Community

The Blender community is one of its greatest assets. Engaging with this community can provide inspiration, support, and networking opportunities. Here's how you can get involved:

- **Forums**: Join discussions on platforms like Blender Artists or the Blender subreddit.
- **Local Meetups**: Attend Blender user group meetings or workshops in your area.
- **Contributing to Open Source**: Blender is open-source software, and you can contribute by reporting bugs, submitting feature requests, or even developing add-ons.

Building relationships within the community not only enhances your learning but also opens doors to collaborations and career opportunities.

Staying Updated with Blender Development

Blender is constantly evolving, with regular updates that introduce new features and improvements. Staying informed about these changes is crucial for keeping your skills relevant. Here's how to stay updated:

1. **Follow Release Notes**: Each new version of Blender comes with detailed release notes highlighting updates and new features.
2. **Subscribe to Blender Newsletters**: Stay informed about upcoming events, releases, and community highlights.
3. **Join Beta Testing**: Participate in testing pre-release versions of Blender to get an early look at new features and provide feedback to the developers.

Setting Personal Projects and Goals

One of the most effective ways to continue learning is by setting ambitious personal projects. These projects allow you to apply your skills, experiment with new techniques, and build a body of work. Examples of personal projects include:

- Creating a short animated film.
- Designing a detailed 3D environment.
- Developing a game-ready character.

Define clear goals for each project and break them down into manageable tasks. Regularly evaluate your progress and adjust your approach as needed.

Teaching and Sharing Your Knowledge

Teaching is a powerful way to reinforce your learning and give back to the community. Consider creating tutorials, writing blog posts, or mentoring beginners. Sharing your knowledge not only helps others but also deepens your understanding of the topics you teach.

You can start by creating simple tutorials on techniques you've mastered and gradually progress to more advanced topics. Platforms like YouTube, Medium, or Blender-focused forums are excellent spaces to share your expertise.

Final Thoughts

Continuous learning is the key to growth in any creative field. By exploring new tools, engaging with the community, and challenging yourself with ambitious projects, you'll not only enhance your Blender skills but also discover new avenues for creative expression. Embrace the journey with curiosity and determination, and you'll continue to evolve as an artist and creator.

Becoming a Part of the Blender Community

Blender is not just software; it's the center of a vibrant, global community of artists, developers, educators, and enthusiasts. Joining this community will provide you with a wealth of resources, support, and opportunities to grow as a 3D artist. This section explores the importance of the Blender community, how you can actively participate, and how becoming an integral member of this ecosystem can shape your Blender journey.

Understanding the Blender Ecosystem

The Blender community operates on several levels, each catering to different interests and skill levels. These include:

- **Forums and Discussion Boards**: Platforms like Blender Artists and Reddit's r/blender are hubs for discussions, questions, and showcase opportunities.
- **Development Channels**: Blender is open-source, and its development is community-driven. Platforms like Blender Chat and the developer forums allow users to contribute ideas or code.
- **Social Media Groups**: Communities on Facebook, Discord, and Twitter cater to Blender users with diverse interests, from general support to niche topics like procedural modeling or Grease Pencil animation.
- **Workshops and Meetups**: Many cities host Blender user groups or workshops where you can connect with like-minded individuals.

Understanding how these components interact will help you choose the avenues most aligned with your interests and goals.

Joining Online Forums and Groups

Online forums are an excellent place to start your community involvement. Here's how you can make the most of them:

1. **Participate Actively**: Regularly visit forums like Blender Artists or Stack Exchange to ask questions, offer solutions, and engage in discussions. Contributing to threads not only builds your reputation but also deepens your understanding of Blender.
2. **Seek Constructive Feedback**: Share your projects and request feedback. Be open to critique—it's one of the fastest ways to improve your skills.
3. **Follow Etiquette**: Respect the rules and culture of the platform. Be polite, avoid spamming, and contribute meaningfully to discussions.

These interactions will help you build relationships with other Blender users while honing your skills.

Contributing to Blender's Development

Blender's open-source nature makes it unique. Anyone can contribute to its development, whether through code, documentation, or bug reporting. Here's how you can get involved:

- **Coding Contributions**: If you're proficient in Python or C++, you can contribute to Blender's codebase or develop add-ons. Start by reviewing Blender's development documentation and joining Blender Chat to connect with other developers.
- **Bug Reports**: Testing Blender and reporting bugs is a valuable way to help improve the software. Use Blender's bug tracker to submit detailed reports.
- **Documentation**: Clear and concise documentation is essential for new users. Contribute by improving existing documentation or creating tutorials for niche topics.

These contributions not only benefit the community but also provide you with valuable experience and recognition.

Participating in Challenges and Contests

Blender challenges and contests are a fantastic way to showcase your work, test your limits, and connect with other artists. Here are some tips for participating:

- **Select the Right Challenge**: Choose contests that align with your skill level and interests. Whether it's a modeling challenge or an animation contest, picking something you're passionate about will keep you motivated.
- **Follow the Rules**: Pay close attention to the guidelines, themes, and deadlines.
- **Engage with Participants**: Use contests as an opportunity to learn from and interact with other artists. Discuss techniques, share tips, and provide feedback.

Winning isn't the only goal—participation itself is a valuable learning experience.

Attending Blender Events

Blender events, both online and offline, are incredible opportunities to network, learn, and share your work. These include:

- **Blender Conference**: This annual event brings together Blender users and developers from around the world for talks, workshops, and networking.

- **Local Meetups**: Many cities host Blender user groups or workshops. These smaller gatherings are excellent for making local connections and getting personalized advice.
- **Online Webinars**: Platforms like YouTube and Discord often host live webinars by Blender experts.

Attending these events will expand your understanding of Blender and expose you to new techniques and ideas.

Creating and Sharing Tutorials

Sharing your knowledge through tutorials is a rewarding way to contribute to the community. Here's how you can start:

1. **Choose a Topic**: Focus on an area you're confident in, whether it's creating realistic materials, mastering UV unwrapping, or using Geometry Nodes.
2. **Plan Your Content**: Break the topic into manageable sections and ensure your tutorial flows logically. Use clear, concise language and avoid assuming prior knowledge.
3. **Share Widely**: Post your tutorials on platforms like YouTube, Medium, or Blender-specific forums.

Not only does this help others, but it also reinforces your own understanding of the subject.

Supporting Others in the Community

Supporting other Blender users is a cornerstone of community involvement. Here's how you can offer support:

- **Answer Questions**: Spend time on forums or social media answering questions from newer users.
- **Mentor Beginners**: Offer one-on-one guidance to those just starting out. This can be as informal as helping a friend or as structured as hosting a workshop.
- **Provide Resources**: Share links to helpful tutorials, scripts, or assets you've created.

By lifting others, you contribute to a culture of generosity and collaboration.

Building Collaborative Relationships

Collaboration is at the heart of many successful Blender projects. Whether you're working on a short film, game assets, or an open-source add-on, teamwork allows you to achieve more than you could alone. Here's how to foster collaborations:

- **Seek Like-Minded Artists**: Join groups or forums that focus on your area of interest, such as character modeling or game design.
- **Define Roles Clearly**: In collaborative projects, ensure each participant understands their responsibilities.

- **Communicate Effectively**: Use tools like Slack, Discord, or Trello to coordinate tasks and share updates.

Collaborations can lead to lasting partnerships and even professional opportunities.

Staying Updated and Informed

The Blender community is dynamic, with constant updates, trends, and discussions. Stay informed by:

- **Subscribing to Newsletters**: Sign up for the Blender Foundation's newsletter or other community-driven updates.
- **Following Social Media**: Follow Blender influencers, developers, and community pages for the latest news and tutorials.
- **Watching Development Streams**: Blender developers often livestream their work, providing insights into upcoming features and changes.

Staying updated ensures your skills remain relevant and that you're aware of opportunities to contribute or learn.

Giving Back to the Community

As you grow more experienced, consider giving back to the community that supported your journey. This might include:

- **Creating Free Resources**: Share models, textures, or scripts you've created.
- **Hosting Workshops**: Teach Blender techniques to others in your local area or online.
- **Supporting Blender Development**: Donate to the Blender Development Fund to help sustain and grow the software.

Giving back strengthens the community and ensures Blender continues to thrive.

Final Thoughts

The Blender community is a rich, supportive ecosystem that offers endless opportunities for growth and collaboration. By actively participating, you not only enhance your own journey but also contribute to the success of others. Embrace the community with an open mind and a willingness to share, and you'll find yourself surrounded by inspiration, support, and camaraderie that will fuel your creative endeavors for years to come.

Chapter 15: Appendices

Glossary of Terms

3D Modeling

The process of creating a three-dimensional representation of an object using specialized software like Blender. It involves constructing a mesh, defining vertices, edges, and faces to form the shape of the object.

Ambient Occlusion (AO)

A shading technique used to calculate how exposed each point in a scene is to ambient lighting. Areas that are occluded, such as corners or tight spaces, appear darker, adding depth and realism to the scene.

Armature

A skeletal structure used for rigging and animating objects, typically characters. It consists of interconnected bones that allow for smooth and realistic movement.

Bake

The process of precomputing certain effects (such as lighting, textures, or simulations) and storing them as fixed data to reduce rendering times.

Bevel

A modeling operation that creates rounded or chamfered edges on an object. This technique is often used to soften hard edges and enhance realism.

Boolean

An operation used to combine or subtract 3D objects based on their overlapping geometry. Blender supports Union, Difference, and Intersection Boolean operations.

Cycles

Blender's ray-trace-based render engine designed for high-quality rendering. It uses physically accurate light simulations to produce realistic results.

Denoising

A process that reduces noise or grain in rendered images, especially in scenes rendered with limited sample counts.

Edge Loop

A continuous series of connected edges in a mesh that forms a loop. Edge loops are essential for efficient topology and smooth deformation in animations.

Eevee

A real-time rendering engine in Blender that balances speed and quality, ideal for quick previews and interactive projects.

Extrude

A modeling technique that creates new geometry by extending the surface of an object. It is commonly used for creating complex shapes from basic ones.

Face

A flat, polygonal surface in a 3D mesh formed by connecting edges. Faces can be triangular, quadrilateral, or composed of more sides (ngons).

IK (Inverse Kinematics)

A rigging system where the movement of a chain's end (e.g., a hand) dictates the position and rotation of intermediate joints (e.g., elbow, shoulder). This technique simplifies animating complex motions.

Keyframe

A marker that defines the value of an animated property (e.g., position, rotation) at a specific point in time. Blender interpolates the values between keyframes to create animation.

Lattice

A deformer object used to modify the shape of other objects. By manipulating the lattice's control points, you can create smooth deformations.

Material

A property applied to 3D objects that defines their appearance, including color, texture, and reflectivity. Materials are created using Blender's Shader Editor.

Mesh

A collection of vertices, edges, and faces that define the shape of a 3D object.

Modifier

A non-destructive operation applied to objects to alter their geometry or properties. Common modifiers include Subdivision Surface, Array, and Boolean.

NLA Editor

The Nonlinear Animation Editor in Blender allows users to combine and layer animation sequences, making it easier to manage complex animations.

Normal

A vector perpendicular to a surface, used in shading calculations to determine how light interacts with the object.

Path Animation

An animation technique where an object follows a predefined path over time.

Physics Simulation

A system in Blender that mimics real-world physical behaviors, such as gravity, collisions, and fluid dynamics.

Procedural Texture

A texture generated mathematically rather than using an image. Procedural textures are highly customizable and resolution-independent.

Render

The process of generating a final image or animation from a 3D scene, considering all objects, lights, and materials.

Rigging

The process of creating a skeletal structure (armature) and binding it to a 3D model, enabling animation through the manipulation of bones.

Sculpting

A modeling method where the mesh is manipulated like digital clay using brushes and tools to create detailed shapes and features.

Shader

A program or set of instructions that defines how light interacts with a surface. Blender uses shader nodes to create complex material effects.

Subdivision Surface

A modeling technique that smoothens a mesh by subdividing its faces into smaller, more detailed polygons.

Texture

An image or procedural map applied to a surface to give it detail, such as color, patterns, or bumpiness.

Topology

The arrangement of vertices, edges, and faces in a mesh. Good topology ensures efficient modeling and animation.

UV Mapping

A process of unwrapping a 3D model onto a 2D plane so textures can be applied correctly.

Vertex

The smallest unit of a 3D object, representing a single point in space. Multiple vertices are connected by edges to form the framework of a mesh.

VFX

Visual Effects; the process of integrating computer-generated elements with live-action footage to create realistic or fantastical scenes.

Viewport

The interactive area in Blender's interface where users can view and manipulate their 3D scene.

Weight Painting

A method of assigning influence values to vertices, typically used in rigging to control how bones affect different parts of a mesh.

World Settings

Global properties in Blender that define environmental lighting, background color, and ambient effects for a scene.

Z-Depth

The depth information of objects in a scene relative to the camera, often used for compositing and creating effects like depth of field.

Resources for Further Learning

Blender is a vast and dynamic software that evolves constantly, with frequent updates introducing new features, tools, and workflows. To stay updated and continue enhancing your skills, tapping into the right resources is essential. This section provides an extensive list of learning materials, communities, and tools to support your Blender journey.

Official Blender Resources

The Blender Foundation and its affiliated platforms are excellent starting points for beginners and experienced users alike. These resources are tailored to provide official, up-to-date information.

- **Blender Documentation**
  The official Blender documentation is an in-depth guide covering every tool, feature, and concept in Blender. It is regularly updated and includes practical examples. Access it here: https://docs.blender.org
- **Blender Manual**
  A comprehensive manual maintained by the Blender Foundation, offering detailed explanations of Blender's interface, tools, and workflows.
- **Blender Release Notes**
  Stay informed about the latest updates and new features with detailed release notes for each version: https://www.blender.org/download/releases
- **Blender Cloud**
  A subscription-based platform providing access to exclusive tutorials, production files, and assets. It also supports Blender's development.
  Visit: https://cloud.blender.org

Online Tutorials and Courses

There are countless online resources offering free and paid tutorials, courses, and learning tracks for Blender. Here are some recommended options:

- **Blender Guru**
  Blender Guru, created by Andrew Price, is one of the most popular platforms for learning Blender. It covers topics like modeling, lighting, texturing, and rendering. Website: https://www.blenderguru.com
- **CG Cookie**
  A paid subscription service offering high-quality Blender tutorials on everything from beginner basics to advanced workflows.
  Website: https://www.cgcookie.com
- **YouTube Channels**
  - **Blender Guru**
  - **Grant Abbitt** – Focuses on modeling, sculpting, and game assets.
  - **Ducky 3D** – Specializes in procedural shading and motion graphics.
  - **Blender Bob** – Great for understanding real-world production techniques.

Books and E-Books

For those who prefer structured learning through written content, consider these popular books:

- *Blender For Dummies* by Jason van Gumster
  A beginner-friendly book offering step-by-step instructions and an approachable introduction to Blender.
- *Blender 3D by Example* by Oscar Baechler and Xury Greer
  Covers hands-on projects to learn Blender's functionalities in context.
- *The Complete Guide to Blender Graphics* by John M. Blain
  An in-depth guide to Blender's tools and workflows, ideal for intermediate users.

Forums and Community Platforms

Engaging with the Blender community is invaluable for troubleshooting, sharing knowledge, and staying motivated.

- **Blender Artists Forum**
  A dedicated forum where artists of all skill levels share their work, ask questions, and provide feedback.
  Visit: https://blenderartists.org
- **Reddit Communities**
  - r/blender – A general Blender community for discussions, tips, and showcases.
  - r/blenderhelp – Focused on answering user questions and solving problems.
- **Discord Servers**
  Many Blender-focused Discord servers offer real-time support and networking opportunities with other artists.

Asset Libraries

Using pre-made assets can speed up your workflow and provide inspiration for your projects.

- **BlenderKit**
  A built-in add-on in Blender that provides access to a vast library of free and paid 3D models, materials, and brushes.
- **Sketchfab**
  An online platform offering thousands of 3D models, many of which are compatible with Blender.
  Website: https://sketchfab.com
- **Poly Haven**
  Free, high-quality assets for use in Blender, including textures, HDRIs, and models.
  Website: https://polyhaven.com

Python and Scripting Resources

For users interested in extending Blender's capabilities through scripting, the following resources are invaluable:

- **Blender Python API Documentation**
  The official documentation for Blender's Python API, providing detailed explanations and code examples.
  Website: https://docs.blender.org/api/current
- **Stack Overflow**
  A great platform for getting help with specific coding problems in Blender scripting.
  Visit: https://stackoverflow.com
- **Online Python Courses**
  Websites like Codecademy and Coursera offer Python courses that are applicable to scripting in Blender.

Real-World Projects and Challenges

Learning is most effective when applied to real-world projects. Consider participating in challenges and contributing to collaborative works.

- **Weekly CG Challenge**
  A regular challenge for 3D artists to create renders based on specific themes.
  Website: https://weeklycgchallenge.com
- **Open Movies by Blender Studio**
  Study Blender's capabilities by exploring files and production techniques from open movie projects like *Sintel*, *Tears of Steel*, and *Spring*.
  Access: https://cloud.blender.org/films

Advanced Tips for Continuous Learning

- **Explore Add-ons**: Experiment with community-created add-ons to extend Blender's capabilities.

Example: Install the Node Wrangler add-on for easier material editing.
python

```
import bpy
bpy.ops.preferences.addon_enable(module="node_wrangler")
```

  o

- **Join Competitions**: Platforms like ArtStation and CGTrader often host 3D design competitions with exciting themes and prizes.
- **Set Personal Goals**: Challenge yourself to create something new, such as modeling a detailed character or designing an architectural scene.

By leveraging these resources and continually experimenting, you can master Blender and remain at the forefront of 3D design and animation.

Sample Projects and Code Snippets

This section provides practical examples and hands-on projects to help you apply what you've learned in Blender. Each project is accompanied by code snippets, techniques, and tips to guide you through the process. These projects are designed to deepen your understanding of modeling, texturing, animation, and scripting in Blender.

Project 1: Creating a Low-Poly Tree

Low-poly art is a popular style in 3D modeling. In this project, you'll create a simple, low-poly tree that can be used in games or stylized environments.

Steps:

1. **Set Up the Scene**:
   - Open Blender and delete the default cube.
   - Add a cylinder (Shift + A > Mesh > Cylinder) for the tree trunk. Scale it down to form a narrow base.
   - Add a cone (Shift + A > Mesh > Cone) for the foliage. Position it above the trunk.
2. **Adjust the Geometry**:
   - Enter Edit Mode (Tab) for the cone.
   - Select the top vertex, scale it slightly (S), and extrude (E) to create additional foliage layers.
3. **Apply Materials**:
   - Create a material for the trunk with a brown color.
   - Create another material for the foliage with a green color.
   - Assign materials to respective parts of the tree.
4. **Finalize the Model**:
   - Use Ctrl + A to apply scale transformations.
   - Duplicate the tree (Shift + D) to create a small forest.

Code Snippet (Optional Automation):

```python
import bpy

# Create the tree trunk
bpy.ops.mesh.primitive_cylinder_add(vertices=16, radius=0.2,
depth=2, location=(0, 0, 1))
trunk = bpy.context.object
trunk.name = "TreeTrunk"
bpy.ops.object.material_slot_add()
trunk.active_material = bpy.data.materials.new(name="TrunkMaterial")
trunk.active_material.diffuse_color = (0.5, 0.25, 0.1, 1)

# Create the foliage
```

```
bpy.ops.mesh.primitive_cone_add(vertices=16, radius1=1, depth=2,
location=(0, 0, 2.5))
foliage = bpy.context.object
foliage.name = "TreeFoliage"
bpy.ops.object.material_slot_add()
foliage.active_material =
bpy.data.materials.new(name="FoliageMaterial")
foliage.active_material.diffuse_color = (0.1, 0.8, 0.1, 1)
```

Project 2: Animating a Bouncing Ball

This project demonstrates the basics of animation, including keyframing and the Graph Editor.

Steps:

1. **Set Up the Ball:**
    o Add a UV sphere (`Shift + A > Mesh > UV Sphere`).
    o Scale it to resemble a ball.
    o Assign a material to the ball, such as a rubbery red.
2. **Animate the Bounce:**
    o Move the ball above the ground plane.
    o Set the first keyframe (`I > Location`) with the ball at its initial height.
    o Move to frame 20, lower the ball to the ground, and add another keyframe.
    o Continue adding keyframes to create a bouncing effect.
3. **Refine the Animation:**
    o Open the Graph Editor and adjust the handles to create smooth motion arcs.
    o Add squash and stretch by scaling the ball slightly at the apex and impact points.

Code Snippet for Keyframe Automation:

```
import bpy

# Create a ball
bpy.ops.mesh.primitive_uv_sphere_add(radius=1, location=(0, 0, 2))
ball = bpy.context.object
ball.name = "BouncingBall"

# Animate the ball
frames = [(1, 2), (20, 0), (40, 1.5), (60, 0), (80, 1)]
for frame, z in frames:
    ball.location.z = z
```

```
ball.keyframe_insert(data_path="location", frame=frame)
```

Project 3: Procedural Shader Creation

Learn to create a procedural material that mimics wood grain using Blender's Shader Editor.

Steps:

1. **Set Up a Plane**:
   - Add a plane (`Shift + A > Mesh > Plane`) to the scene.
2. **Open the Shader Editor**:
   - Assign a new material to the plane.
   - Add a **Wave Texture** node and connect it to the **Base Color** of the material.
   - Adjust the scale, distortion, and detail settings to create a wood grain pattern.
3. **Enhance the Material**:
   - Add a **ColorRamp** node to modify the wave texture's colors.
   - Mix the wave texture with a noise texture to add imperfections.

Code Snippet for Material Creation:

```python
import bpy

# Create a plane
bpy.ops.mesh.primitive_plane_add(size=2, location=(0, 0, 0))
plane = bpy.context.object

# Create and assign a procedural wood material
material = bpy.data.materials.new(name="WoodMaterial")
material.use_nodes = True
nodes = material.node_tree.nodes
links = material.node_tree.links

# Add texture nodes
wave = nodes.new("ShaderNodeTexWave")
wave.location = (-300, 0)
color_ramp = nodes.new("ShaderNodeValToRGB")
color_ramp.location = (-100, 0)
bsdf = nodes["Principled BSDF"]

# Connect nodes
links.new(wave.outputs["Color"], color_ramp.inputs["Fac"])
links.new(color_ramp.outputs["Color"], bsdf.inputs["Base Color"])
```

```
plane.data.materials.append(material)
```

Project 4: Exporting Game Assets

Exporting optimized assets for game engines like Unity or Unreal is a critical skill. In this project, you'll prepare and export a character model.

Steps:

1. **Prepare the Model**:
   - Use modifiers like Decimate to reduce polygon count.
   - Bake high-resolution textures into a low-poly model.
2. **Apply Transformations**:
   - Apply all transformations (`Ctrl + A`) to reset the scale and orientation.
3. **Export Settings**:
   - Go to `File > Export > FBX`.
   - Configure settings: Check "Selected Objects" and enable "Apply Modifiers."
   - Export with the appropriate scale for your game engine.

These projects are just the beginning. Each example can be expanded and customized to match your artistic vision. Dive into these exercises to hone your skills, experiment with Blender's features, and build a diverse portfolio of 3D creations.

Reference Guide

This section provides a detailed reference guide for Blender's core tools, shortcuts, and settings. It is designed to be a quick-access resource for users to streamline their workflows and enhance their efficiency. Whether you are modeling, animating, or rendering, these references cover essential commands and techniques.

General Shortcuts

Navigation:

- **Middle Mouse Button (MMB)**: Rotate the viewport.
- **Shift + MMB**: Pan the viewport.
- **Scroll Wheel**: Zoom in and out.
- **Numpad 1**: Front view.
- **Numpad 3**: Side view.
- **Numpad 7**: Top view.
- **Numpad 0**: Camera view.

- **Shift + (Grave/Tilde)**: Fly navigation mode.

Object Manipulation:

- **G**: Grab (move) the object.
- **S**: Scale the object.
- **R**: Rotate the object.
- **Ctrl + A**: Apply transformations (scale, rotation, location).
- **Shift + D**: Duplicate selected object.
- **Ctrl + Z**: Undo.
- **Ctrl + Shift + Z**: Redo.

Viewport Controls:

- **Z**: Toggle shading modes (Wireframe, Solid, Material Preview, Rendered).
- **Shift + Spacebar**: Maximize/minimize the current viewport.

Modeling Tools

Basic Tools:

- **Tab**: Toggle between Object Mode and Edit Mode.
- **Ctrl + R**: Add an edge loop (Loop Cut).
- **E**: Extrude selected geometry.
- **I**: Inset faces.
- **K**: Knife tool for cutting geometry.
- **M**: Merge vertices.
- **Alt + M**: Collapse vertices into one.

Advanced Modeling:

- **Shift + Alt + S**: Shrink/Fatten vertices for organic shapes.
- **Ctrl + Shift + B**: Bevel vertices.
- **Ctrl + Shift + X**: Mirror an object on a specific axis.

Modifiers:

- **Ctrl + 1/2/3**: Add Subdivision Surface modifier.
- **Ctrl + A > Apply**: Apply all modifiers to finalize the geometry.

UV Mapping Reference

Unwrapping:

- **U**: Open the UV Mapping menu.
  - **Smart UV Project**: Quick automatic unwrapping.

- ○ **Unwrap**: Use marked seams to unwrap manually.
- ○ **Lightmap Pack**: Organize UV islands for baking.

Shortcuts in UV Editor:

- **A**: Select all UV islands.
- **L**: Select linked UV islands.
- **S**: Scale UV islands.
- **R**: Rotate UV islands.
- **G**: Move UV islands.

Tools:

- **Ctrl + E**: Mark Seam/Clear Seam.
- **P**: Pin vertices in the UV layout.
- **Ctrl + P**: Pack UV islands automatically.

Shader and Material Nodes

Frequently Used Nodes:

- **Principled BSDF**: A versatile shader for most materials.
- **Image Texture**: For applying texture maps.
- **Mix Shader**: Combine two shaders for complex materials.
- **Bump**: Add surface details using height maps.
- **Texture Coordinate**: Control how textures are mapped onto objects.

Shader Editor Shortcuts:

- **Shift + A**: Add a new node.
- **Ctrl + Shift + Click (Node Wrangler)**: Preview node outputs.
- **G**: Move nodes.
- **F**: Connect two nodes.
- **Ctrl + X**: Delete a node but retain its connections.

Example Material Node Setup:

```python
import bpy

# Create a new material
material = bpy.data.materials.new(name="ExampleMaterial")
material.use_nodes = True
nodes = material.node_tree.nodes

# Add a Principled BSDF shader
principled = nodes.get("Principled BSDF")
```

```
# Add an Image Texture node
texture = nodes.new(type="ShaderNodeTexImage")
texture.image = bpy.data.images.load("path_to_texture.jpg")

# Connect the nodes
links = material.node_tree.links
links.new(texture.outputs["Color"], principled.inputs["Base Color"])
```

Animation Reference

Keyframes:

- **I**: Insert keyframe for selected property.
- **Alt + I**: Clear keyframe.
- **Shift + Alt + I**: Clear all keyframes.

Timeline Navigation:

- **Spacebar**: Play/Pause animation.
- **Up/Down Arrow**: Jump between keyframes.
- **Left/Right Arrow**: Move frame by frame.

Graph Editor:

- **G**: Move keyframes.
- **R**: Rotate Bezier handles.
- **Shift + H**: Hide selected curves.
- **Alt + H**: Unhide all curves.

Drivers (Advanced):

Drivers allow for creating dynamic relationships between object properties.

Example: Linking Object Rotation:

```
import bpy

# Create a driver for the rotation of Cube.001 based on Cube
cube_1 = bpy.data.objects['Cube.001']
cube = bpy.data.objects['Cube']

driver = cube_1.driver_add("rotation_euler", 2)  # Z-axis
driver.driver.type = 'SCRIPTED'
```

```
driver.driver.expression = "var * 2"

var = driver.driver.variables.new()
var.name = "var"
var.targets[0].id = cube
var.targets[0].data_path = "rotation_euler[2]"
```

Rendering Tips

Render Engines:

- **Eevee**: Use for real-time rendering.
- **Cycles**: Use for physically accurate rendering.

Common Settings:

- **Ctrl + B**: Render a specific region.
- **F12**: Render the current frame.
- **Shift + F12**: Render the entire animation.
- **Shift + Z**: Toggle between rendered and solid viewport shading.

Optimizing Renders:

- Lower **Samples** for preview renders.
- Enable **Denoising** in Cycles for faster results.
- Use **Compositor** for post-processing (e.g., color correction, glare).

Physics Simulations Reference

Simulation Types:

- **Rigid Body**: Use for solid objects (e.g., boxes, balls).
- **Soft Body**: Simulate flexible objects.
- **Fluid**: Create water or other liquid effects.
- **Smoke/Fire**: Add atmospheric effects.

Common Physics Settings:

- **Ctrl + A > Apply Scale**: Ensure scale is applied to avoid simulation issues.
- **Domain**: The area containing the simulation.
- **Resolution Divisions**: Increase for better quality.

This comprehensive reference guide ensures that you have the essential tools and workflows at your fingertips, enabling you to tackle projects more efficiently and effectively. With practice, these references will become second nature.

Frequently Asked Questions

Blender's versatility can sometimes make it overwhelming for beginners and even seasoned users. This FAQ section addresses common questions to help troubleshoot issues, clarify concepts, and enhance your understanding of the software.

General Blender Questions

Q: Is Blender completely free?
A: Yes, Blender is an open-source software licensed under the GNU General Public License (GPL). This means you can use, modify, and distribute it without any cost. Donations to support its development are welcome but not required.

Q: What are the system requirements for Blender?
A: While Blender is lightweight compared to other 3D software, the following are recommended for optimal performance:

- **Processor**: Quad-core CPU, 64-bit.
- **RAM**: 16 GB or more.
- **Graphics Card**: Dedicated GPU with 4 GB VRAM or higher (NVIDIA RTX/GTX or AMD equivalent).
- **Storage**: SSD for faster loading times.
- **Operating System**: Windows 10/11, macOS, or a Linux-based OS.

Q: Can I use Blender for commercial projects?
A: Absolutely. Blender is frequently used in industries like film, gaming, and product design. Its license imposes no restrictions on commercial use.

Interface and Workflow

Q: How can I reset the Blender interface to default?
A: If you've made changes to the interface and want to reset it:

1. Go to `Edit > Preferences > Load Factory Settings`.
2. Restart Blender.
3. Save the default layout with `File > Defaults > Save Startup File`.

Q: How do I navigate large scenes efficiently?
A: Use these tips for better scene management:

- Organize objects into **Collections** (Outliner > Right-click > New Collection).
- Use **View Layers** to toggle visibility for specific elements.
- Utilize the **Numpad period (.)** to focus on a selected object.

Q: Why can't I see my object in the viewport?
A: Check the following:

- Ensure the object is not hidden (Alt + H to unhide all).
- Confirm that it is within the camera's clipping range (N > View > Clip Start/End).
- Verify that the object is not in a disabled collection.

Modeling and Texturing

Q: How can I fix distorted UV maps?
A: Distortions often arise from poor topology or uneven scaling. Follow these steps:

1. In Edit Mode, select the model and apply **Ctrl + A > Apply Scale**.
2. Use **Smart UV Project** for a quick solution or manually mark seams with **Ctrl + E > Mark Seam**.
3. Open the UV Editor and adjust the islands as needed.

Q: What is the difference between procedural and image textures?
A:

- **Procedural Textures**: Generated mathematically and are resolution-independent (e.g., wood grain, noise).
- **Image Textures**: Based on image files, requiring higher resolutions for detail but easier to customize.

Q: Why does my model look jagged after applying a Subdivision Surface modifier?
A: Ensure proper topology:

- Avoid long, stretched faces. Use quads where possible.
- Add supporting edge loops to control smoothing.
- Check for overlapping or duplicate vertices (M > Merge By Distance).

Animation and Rigging

Q: How do I animate an object following a path?
A:

1. Create a curve (Shift + A > Curve > Path).
2. Select the object and apply a **Follow Path** constraint.
3. Assign the curve as the target in the constraint settings.

4. Animate the **Offset** value over time to move the object.

Q: What are IK and FK in rigging?
A:

- **Inverse Kinematics (IK)**: Moves the end of a chain (e.g., hand) and calculates joint positions automatically. Ideal for foot placement or hand movements.
- **Forward Kinematics (FK)**: Requires manual adjustment of each joint. Useful for precise, sequential motions.

Q: My animation looks stiff. How can I make it smoother?
A:

- Use the **Graph Editor** to adjust interpolation curves.
- Add subtle secondary motions like overlapping actions or follow-through.
- Enable motion blur in the render settings for added realism.

Rendering and Lighting

Q: Which render engine should I use: Eevee or Cycles?
A:

- **Eevee**: Best for real-time previews and stylized projects. Faster but less realistic.
- **Cycles**: Ray-traced and more realistic. Ideal for high-quality rendering but requires more computing power.

Q: Why is my render taking so long?
A: Rendering time depends on scene complexity. Optimize with these tips:

- Lower the **Sample Count** (Render Properties > Sampling).
- Enable **Denoising** to reduce grain.
- Use **Render Regions** (Ctrl + B) to focus on specific areas.
- Simplify materials by avoiding excessive reflection and translucency.

Q: How do I fix fireflies (bright specks) in my render?
A: Fireflies occur due to high-contrast lighting. To reduce them:

- Enable **Denoising** in the render settings.
- Increase the **Clamp Direct/Indirect** values under Light Paths.
- Use a more even lighting setup.

Scripting and Automation

Q: How do I access the Python Console in Blender?
A: Go to `Scripting > Python Console`. Here, you can test commands and debug scripts interactively.

Q: Can I automate repetitive tasks in Blender?
A: Yes, Python scripting is perfect for automation. Example: Automatically adding multiple lights.

```python
import bpy

# Add three point lights
locations = [(2, 2, 3), (-2, -2, 3), (0, 0, 5)]
for loc in locations:
    bpy.ops.object.light_add(type='POINT', location=loc)
    light = bpy.context.object
    light.data.energy = 1000
```

Q: How can I create a custom add-on?
A: Create a Python script and save it in Blender's add-ons directory. Example structure:

```python
bl_info = {
    "name": "My Add-On",
    "description": "Custom Blender Add-On",
    "version": (1, 0, 0),
    "blender": (3, 0, 0),
    "category": "Object",
}

import bpy

def menu_func(self, context):
    self.layout.operator("mesh.primitive_cube_add")

def register():
    bpy.utils.register_class(menu_func)

def unregister():
    bpy.utils.unregister_class(menu_func)

if __name__ == "__main__":
    register()
```

Common Errors

Q: Why does my viewport freeze or lag?
A: Blender might be running out of system resources. To fix this:

- Use **Wireframe Mode** to reduce rendering in the viewport.
- Limit the **Viewport Subdivision Level** in the Subdivision Surface modifier.
- Hide heavy geometry objects in the Outliner.

Q: Why does my imported model have missing textures?
A: Ensure the textures are packed or located in the specified directory. Use `File > External Data > Pack Resources` to bundle them into the .blend file.

Q: How do I recover a file after a crash?
A: Blender auto-saves periodically. Check the auto-save directory:

- **Windows**: `C:\Users\<User>\AppData\Local\Temp`
- **Mac/Linux**: `/tmp/`
  Load the `.blend1` file as your recovery file.

This FAQ section is a starting point for resolving common issues and improving your understanding of Blender's tools and features. Refer back to it whenever you encounter challenges or want to explore new possibilities.